D1314582

American Heart Association

AROUND THE WORLD COOKBOOK

American Heart
Association℠
*Fighting Heart Disease
and Stroke*

AROUND THE

WORLD COOKBOOK

Healthy Recipes with International Flavor

American Heart Association

TIMES 📖 BOOKS

RANDOM HOUSE

Your contribution to the American Heart Association supports research that helps make publications like this possible. For more information, call 1-800-AHA-USA1 (1-800-242-8721) or contact us online at http://www.americanheart.org.

Originally published in hardcover by Times Books, a division of Random House, Inc., in 1996.

Library of Congress Cataloging-in-Publication Data

American Heart Association around the world cookbook: healthy recipes with international flavor / American Heart Association.—1st ed.

p.   cm.

Includes index.

ISBN 0-8129-3307-9

1. Low-fat diet—Recipes. 2. Low-cholesterol diet—Recipes. I. American Heart Association.

RM237.7.A437 1996

641.5′638—dc20   95-46754

Random House website address: www.randomhouse.com

Printed in the United States of America on acid-free paper

9 8 7 6 5 4 3 2

First Paperback Edition

ART DIRECTION: NAOMI OSNOS

BOOK DESIGN: CHRIS WELCH

ILLUSTRATIONS: DAVID CAIN

PHOTOGRAPHY ART DIRECTION: ROBBIN SCHIFF

PHOTOGRAPHS: ELLEN SILVERMAN

Front cover: Red Snapper in Spicy Tomato Sauce (pages 152–53)

SPECIAL SALES

Times Books are available at special discounts for bulk purchases for sales promotions or premiums. Special editions, including personalized covers, excerpts of existing books, and corporate imprints, can be created in large quantities for special needs. For more information, write to Special Markets, Times Books, 201 East 50th Street, New York, New York 10022, or call 800-800-3246.

ACKNOWLEDGMENTS

Creating this cookbook brimming with flavorful, heart-healthful recipes took the joint efforts and expertise of a number of people.

The talented recipe developers for this project were Anita Frank, Carol Ritchie, and Linda Foley Woodrum. Much of the writing of the text you will find on the following pages came from the creative mind of Pat Naegele.

Janice Roth Moss and Jane Anneken Ruehl transformed the developers' recipe ideas and diverse writing styles into a unified cookbook. Much-appreciated help toward that end came from Sarah Flaherty Johnson and Amy Lindsly. Debra Bond, Gerre Gilford, and Michele Frye performed the task of word processing the entire manuscript.

Mary Winston, Ed.D., R.D., performed the paramount task of assuring scientific accuracy of the recipes and the text. The Nutrition Coordinating Center at the University of Minnesota at Minneapolis analyzed each recipe.

All of us hope you enjoy trying the international cuisines you will find in this book.

CONTENTS

INTRODUCTION

I t used to be that most American cooks prepared only one cuisine—American.

Today things are different. Ethnic foods abound, and Americans have embraced them happily. Many local grocery stores carry exotic spices and other ingredients from around the world. If yours doesn't, look for them at gourmet stores or order what you need by mail (see Appendix H, page 281). You don't have to go to the Caribbean for jerked chicken. It's as near as your corner supermarket (and page 195 of this book).

Food experts call this the global kitchen: International foods are available to almost everyone. Not only are U.S. restaurants serving crêpes suzette and chicken Kiev, but our own crayfish étouffée and New England clam chowder are on the menu in Paris and Moscow! One survey showed that 98 percent of all U.S. restaurants offer some form of ethnic cuisine.

In this cookbook, we started with some of the world's best recipes, altering them only slightly so we could keep the authenticity but lower the fat. Then we grouped them according to a number of factors, including ingredients, cooking methods, and general approach to eating and hospitality. Sometimes this resulted in a chapter about countries in the same geographical region, such as the Middle East. Sometimes the resulting chapter includes countries half a world away, such as the section on Hispanic cuisine. It features dishes from Spain, Mexico, and Latin America.

Serving Up Advice for a Healthy Heart

Although we all want nonstop taste and flavor, the world is turning away from high-fat foods. That's because the global community is wising up. Everyone knows that one of the major risk factors for heart attack is high blood cholesterol. So one of the best ways to reduce your risk of heart attack is to eat foods low in total fat, saturated fat, and cholesterol.

You'll find that the recipes in this book are heart-friendly. Of course, some foods are higher in fat and cholesterol than others, so it's important to know the basics of a healthful diet. The American Heart Association Dietary Guidelines on page 249 will show you how to build an eating plan that will stimulate your taste buds but help protect your heart.

Living High on Low–Fat Foods

It's universal: The world is full of skeptics where low-fat food is concerned. It's difficult to convince doubters that low-fat foods can be truly tantalizing. But it's true!

Why the perception problem? Because many people don't know one simple fact: Fat is an acquired taste. People who aren't used to eating high-fat food don't crave it. For example, talk to people who drink skim milk. If they switched from whole milk, they'll probably tell you that the change seemed undesirable at first, but skim milk soon began to taste rich and totally satisfying to them. In fact, they probably prefer skim milk now. And people who gave up fried food often report that if they try to eat fried chicken or fried fish now, it tastes heavy, greasy, and unnatural. After a while, they simply *prefer* fresh, natural, low-fat foods. At last, they're hooked on *flavor,* not fat.

Creative Cooking—and Tasting

If you're in a hurry, like most of us, you'll want to try the easy recipes, with few ingredients and short preparation times. Other recipes are more elaborate, with more ingredients and more steps. But, oh, the results!

With international food, what's really important is to *try every-thing*. At one of our recipe tastings, a tester swore she hated liver, yet rated our Poultry Pâté (page 37) the number-one dish of the day! Another tester simply would not eat cherries in any form—until someone sneaked her a piece of Black Forest Cake with cherry filling (page 89). She ate that piece and was ready for more! Our international food motto: Try it, you'll like it.

The World on Your Dinner Plate

These inspired recipes speak a universal language. Who wouldn't love and understand the vibrant zest of Meaty Black Beans and Rice (page 160) and the temptation of a Puffed Pancake with Apple-Cranberry Sauce (page 91)? They're here, your passport to fun and flavor.

We invite you to relish our Chicken in Garlic Sauce from China (page 229), savor Italy's Fettuccine Alfredo (page 23), and tantalize your taste buds with Normandy Pork with Calvados Cream Sauce from France (page 53).

This cookbook brings you some of the world's most delectable and heart-healthy offerings. From the glittering lights of Paris to the farthest Chinese province and the Caribbean's pristine beaches, you hold a world of food pleasures right here in your hands.

HOW TO USE THE NUTRIENT ANALYSES

A world of healthful international cuisine awaits. But first, take a minute to learn how to use these recipes.

Beside each recipe, you'll find its nutrition breakdown—calorie count and the amounts of protein, carbohydrate, cholesterol, sodium, total fat, saturated fat, polyunsaturated fat, and monounsaturated fat. This analysis will help you decide whether the recipe fits into your eating plan. The amount of each nutrient can vary widely from one recipe to another. If you're on a restricted diet, reading these analyses carefully can help you choose recipes that best meet your needs. For example, if you are watching your sodium intake, pay particular attention to the sodium listings. Choose recipes in which the sodium content is low enough to fit into your daily eating plan.

Keep the following information in mind as you review the nutrient analyses of the recipes:

- Garnishes (unless you'd eat them) and optional ingredients were not included in the nutrient analysis. Garnishes and optional ingredients add flavor and texture, but some, such as soy sauce, also add sodium. So if you're trying to cut down on sodium, skip such toppings or use them sparingly. The food will still taste great.

- Ingredients with a weight range (a 2- to 3-pound chicken, for example) were analyzed at the average weight.

- The analysis of meat dishes was based on cooked lean meat with all visible fat removed.

- When a recipe lists two or more ingredient options (1 cup non-fat or low-fat yogurt, for example), the first was used in the nutrient analysis.

- Each analysis is based on a single serving, unless otherwise indicated.

- The specific amounts of the ingredients listed, not the amounts sometimes shown in parentheses, were analyzed. The amounts in parentheses are guidelines for the quantities to purchase to get at least what the recipe requires. For example, when a recipe calls for 2 tablespoons lime juice (2 limes), we analyzed the 2 tablespoons of juice, not the 2 limes. (We do not list the quantity in parentheses if 1 or only part of the item is needed.)

- When a recipe calls for low-fat cheese, it was analyzed using cheese that has 33 percent less fat than regular cheese. If you want to reduce the fat even further, choose a cheese that has 50 percent less fat than regular cheese. For cold dishes, you might want to use nonfat cheese products. If you're watching your sodium intake, be aware that the nonfat cheeses are typically higher in sodium than the low-fat cheeses.

- The values for saturated, monounsaturated, and polyunsaturated fatty acids may not add up precisely to the total fat in the recipe. That's because the total fat includes not only the fatty acids that are reflected in the analyses but also other fatty substances and glycerol that aren't. It's also because all values are rounded to the nearest whole number.

- When a recipe calls for acceptable margarine, we used corn-oil margarine for the analysis. Remember to choose a margarine that lists liquid vegetable oil as the first ingredient. It should contain no more than 2 grams of saturated fat per tablespoon.

- When a recipe calls for acceptable vegetable oil, we used corn oil. Other examples of acceptable vegetable oils are safflower, soybean, sunflower, sesame, canola, and olive oils. Use peanut oil only occasionally for a flavor change.

- The abbreviation for gram is "g"; the abbreviation for milligram is "mg."

- If a meat marinade was used, the nutrient analysis includes only the amount absorbed by the meat, based on U.S. Department of Agriculture (USDA) data on absorption.

- Absorption data is not available for vegetable marinades, so we added in the total amount of marinade used in the recipe.

- Feel free to make any creative substitutions that won't affect the recipe's nutrition profile. For example, you could use basil instead of thyme or try tarragon vinegar instead of white wine vinegar.

- We analyzed whole carrots with peel. Unless carrots are very old or the peel is discolored, simply scrub them and leave the peel on. That way, you'll get all the flavor and nutrients the carrots contain.

- We analyzed the entire green onion unless only the white or only the green was specified. Use the part you like best—or the whole onion.

- According to the USDA, there is virtually no difference in the nutritional values of fresh, frozen, and canned food when prepared for the table. When using frozen or canned foods, however, be sure to watch for added ingredients, such as salt, that may change the analysis.

American Heart Association

AROUND THE WORLD COOKBOOK

ITALIAN CUISINE

Chicken Soup with Pasta and Cheese

Tomato-Mozzarella Salad
Fennel-Orange Salad

Baked Fish Steak with Capers
Mussels Steamed in Wine

Chicken Piccata
Turkey Rolls with Prosciutto and Cheese
Two-Sauce Turkey Cannelloni

Pot-Roast-Style Steak with Tomatoes

Pasta Primavera

Peas with Pine Nuts
Fettuccine Alfredo

Herbed Batter Bread
Tuscan Peasant Bread

Biscotti
Cannoli Cream
Tiramisù

I talians have an intense love affair with food. No family get-together would be complete without gathering around a table near collapse under the weight of enough food to feed everyone at least twice.

Garlic, the quintessential Italian seasoning, made its way through Europe with help from the militia of ancient Rome. Their love of this member of the lily family actually caused some outright revolts against military authority. According to local legend, soldiers who deserted when the supplies of garlic, onions, and salt ran out built the Roman villas and roads now in ruins north of Italy.

Northern Italy gets its love of dairy products from its Swiss neighbor. Cheese in myriad forms graces every table, butter abounds, and there's hardly a tomato in sight. The tomato was originally a gift of conquest brought from the New World by the Spanish conquistadors. Europeans regarded it primarily as an ornamental plant. Even now, when tomatoes are used in the north, they're usually lightly cooked. The southern Italians, however, brought the tomato to life by stewing and seasoning it, turning it into the sauce we Americans know and love.

Homemade Pasta: That's Amore!

Usually thought of as uniquely Italian, pasta has a convoluted history. Early forms were similar to the spaetzle made by the Swiss. The Italian version of spaetzle, gnocchi (NYO-ki), is made of flour, water, potato, and cheese or herbs. This mixture is hand molded into bite-size dumplings that are boiled in water. One story holds that Marco Polo introduced the true noodle to Italy after observing the Chinese rolling and stretching dough during his travels to the Orient. And the Italians have indisputably raised pasta to an art form. Italian pasta shapes resemble ears (orrechiette), thimbles (ditalini), butterflies (farfalle), seashells (conchiglie), pens (penne), radiator grills (radiatore), and even little worms (vermicelli)—to name but a few of the dozens of shapes available.

Italians in the coastal cities revere the gifts of the Mediterranean, and seafood in all its varieties finds its way to the Italian table. Clams, mussels, octopus, and squid are delicious when properly prepared, but some Western diners don't like their looks and names. Ironically, Americans tend to shun menu items that include squid but devour dishes featuring calamari, the Italian word for squid. To paraphrase Juliet: What's in a name? Forsake your preconceptions and try the mussels! A good place to start might be the Mussels Steamed in Wine on page 10.

War and the Olive Branch

No chronicle of Italian cuisine would be complete without honoring the olive. In ancient Rome, an offering of bread and olives meant you extended the hospitality of your house to your guest. During the civil wars, when the fiercely independent city-states of Italy struggled for supremacy, a handful of olives kept many a person from starving. And today in almost every part of Italy, you'll find a few friends gathered in the late afternoon, sharing a bottle of wine and dipping morsels of good country bread in the very best extra-virgin olive oil.

With olives, the choices are endless, but with oil, don't settle for less than the best if you want authentic Italian taste. Extra-virgin olive oil has less than 1 percent acidity. Its smoothness and flavor are unsurpassed. Lesser grades are readily available, but in an Italian kitchen, the results rest on the quality of the ingredients—no scrimping allowed!

An Italian meal almost always centers on at least one pasta dish. Meat or fish—roasted, stewed, or combined with the pasta—is often served, as is a loaf of fresh, crusty bread. Cooks in Italy usually prepare vegetables quite simply, often grilled or sautéed with a drizzle of olive oil. A glass of wine may be served before, during, or after the meal. Fresh fruit, always available, makes a light, refreshing dessert. Italians usually buy the more complex desserts at pastry shops, because few households have the tools or the time to make fancy concoctions. Often dessert is simply coffee or espresso, or a glass of sherry or sweet wine, perhaps for dunking biscotti (page 27). The diners linger at the table, chatting into the evening.

What are you waiting for? *Mangia!* Eat!

Chicken Soup with Pasta and Cheese

Zuppa di Pollo

L ight but filling, this soup is good year-round. Leftover chicken can be added to the dish to turn it into a satisfying main course. Best of all, it takes only a few minutes to prepare.

Egg substitute equivalent to 2 eggs, or 2 eggs
4 cups low-sodium chicken broth
1 cup pastina or any crushed macaroni
¼ cup grated Parmesan cheese
1 tablespoon chopped fresh parsley

Whisk the egg substitute in a small mixing bowl until thoroughly blended. Set aside.

Bring the broth to a simmer in a medium saucepan over medium heat. Add the pastina and return the broth to a simmer. Simmer until pastina is tender, about 10 minutes. Whisk in egg substitute and continue to cook for 1 minute.

Ladle into soup bowls and sprinkle with Parmesan and parsley.

Serves 6; about ¾ cup per serving

Nutrient
Analysis
(per serving)

Calories 124
Protein 8 g
Carbohydrate 18 g
Cholesterol 3 mg
Sodium 128 mg
Total fat 2 g
  Saturated 1 g
  Polyunsaturated 0 g
  Monounsaturated 1 g

Tomato–Mozzarella Salad

Insalata di Pomodori

*O*ne *of the delights of summer, this salad is perfect as a light lunch or supper for those days when it's just too hot to cook.*

1 medium red onion, very thinly sliced
4 large tomatoes, preferably vine-ripened or
  greenhouse, sliced about $^1/_2$ inch thick
$^1/_2$ pound nonfat or part-skim mozzarella, thinly
  sliced or shredded
$^1/_4$ cup chopped fresh parsley
2 teaspoons finely chopped fresh basil
3 to 4 cloves garlic, minced
Black pepper to taste
2 tablespoons extra-virgin olive oil
2 teaspoons red wine vinegar, or to taste

Serves 4

Nutrient
Analysis
(per serving)

Calories 210
Protein 20 g
Carbohydrate 16 g
Cholesterol 1 mg
Sodium 418 mg
Total fat 8 g
  Saturated 1 g
  Polyunsaturated 1 g
  Monounsaturated 5 g

Place a layer of onion in a glass or ceramic serving dish. Cover with a layer of tomatoes and a layer of mozzarella. Sprinkle with some of the parsley, basil, garlic, and pepper. Drizzle with a little oil and a splash of vinegar. Continue layering the rest of the ingredients (the number of layers will depend on the size of your dish). Refrigerate until well chilled.

Fennel–Orange Salad

Insalata di Finocchio

A flavorful dressing that incorporates the feathery tops of the mildly licorice-flavored fennel bulb enhances this crispy salad.

Dressing

3 tablespoons white wine vinegar
1 tablespoon extra-virgin olive oil
2 teaspoons honey
1 teaspoon chopped fennel leaves (optional)
1 clove garlic, minced
$\frac{1}{2}$ teaspoon grated orange zest
$\frac{1}{4}$ teaspoon salt
$\frac{1}{8}$ teaspoon black pepper

Salad

4 cups torn romaine lettuce (4 ounces)
1 cup torn radicchio leaves (1 ounce)
2 fennel bulbs, ends trimmed and thinly sliced
2 medium oranges, peeled and sliced crosswise, seeds removed (about 2 cups)

Serves 4; 2¼ cups salad and 1 tablespoon dressing per serving

Nutrient Analysis (per serving)

Calories 118
Protein 3 g
Carbohydrate 21 g
Cholesterol 0 mg
Sodium 211 mg
Total fat 4 g
   Saturated 0 g
   Polyunsaturated 0 g
   Monounsaturated 3 g

Combine dressing ingredients in a small non-metallic bowl. Set aside.

For the salad, place romaine and radicchio in a large bowl. Scatter fennel on top and pour dressing over all. Toss lightly. Arrange oranges over salad and serve.

COOK'S TIP ON RADICCHIO: Radicchio adds color to green salads. This member of the chicory family has small, delicate leaves that range in color from purple to red with white accents. It has an assertive flavor, so you'll need only a few leaves to perk up your salads.

Discard any mussels that have not opened. Spoon some of the juices over the mussels and serve immediately.

COOK'S TIP ON MUSSELS: Most Americans haven't grown up eating mussels, so they are unsure of how—and even whether—to eat them. A great pity, because mussels are the sweetest of the shellfish and are perfectly acceptable as a finger food. Simply pick up a cooked mussel in your fingertips and pull the halves of the shell apart. Use the empty half like a spoon to scoop the mussel out of the other half, then eat it right from the shell. Or scoop the meat out of all the mussels onto the plate and then proceed with more "civilized" utensils.

Chicken Piccata

Pollo Piccata

Refreshingly tart, this dish tastes a lot more complicated than it is.

6 boneless, skinless chicken breast halves (about 4 ounces each)
1 teaspoon extra-virgin olive oil
8 green onions, thinly sliced on the diagonal
2 cloves garlic, crushed or minced
½ cup all-purpose flour
2 to 3 teaspoons extra-virgin olive oil
2 tablespoons low-sodium chicken broth
2 tablespoons fresh lemon juice
2 tablespoons capers, rinsed, drained, and chopped if very large
2 tablespoons dry white wine (optional)
2 tablespoons dry sherry (optional)
Black pepper to taste
1 small lemon, thinly sliced (optional)
2 tablespoons chopped parsley (optional)

Serves 6; 1 breast half per serving

Nutrient Analysis (per serving)

Calories 212
Protein 28 g
Carbohydrate 10 g
Cholesterol 66 mg
Sodium 72 mg
Total fat 6 g
   Saturated 1 g
   Polyunsaturated 1 g
   Monounsaturated 3 g

Rinse the chicken breasts and pat dry with paper towels. Place between sheets of plastic wrap and flatten slightly with a meat mallet or rolling pin. Set aside.

Heat a large skillet over medium heat, add 1 teaspoon olive oil, and sauté the green onions and garlic just until tender, about 2 minutes. Remove from the pan and set aside.

Put the flour on a plate and lightly coat both sides of the chicken. Shake off excess flour.

Lightly brown chicken in the skillet over medium heat, adding a small amount of oil as needed. Return the green onions and garlic to the pan. Add the broth, lemon juice, and capers, and the wine and sherry, if using. Sauté over high heat until heated through, about 2 minutes. Stir in the pepper.

Serve on a warmed platter and garnish with lemon slices and chopped parsley, if using.

Turkey Rolls with Prosciutto and Cheese

This dish traditionally uses chicken breasts, but our convenient method uses turkey cutlets (sliced turkey breast). After you roll them up with the prosciutto and mozzarella inside, all you need to do is quickly cook them with some meaty portobello mushrooms. Serve with vermicelli pasta for a sumptuous and elegant feast.

4 turkey cutlets (8 ounces) or 4 small boneless, skinless chicken breast halves (8 ounces), all visible fat removed (you can parallel cut 2 large boneless, skinless chicken breast halves to make 4 pieces)

2 teaspoons chopped fresh rosemary or $^1/_2$ teaspoon dried, crushed using mortar and pestle

$^1/_8$ teaspoon black pepper

4 thin slices part-skim mozzarella cheese (1 ounce)

4 thin slices prosciutto or lean ham (1 ounce)

2 tablespoons all-purpose flour

Egg substitute equivalent to 1 egg

$^1/_2$ cup plain dry bread crumbs

Water as needed

8 ounces dried vermicelli

1 tablespoon extra-virgin olive oil

1 clove garlic, minced

$^1/_2$ teaspoon dried oregano, crumbled

$^1/_2$ teaspoon dried basil, crumbled

4 ounces portobello mushrooms, sliced

2 tablespoons marsala wine, white wine, nonalcoholic white wine, or low-sodium chicken broth

2 tablespoons water

Rinse turkey and pat dry with paper towels. Place cutlets on a flat surface. Cover with a sheet of plastic wrap. With the smooth side of a meat

Serves 4; 1 roll and 1 cup cooked pasta per serving

Nutrient Analysis (per serving)

Calories 408
Protein 26 g
Carbohydrate 53 g
Cholesterol 42 mg
Sodium 515 mg
Total fat 8 g
  Saturated 2 g
  Polyunsaturated 1 g
  Monounsaturated 4 g

mallet, lightly flatten the cutlets, being careful not to tear the meat. Sprinkle the top of each cutlet with chopped rosemary and black pepper. Place a slice of cheese and prosciutto in the center of each cutlet. Starting at a short end, roll up each cutlet, jelly-roll style. Fasten seams with wooden tooth-picks.

Lightly sprinkle flour over each roll; pat flour into surface of turkey with your hands. Pour egg substitute into a shallow bowl; spread bread crumbs onto a plate. Dip each roll into egg substitute and then lightly coat with bread crumbs. Set aside.

Following manufacturer's directions, cook vermicelli. (Don't add salt or oil, however.)

Meanwhile, heat a nonstick skillet over medium-high heat. Add the olive oil, garlic, oregano, and basil. Cook for 30 seconds. Brown the turkey rolls on all sides (approximately 1 minute on each side). Reduce heat to medium-low. Add mushrooms and cook for 1 minute. Add marsala and 2 tablespoons water; cook, covered, for 3 to 4 minutes, or until turkey is no longer pink when tested with a knife (do not overcook).

Remove skillet from heat. Pull toothpicks from rolls. Let cool slightly and slice crosswise. To serve, place 1 cup cooked vermicelli on each serving plate. Place the turkey slices from one roll on top or to one side, and top with a quarter of the mush-rooms or place them to the side. Repeat with remaining pasta, turkey, and mushrooms.

COOK'S TIP ON PORTOBELLO MUSHROOMS: Portobello mushrooms are very large, dark brown, and meaty tasting. Grilling is an easy way to fix these flavorful favorites. Clean 8 ounces of portobellos as you would button mushrooms—wipe with a clean, damp cloth or brush gently with a mushroom brush. Lightly spray them with vegetable oil spray or olive oil spray; sprinkle with 1 to 2 tablespoons chopped fresh herbs (basil, oregano, or your own favorite) or 1 to 2 teaspoons dried. Grill over medium-hot coals for 3 to 4 minutes, then turn and cook on the other side for another 3 to 4 minutes. Serve hot or cold with your favorite main dish.

Two-Sauce Turkey Cannelloni

Cannelloni

This perennial favorite gets an update but keeps its familiar highlights. Homemade pasta filled with rich-tasting turkey and ricotta cheese bakes under not one sauce, but two. This savory sensation is even better when made ahead, then reheated the next day.

Pasta Dough

½ cup all-purpose flour
½ cup semolina or all-purpose flour
Egg substitute equivalent to 1 egg
2 tablespoons skim milk

Seasoned Turkey

8 ounces ground skinless turkey breast (fat free)
*   or 8 ounces boneless, skinless chicken breast,*
*   all visible fat removed, finely minced*
Vegetable oil spray
¼ cup finely chopped onion (about ½ medium)
1 clove garlic, minced (about ½ teaspoon)
1 tablespoon marsala or nonalcoholic white wine
1 teaspoon cornstarch
½ teaspoon dried oregano, crumbled
¼ teaspoon fennel seeds
⅛ teaspoon black pepper

Filling

1 cup fat-free ricotta cheese (8 ounces)
½ cup chopped fresh spinach (about 1 ounce)
Egg substitute equivalent to 1 egg

Tomato Sauce

Vegetable oil spray
¼ cup chopped onion
2 cloves garlic, crushed or minced
¼ teaspoon crushed red pepper flakes
15-ounce can no-salt-added crushed tomatoes
½ teaspoon dried oregano, crumbled
½ teaspoon dried basil, crumbled

Serves 4; 2 stuffed shells per serving

Nutrient Analysis (per serving)

Calories 332
Protein 31 g
Carbohydrate 42 g
Cholesterol 37 mg
Sodium 388 mg
Total fat 3 g
  Saturated 1 g
  Polyunsaturated 1 g
  Monounsaturated 1 g

¹/₂ teaspoon sugar
¹/₈ teaspoon black pepper

Pimiento-Béchamel Sauce
1 cup skim milk
2-ounce jar sliced pimientos, rinsed and drained
¹/₈ teaspoon black pepper
3 tablespoons water
2 tablespoons all-purpose flour

Vegetable oil spray
2 tablespoons Parmesan cheese

For the pasta dough, place all-purpose and semolina flours in a medium mixing bowl. Add the egg substitute and milk. Stir with a fork until mixture is moistened. With your hands, form mixture into a ball. On a lightly floured flat surface, knead dough until smooth and elastic, about 2 to 3 minutes. Place dough back in bowl and cover with a dish towel. Let dough rest about 15 minutes. Roll dough out on a floured surface to a 15-inch square. With a sharp knife, cut square into quarters; cut each quarter in half (you will have 8 rectangular pieces of dough). Cover with plastic wrap and set aside. (Dough can be kept, refrigerated in an airtight plastic bag, for up to 10 hours.)

For the seasoned turkey, cook ground turkey over medium heat in a medium nonstick skillet, stirring occasionally, for 5 minutes, or until no longer pink. Place turkey in a colander, rinse under hot water, and drain. Set aside in a nonmetallic bowl. Wipe skillet with paper towels, coat lightly with vegetable oil spray, and heat over medium heat. Sauté the onion and garlic in the hot skillet for 2 to 3 minutes, or until onion is tender. Add to bowl with ground turkey. Add marsala, cornstarch, oregano, fennel seeds, and black pepper and mix well. Cover bowl and let sit for 15 to 20 minutes. (You can prepare sauces while turkey mixture sits.) Add filling ingredients to turkey mixture and mix with a spoon. Set aside.

For the tomato sauce, spray a medium nonstick saucepan with vegetable oil spray. Heat pan over medium heat. Sauté onion, garlic, and red pepper, stirring constantly, until onion is tender, about 2 to 3 minutes. Add remaining tomato sauce ingredients. Bring to a boil over high heat. Reduce heat to medium-low and cook, uncovered, for 20 minutes, stirring occasionally. Remove from heat and set aside.

For the pimiento-béchamel sauce, place milk, pimientos, and pepper in a small saucepan. Bring to a simmer over medium-high heat. Place water and flour in a container with a tight-fitting lid. Shake mixture until smooth. Stir flour mixture into milk mixture. Cook over medium-high heat, stirring occasionally, until mixture thickens, about 2 to 3 minutes. Remove from heat and set aside.

Preheat oven to 375° F.

To assemble dish, spray a 9×13-inch baking dish with vegetable oil spray. Ladle $\frac{1}{2}$ cup tomato sauce into the dish; spread evenly to coat (mixture may not cover the bottom entirely). Spoon $\frac{1}{4}$ cup turkey mixture down the middle of a piece of pasta dough. Roll pasta up and place seam side down in prepared baking dish. Repeat with remaining pasta and filling. Spread the pimiento-béchamel sauce evenly over pasta rolls. Spread the remaining tomato sauce over all. Cover pan with aluminum foil and bake for 1 hour, or until pasta is tender to the bite. Remove from oven and sprinkle with Parmesan cheese.

COOK'S TIP: Because of the many steps required in this dish, here are some suggestions to make preparation a bit easier. For the pasta: You can substitute 8 ounces manicotti shells, cooked and cooled according to package directions. (Don't add salt or oil, however.) This will yield about 3 shells per serving. Prepare baking dish as directed above. Fill shells using about 3 tablespoons filling for each. Top with sauces and bake as directed, except cut baking time to 40 minutes. For the filling: If you have 1 cup of plain cooked turkey or chicken, mix it with the ingredients for the seasoned turkey (omit cornstarch) and combine with the filling ingredients. For the tomato sauce: You can substitute 1¾ cups of your favorite low-fat, low-sodium prepared spaghetti sauce.

Pot–Roast–Style Steak with Tomatoes

Manza Stufato

Since this dish is cooked for a short time, the flavors of the meat and seasonings remain distinct. You can also stew the meat for a much longer time, melding the flavors to create a melt-in-your-mouth feast.

1½ teaspoons extra-virgin olive oil
1 pound sirloin or lean steak of choice, all visible
   fat removed, cut into serving-size pieces
2 cloves garlic, crushed or minced
2 Italian plum tomatoes, chopped
1 teaspoon fresh lemon juice
¼ teaspoon dried oregano, crumbled
Black pepper to taste
Pinch of salt

Serves 4; 3 ounces per serving

Nutrient Analysis (per serving)

Calories 157
Protein 23 g
Carbohydrate 3 g
Cholesterol 60 mg
Sodium 49 mg
Total fat 5 g
   Saturated 1 g
   Polyunsaturated 0 g
   Monounsaturated 3 g

Heat the oil in a large skillet over medium heat and sear the steak pieces until they reach desired doneness, about 10 minutes for rare. Transfer the meat to a serving platter and cover with foil or a lid to keep warm. Set aside.

Add the garlic to the skillet and sauté over low heat until golden, about 2 minutes, being careful not to burn it. Add the rest of the ingredients except the meat. Cook over medium heat until the tomatoes are tender but still have texture, about 5 minutes. Return the meat to the skillet, along with any juices, and cook gently for a few minutes to combine flavors.

Transfer meat and sauce to the platter and serve immediately.

COOK'S TIP: Keep in mind that the meat will continue to cook slightly both when covered on the platter and when returned to the sauce. If you like your steak on the pink side, you might want to undercook it a bit to ensure desired doneness.

Pasta Primavera

Pasta primavera simply means spring pasta, and the only criterion is that you use fresh vegetables when you assemble your choices. You can easily modify this simple recipe to accommodate 2 to 20.

3 ounces dried pasta, such as rotelli, penne, ziti, or radiatore
1 teaspoon extra-virgin olive oil
1 clove garlic
6 ounces fresh mixed vegetables, such as shredded zucchini or other summer squash, shredded carrot, broccoli florets, cauliflower florets, thinly sliced red bell pepper, snow peas, or sliced mushrooms
2 teaspoons fresh lemon juice, or to taste
Black pepper to taste

Cook pasta according to package instructions until desired doneness is reached. (Don't add salt or oil, however.) Add a cup or so of cold water to stop the cooking process; allow pasta to remain in hot water until needed.

Heat 1 teaspoon oil in a large skillet over medium heat and sauté the garlic until golden, taking care not to let it brown. Add the vegetables and cook until just tender, about 2 to 3 minutes, stirring occasionally. Season with lemon juice and pepper.

Drain the pasta and add to the skillet. Stir and toss until the pasta is blended with the vegetable mixture. Transfer to a plate and serve.

COOK'S TIP: Leftovers make a delicious cold pasta salad, so you might want to make extra!

Serves 1

Nutrient Analysis (per serving)

Calories 420
Protein 15 g
Carbohydrate 77 g
Cholesterol 0 mg
Sodium 48 mg
Total fat 6 g
    Saturated 1 g
    Polyunsaturated 1 g
    Monounsaturated 4 g

Peas with Pine Nuts

Piselli con Pignoli

I f you think you don't care for peas, try them this way. We think you'll change your mind! You can find pine nuts, or pignoli, in larger supermarkets and most Italian grocery stores.

½ **cup low-sodium chicken broth**
½ **medium onion, sliced**
½ **teaspoon sugar**
3 **pounds fresh peas, shelled, or 20 ounces**
   frozen peas
1 **teaspoon extra-virgin olive oil**
¼ **cup pine nuts (about 1 ounce)**
1 **teaspoon dried rosemary, crushed using a**
   mortar and pestle, or Italian seasoning,
   crumbled
¼ **teaspoon salt**
Black pepper to taste

Serves 8; ½ cup per serving

Nutrient Analysis (per serving)

Calories 75
Protein 4 g
Carbohydrate 10 g
Cholesterol 0 mg
Sodium 130 mg
Total fat 3 g
   Saturated 0 g
   Polyunsaturated 1 g
   Monounsaturated 1 g

Bring broth, onion, and sugar to a boil over high heat in a medium saucepan. Add peas and cook until tender, about 5 minutes for fresh peas or 3 minutes for frozen. Drain. Discard liquid and onion slices. Set peas aside.

Heat oil in a large skillet over medium heat. Add the pine nuts and cook, stirring, for about 3 minutes, or until golden. Add rosemary, then peas, and sauté until heated through, about 2 minutes. Season with salt and pepper and serve.

COOK'S TIP ON FROZEN PEAS: If you use frozen peas, don't bother to thaw them. A few seconds in the pan is all it takes.

Fettuccine Alfredo

Thanks go to Alfredo DiLelio for his 1914 creation of the classic dish known as fettuccine Alfredo. No thanks to him, though, for all the fat it usually contains. This lightened version is considerably lower in fat than the traditional version. Nevertheless, you need to eat low-fat accompaniments with it for balance.

1 cup evaporated skim milk
1 teaspoon acceptable margarine
¼ cup reduced-fat cream cheese
8 ounces dried fettuccine
⅔ cup grated Parmesan cheese
Black pepper (freshly ground preferred)

Serves 6; ½ cup per serving

Nutrient Analysis (per serving)

Calories 242
Protein 14 g
Carbohydrate 30 g
Cholesterol 46 mg
Sodium 327 mg
Total fat 7 g
  Saturated 4 g
  Polyunsaturated 1 g
  Monounsaturated 2 g

In a large saucepan or Dutch oven, combine milk and margarine. Cook over medium heat until milk mixture simmers, about 7 minutes. Add cream cheese. Cook and stir with a wire whisk until cream cheese melts and mixture is smooth, about 3 to 4 minutes. Cover and remove from heat.

Meanwhile, cook fettuccine in a large stockpot of boiling water according to package directions or until desired doneness. (Don't add salt or oil, however.) Drain thoroughly.

Add fettuccine to pan with milk mixture. Cook over low heat, tossing fettuccine until well coated, about 1 minute. Add Parmesan cheese and season with pepper. Toss lightly to combine.

Remove from heat, cover, and let stand 1 to 2 minutes (this gives liquid a chance to be slightly absorbed into the pasta). Serve immediately.

Herbed Batter Bread

Pannetone Piati

This easy bread tastes wonderful toasted. If there's any left, it makes terrific bread crumbs once stale.

Serves 32; 1 slice per serving

Nutrient Analysis (per serving)

Calories 75
Protein 2 g
Carbohydrate 14 g
Cholesterol 0 mg
Sodium 93 mg
Total fat 1 g
  Saturated 0 g
  Polyunsaturated 0 g
  Monounsaturated 0 g

1 package (1 tablespoon) active dry yeast
½ cup warm water (105° F)
1 cup skim milk
2 tablespoons acceptable margarine
Egg substitute equivalent to 2 eggs, or 2 eggs, lightly beaten
3 tablespoons honey
2 tablespoons nonfat plain yogurt
1 tablespoon Italian seasoning
1 teaspoon salt
4 cups all-purpose flour
Vegetable oil spray

Combine yeast and warm water in a large mixing bowl. Set aside.

In a small saucepan over low heat, heat milk and margarine just long enough to melt margarine.

Add egg substitute, honey, yogurt, Italian seasoning, and salt to yeast mixture and blend thoroughly. Stir in the flour. When combined, beat at least 100 strokes by hand or for 1 minute with an electric mixer. Please note that this is a batter, not a solid dough.

Cover with plastic wrap and let stand in a warm place until batter is almost tripled in bulk, about 1 hour. Spray four 5½-inch loaf pans with vegetable oil spray. Set aside. Stir the batter down and divide evenly among the loaf pans. Cover and let rise until almost to top of pans, about 20 to 25 minutes.

Meanwhile, preheat oven to 350° F. Bake for 35 minutes, or until a cake tester inserted near the center of the loaf comes out clean. Let cool for about 15 minutes before removing from pan. Cut into 8 slices per loaf and serve hot, warm, or cool.

Tuscan Peasant Bread

Pane Contadina Toscana

The traditional bread of Tuscany is usually made without any added salt, which earns it a place on the heart-healthy table. Don't skimp on the kneading; listen to your favorite CD or watch a half-hour television show to keep occupied. A baking stone gives the best crust. If you don't have one, go to a tile store or home center and buy a few terra-cotta tiles to place on your oven rack. Just be sure you leave at least 1 inch between the tiles and the walls of the oven so heat can circulate properly.

1 cup whole-wheat bread flour
1 cup unbleached white bread flour
2 cups warm water (105° F)
2 teaspoons active dry yeast
2½ to 3½ cups unbleached all-purpose flour
1 tablespoon extra-virgin olive oil
About ½ tablespoon extra-virgin olive oil
Coarse stone-ground cornmeal

Makes 1 large loaf. Serves 10; 1 wedge per serving

Nutrient Analysis (per serving)

Calories 247
Protein 7 g
Carbohydrate 48 g
Cholesterol 0 mg
Sodium 2 mg
Total fat 3 g
   Saturated 0 g
   Polyunsaturated 0 g
   Monounsaturated 2 g

Combine the whole-wheat and white flours, the warm water, and the yeast in a large mixing bowl and stir until well combined. Cover with plastic wrap and let stand at room temperature overnight. The batter will ferment slightly and smell a bit like sourdough.

Stir 2½ cups all-purpose flour and 1 tablespoon olive oil into the yeast mixture. Add enough of the remaining all-purpose flour to form a soft, slightly sticky dough. Turn out dough onto a floured board and knead with floured hands until dough is smooth and elastic, about 20 minutes, adding remaining flour as necessary. Dough should be slightly sticky.

Clean the bowl. Using the ½ tablespoon olive oil, coat the bowl. Transfer the kneaded dough back to the bowl, turning to coat all surfaces. Cover with plastic wrap and let the dough stand at room temperature until doubled in volume, about 2 hours. Punch dough down. Cover and let rise again until doubled, $1\frac{1}{2}$ to 2 hours.

Generously sprinkle a baker's peel (or the back of a baking sheet) with cornmeal. Punch the dough down again and turn out onto a lightly floured surface. Form the dough into a large circle, about 10 inches in diameter, and transfer the loaf to the prepared peel. Dust dough lightly with flour. Cover with a clean dish towel and let rise in a warm, draft-free place until more than doubled in bulk, about $1\frac{1}{2}$ to 2 hours.

About 30 minutes before dough has finished rising, position a rack in the center of the oven and arrange the baking stone on the rack. Set a broiler pan with several inches of water in it on a rack in the bottom of the oven and preheat oven to 425° F.

Using a single-edged razor blade, carefully slash the dough in a pattern, such as a tic-tac-toe design. The slashes should be about $\frac{1}{2}$ inch deep—they will spread decoratively while the loaf bakes.

Sprinkle the loaf with more flour if the flour has been absorbed. Generously sprinkle the baking stone with cornmeal. Transfer the loaf to the stone by shaking the peel to make sure the loaf isn't stuck to it, carefully lifting the edges of the loaf and putting a little more cornmeal under it if necessary. Hold the peel over the hot baking stone, then whip the peel out from under the loaf.

Bake for about 40 minutes. The bottom of the loaf should sound hollow when thumped. Remove the bread from the oven and cool on a rack for about 10 minutes. Serve hot, warm, or cool.

Biscotti

Biscotti are designed as dipping cookies for coffee, but they can be dipped in just about everything, including a glass of red wine! Italian mothers leave out the nuts when making these for their babies to teethe on.

2½ cups all-purpose flour
1 cup sugar
Egg substitute equivalent to 2 eggs, or 2 eggs
⅓ cup whole almonds or hazelnuts (about 4 ounces)
1 teaspoon baking soda
Pinch of salt
Egg substitute equivalent to 1 egg, or 1 egg, beaten

Serves 20; 2 cookies per serving

Nutrient Analysis (per serving)

Calories 113
Protein 3 g
Carbohydrate 23 g
Cholesterol 0 mg
Sodium 76 mg
Total fat 1 g
  Saturated 0 g
  Polyunsaturated 0 g
  Monounsaturated 1 g

Preheat oven to 350° F.

Place the flour in a medium mixing bowl and make a well in the center. Add the remaining ingredients except the egg substitute equivalent to 1 egg and stir into the flour. When the dough gets too stiff to stir, use your hands to work in the rest of the flour until thoroughly combined.

Divide the dough into quarters and roll each piece into a log about 1 inch thick. Place 2 rolls on each of 2 baking sheets lined with baking parchment. Brush the dough with the beaten egg substitute. Bake for about 30 minutes, or until lightly browned.

Leave oven on. Remove the rolls from the baking sheets and cut into ½-inch slices while still warm and pliable. Return the slices to the baking sheets. Bake for 10 minutes, or until cookies are crisp and golden brown. Cool completely on wire racks and store in an airtight container. Biscotti keep well for several weeks.

COOK'S TIP: You can crush or even grind the nuts to vary the texture.

Cannoli Cream

A dollop of this dessert cream on a bowl of fresh fruit or as a dip for fresh strawberries is the perfect summer treat. Layer the creamy mixture and the fruit in pretty parfait glasses for a change. Save some of the fruit to use as a garnish or try some Candied Citrus Peel (recipe below).

2 cups nonfat ricotta cheese
½ cup powdered sugar
2 teaspoons vanilla
¼ cup mini chocolate chips
3 cups berries or sliced fruit
Candied Citrus Peel, for garnish (optional)
  (recipe follows)

Using an electric mixer or in the work bowl of a food processor fitted with a metal blade, whip the ricotta cheese until fluffy. Beat in powdered sugar and vanilla. Whip until smooth and light. Stir in the chocolate chips.

Place fruit in a serving bowl and spoon the dessert cream over all. Garnish with candied citrus peel, if desired.

Candied Citrus Peel

Citrus fruits, any variety
Sugar

With a small, sharp knife, trim off the ends of the fruits and make 4 deep vertical cuts in the skins, cutting through to the fruit. Peel off the skin and trim away as much of the bitter pith as possible. Cut the skin into narrow strips.

In a small saucepan, cover the citrus strips with cold water and bring to a boil over high heat. Reduce heat and simmer for 5 minutes. Drain and

Serves 4; ½ cup cannoli cream plus ¾ cup fruit per serving

Nutrient Analysis (per serving)*

Calories 219
Protein 14 g
Carbohydrate 33 g
Cholesterol 1 mg
Sodium 423 mg
Total fat 4 g
  Saturated 2 g
  Polyunsaturated 0 g
  Monounsaturated 1 g
*Without optional Candied Citrus Peel

return the citrus strips to the pan. Cover with cold water and repeat the blanching process 2 more times.

Drain the citrus strips and return them to the saucepan. Sprinkle the drained, softened strips with just enough sugar to cover and enough water to just dissolve the sugar. Bring to a boil over high heat, then reduce the heat to maintain a gentle boil until the strips are glazed and translucent, about 10 minutes. Do not let the sugar caramelize; if it starts to turn brown, remove pan from the heat immediately.

Remove the strips with a fork and place on a rack to dry overnight. If you like, roll the dried strips in sugar. Keeps for months in an airtight container.

COOK'S TIP: Nibble some of the extra citrus strips with espresso and biscotti (page 27). For a holiday treat, dip the strips in chocolate if your food plan allows the extra fat.

Tiramisù

The name tiramisù *means "pick me up," and this version of Venice's favorite dessert will certainly lift your spirits. Not only are you getting a rich-tasting classic dessert, but you don't have to worry about skyrocketing fat grams.*

6 ounces light cream cheese
6 ounces nonfat cream cheese
⅓ cup sugar
2 tablespoons skim milk
10 ladyfingers
½ cup strong coffee or espresso, chilled
2 tablespoons dark rum or ½ teaspoon rum extract
1 tablespoon unsweetened cocoa powder
Grated semisweet chocolate (optional)

Serves 6; ½ cup per serving

Nutrient Analysis (per serving)

Calories 181
Protein 8 g
Carbohydrate 22 g
Cholesterol 32 mg
Sodium 342 mg
Total fat 6 g
  Saturated 4 g
  Polyunsaturated 0 g
  Monounsaturated 2 g

In a medium mixing bowl, beat the cream cheeses and sugar with an electric mixer until well combined. Add milk and beat for 2 to 3 minutes, or until mixture is light and fluffy.

Break ladyfingers into bite-size pieces and arrange half in a 1½-quart glass bowl. Stir together coffee and rum. Drizzle half the coffee mixture over ladyfingers. Spoon half of the cream cheese mixture on top; smooth with the back of a spoon or a metal spatula. Sprinkle with half the cocoa powder. Repeat layers.

Cover and chill for 2 to 24 hours before serving. Spoon tiramisù into dessert dishes and garnish each serving with grated chocolate, if desired.

COOK'S TIP: Ladyfingers are small, spongy cookies that readily absorb liquid. Look for them in the frozen-foods area of your supermarket or in gourmet shops.

For a different taste, substitute 18 coarsely crumbled vanilla wafers for the ladyfingers. Since vanilla wafers do not absorb liquid as easily as the ladyfingers, reduce the coffee to $1/3$ cup.

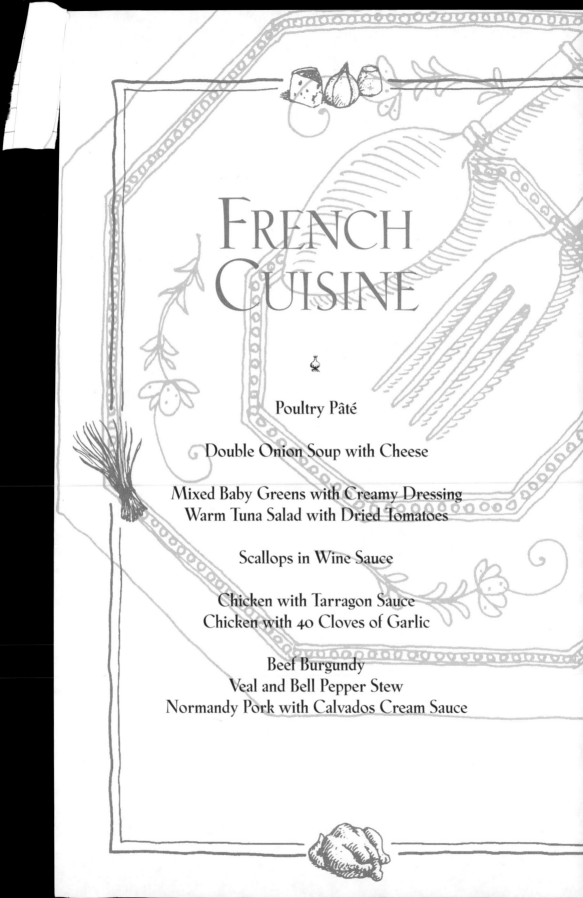

French Cuisine

Poultry Pâté

Double Onion Soup with Cheese

Mixed Baby Greens with Creamy Dressing
Warm Tuna Salad with Dried Tomatoes

Scallops in Wine Sauce

Chicken with Tarragon Sauce
Chicken with 40 Cloves of Garlic

Beef Burgundy
Veal and Bell Pepper Stew
Normandy Pork with Calvados Cream Sauce

Vegetable Quiche in Brown Rice Crust
Watercress–Cheese Soufflé
Meatless Cassoulet

Roasted Asparagus with Dijon Vinaigrette
Young Minted Peas with Radicchio

Crêpes Suzette with Raspberries
Chocolate–Strawberry Meringue Shells

Surely the most celebrated of all cuisines comes from France, where cooking is looked upon as a fine art. And what an art form it is! Consider such masterpieces as an airy soufflé, a hearty coq au vin, a colorful ratatouille, or a rich, silky mousse. To appreciate these "works of art," it helps to know how the foods of France evolved.

France is the home of classic, nouvelle, and provincial cooking. Classic cuisine (also called haute or grande cuisine) is the oldest of these forms of cooking. Sauces are the hallmark of this cuisine. Classic French cooking is based on five sauces and the meticulous preparation of each dish. You're likely to find classic French cooking today in the sophisticated restaurants throughout France. Everything must be cooked perfectly—never undercooked or overcooked. Hot dishes must be served hot, not warm, and cold dishes must be served cold, not cool. Raw food is rarely served except in salads. Menus are carefully planned, taking into consideration the flavors, textures, temperatures, and visual appeal of the dishes featured. Serving the food in classic French cooking is just as important as the food itself. The carefully prepared food should be served in small portions, never piled unattractively on a plate. These exhaustive details might leave you thinking that the French are food snobs. Not so. They believe these details are important to do justice to the food they dearly love.

France's nouvelle cuisine (new cookery) is a lighter, more contemporary version of classic cuisine. This new way of cooking is inventive, with a simple presentation, light sauces, and often exotic ingredients.

Provincial cooking (also called French country cooking or cuisine bourgeois) is the wonderful, soul-satisfying cooking of the home, bistro, and café. It relies on local ingredients and simple recipes. It requires no highly technical cooking skills or rigid recipes. Instead, provincial cooking is based on indigenous seasonal foods that are prepared to suit the tastes of the cook. Aptly named the people's cuisine, it features long-simmered stews, fricassees, and simple pastries.

To understand the foods of France, you must understand its regional flavors. France boasts more fertile soil in temperate regions than any other European country. It produces a remarkable variety of foods: butter, cream, poultry, lamb, veal, fruits, and vegetables. An abundance of fresh fish and other seafood comes from the Mediterranean, the Atlantic, the English Channel, and the North Sea.

A Culinary Tour de France

The first stop on our city-by-city tour of French cuisine is Paris, the City of Light, where the first restaurant opened in 1765. Since then, Paris has been awash with restaurants, bistros, and cafés that serve everything from classic duck à l'orange to home-style onion soup. Paris, the melting pot of French cooking, is a gathering place for world-class chefs and gourmets.

Normandy, on the northern coast of France, is overflowing with cattle and apple orchards. The Normans' dairy cattle produce the rich milk and cream fundamental to their cooking. One of Normandy's most famous products is Camembert cheese. Coastal Normandy is famous for its Dover sole.

Brittany, a province on the northwest coast, gets its riches from the sea. The cooks of Brittany, who prepare simple, hearty fare, are credited with the invention of the crepe.

The most famous product from Champagne is, of course, the bubbly beverage that goes by the same name. But this flatland of northern France also grows potatoes, beets, grains, cabbage, and garlic, and sheep graze on its pastures.

Burgundy, considered by some to be the true seat of French gastronomy, uses poultry, beef, root vegetables, cream, cheese, snails, black currants, morels, wild game, and freshwater fish in its cooking. The liberal use of garlic, Dijon mustard, lard, thick cream, and the region's famous wine makes cooking in this region robust.

Inland around Lyons is an area blessed with the best chickens in France, and perhaps the world. Local markets offer a selection of potatoes, onions, salad greens, cheeses from both goat's and cow's milk, fruits, beef, poultry, game, and freshwater fish. Chicken or fish prepared in the Lyonnaise manner often sports a dash of vinegar.

A Year in Provence

In Provence in southern France, olive trees flourish in the warm sunshine and influence the cooking. Like cooks in other areas that border the Mediterranean, the cooks of Provence prefer to use olive oil, olives, garlic, tomatoes, saffron, sweet and hot peppers, and herbs. Fish stews, such as bouillabaisse, are popular here.

The Basque country, which borders Spain, and the Alsace-Lorraine area, which borders Germany, are strongly influenced by the cooking of their neighbors. Those French cooks prepare meals much the same way their ancestors did centuries ago. Like the Spanish, the Basques specialize in fish and seafood, Bayonne ham, mutton, and goat dishes that are flavored with onions, tomatoes, and red peppers. The Alsatians use geese, beer, cabbage, Brussels sprouts, and root vegetables in their cooking. They also eat large amounts of pork—roasted, salted, smoked for bacon, or formed into sausages.

Thanks to the sea, rivers, forested mountains, and grassy plains, cooks in Bordeaux are never without fresh fish, game, and produce. Many local specialties use the renowned Bordeaux wines as a cooking liquid.

Then there is Périgord, the region of the truffle and foie gras. The cooking here incorporates poultry, mushrooms, goat cheese, game, and fresh fish.

Auvergne, located in central France, suffers from long, cold winters. For this reason, the local cooks favor a hearty cuisine emphasizing soups, stews, and casseroles. They use local grains, cherries, peaches, apricots, nuts, salted hams, dried sausages, and many varieties of cheese.

Cooking à la Heart

French cooking sounds rich, doesn't it? So how does this cuisine fit into a heart-healthy eating plan? Easily, as long as you're eating the revised French fare you'll find in this chapter. Try the tempting example of coquilles Saint-Jacques (Scallops in Wine Sauce, page 44) or sample the provincial French recipes, such as Meatless Cassoulet on page 58 or Veal and Bell Pepper Stew, page 52. Starting with the first recipe, you'll be able to appreciate fine French cooking without sabotaging your heart's good health.

Poultry Pâté

Pâté de Poulet

This smooth pâté is made with ground chicken breast and just a touch of liver to give it the proper taste and texture. Serve with nonfat crackers or melba toast and sparkling water or a crisp white wine.

1 pound ground skinless chicken breast or turkey breast
Vegetable oil spray
$\frac{1}{2}$ cup chopped onion (about 1 medium)
1 clove garlic, crushed or minced
2 ounces chicken livers, coarsely cut and connective tissue removed (3 tablespoons)
$\frac{1}{2}$ cup evaporated skim milk
2 egg whites
2 tablespoons plain dry bread crumbs
2 teaspoons cornstarch
$\frac{1}{2}$ teaspoon ground sage
$\frac{1}{2}$ teaspoon salt
$\frac{1}{8}$ teaspoon black pepper
Vegetable oil spray
2 large lettuce leaves
Fresh sage (optional)

Cook the ground chicken in a medium nonstick skillet over medium heat for 5 minutes, or until no longer pink. Place in a colander and rinse with hot water. Drain well and set aside. Wipe skillet with a paper towel and spray with vegetable oil spray. Sauté onion and garlic over medium heat for 3 minutes, stirring occasionally. Return cooked chicken to skillet with the onions and garlic and add the chicken livers. Cook for 3 minutes over medium heat, or until livers are done. Let cool for 5 minutes.

Transfer the chicken mixture to a blender or to the work bowl of a food processor fitted with a metal blade. Add the milk. Cover and process until

Serves 32; 2 tablespoons per serving

Nutrient Analysis (per serving)

Calories 26
Protein 4 g
Carbohydrate 1 g
Cholesterol 15 mg
Sodium 56 mg
Total fat 0 g
 Saturated 0 g
 Polyunsaturated 0 g
 Monounsaturated 0 g

well combined. Add the egg whites, bread crumbs, cornstarch, ground sage, salt, and pepper. Cover and process until well combined.

Preheat oven to 325° F. Spray a $7\frac{1}{2} \times 3\frac{1}{2} \times 2$-inch or an $8 \times 4 \times 3$-inch loaf pan with vegetable oil spray. Spoon chicken mixture into loaf pan. Cover with foil and place in a shallow baking pan. Pour hot water around loaf pan to a depth of $\frac{1}{2}$ inch.

Bake for $1\frac{1}{4}$ to $1\frac{1}{2}$ hours, or until a knife inserted near the center comes out clean. Let cool. Cover and chill for 2 to 24 hours.

To serve, unmold pâté onto a lettuce-lined serving plate. Garnish with fresh sage, if desired.

COOK'S TIP ON GROUND POULTRY: Prepackaged ground poultry may include high-fat skin, so ask your butcher to grind a package of boneless, skinless chicken or turkey breasts for you.

Double Onion Soup with Cheese

Soupe à l'oignon Gratiné

This classic soup, one of France's best-known specialties, comes from the picturesque Burgundy and Lyons regions. Don't rush this soup—the key to its authentic flavor lies in slow cooking the onions until they turn amber. The sugar helps to caramelize and brown the onions even more.

Vegetable oil spray
1 teaspoon acceptable margarine
2 cups thinly sliced yellow onions (about 2 medium)
1 cup thinly sliced red onion (about 1 medium)
3 cloves garlic, crushed or minced
½ teaspoon sugar
4 cups low-sodium chicken broth
2 tablespoons dry sherry or white wine vinegar
1 tablespoon Worcestershire sauce
½ teaspoon salt
2 tablespoons shredded part-skim mozzarella cheese
2 tablespoons grated or shredded Parmesan cheese
1 teaspoon chopped fresh oregano or ¼ teaspoon dried oregano, crumbled
Black pepper to taste
4 slices French bread, lightly toasted

Spray a large saucepan with vegetable oil spray. Add margarine and melt over medium-low heat. Add yellow and red onions. Cook for about 20 minutes, or until yellow onions are tender and light brown, stirring occasionally. Add garlic and sugar. Increase heat to medium and cook for 5 minutes, stirring occasionally.

Stir in chicken broth, sherry, Worcestershire sauce, and salt. Bring to a boil, reduce heat, and simmer, covered, for 20 minutes.

Serves 4; 1 cup per serving

Nutrient Analysis (per serving)

Calories 180
Protein 8 g
Carbohydrate 27 g
Cholesterol 4 mg
Sodium 611 mg
Total fat 4 g
  Saturated 2 g
  Polyunsaturated 1 g
  Monounsaturated 1 g

Meanwhile, preheat broiler.

In a small mixing bowl, toss together the remaining ingredients except bread. Sprinkle cheese mixture evenly on toasted bread. When soup is almost done, place bread on the unheated rack of a broiler pan. Broil about 4 inches from the heat for 1 to 2 minutes, or until cheese melts and turns light brown.

To serve, ladle soup into bowls and top each serving with a bread slice.

Mixed Baby Greens with Creamy Dressing

Mesclun avec Vinaigrette à la Crème

I n France, mesclun, or a mixture of baby greens, is
taken from the first cuttings of a summer garden.
If your grocery store produce department or local
market doesn't carry mesclun, you can use any
mixture of fresh salad greens. This recipe may not
seem to make much dressing for the amount of
greens, but it's enough to coat the greens nicely. Too
much dressing can wilt a good salad.

**6 cups mixed baby greens or desired salad greens,
torn into bite-size pieces**
**2 tablespoons white wine vinegar or tarragon
vinegar**
2 tablespoons olive oil (extra-virgin preferred)
2 tablespoons low-sodium chicken broth
**1 tablespoon minced fresh herbs (such as basil,
dill, chives, or marjoram)**
1 tablespoon nonfat or low-fat sour cream

Place baby greens in a salad bowl. Cover with
plastic wrap and chill until serving time.

For the dressing, combine the remaining ingredients, except sour cream, in a jar with a tight-
fitting lid. Cover and shake until well combined.
Add sour cream. Cover and shake well. Dressing
can be chilled, covered, until serving time or used
right away.

Before serving, drizzle dressing over greens. Toss
gently until well coated. Serve immediately.

COOK'S TIP: Even if you're not serving 8
people, go ahead and make the entire amount of
dressing and use only what you need. You can
refrigerate the remaining dressing in the jar for up
to 3 days. Shake dressing well before using.

Serves 8; ¾ cup
per serving

Nutrient
Analysis
(per serving)

Calories 41
Protein 1 g
Carbohydrate 2 g
Cholesterol 0 mg
Sodium 36 mg
Total fat 4 g
  Saturated 0 g
  Polyunsaturated 0 g
  Monounsaturated 3 g

Warm Tuna Salad with Dried Tomatoes

Salade Niçoise

This well-known potato-and-tuna salad originated in the region of Provence. Our warm, low-fat version features robust dried tomatoes that soften while the potatoes and green beans cook.

¾ pound small red potatoes, cut into bite-size pieces

8 ounces haricots verts or fresh green beans, trimmed and cut into 1-inch pieces

⅓ cup small dried tomatoes

1 pound tuna or swordfish steaks

Vegetable oil spray

2 tablespoons fresh orange juice

2 tablespoons fresh lemon juice

1 tablespoon low-sodium chicken broth

1 teaspoon brown sugar

1 teaspoon olive oil

1 teaspoon anchovy paste

1 clove garlic, crushed or minced

¼ teaspoon dried thyme, crumbled

4 cups torn Boston or Bibb lettuce

Serves 6; 1½ cups per serving

Nutrient Analysis (per serving)

Calories 184
Protein 17 g
Carbohydrate 18 g
Cholesterol 45 mg
Sodium 129 mg
Total fat 5 g
 Saturated 1 g
 Polyunsaturated 1 g
 Monounsaturated 2 g

Bring a medium saucepan of water to a boil over high heat. Add potatoes, haricots verts, and tomatoes. Reduce heat and simmer, covered, for 15 to 20 minutes, or until potatoes are just tender. Drain.

Meanwhile, rinse fish and pat dry with paper towels. Cut fish into ½-inch cubes. Spray a medium skillet with vegetable oil spray and place over medium-high heat. Cook fish for 2 to 4 minutes, or until tender, stirring gently.

In a large mixing bowl, combine warm potatoes, haricots verts, and cooked fish. Coarsely chop tomatoes and add to potato mixture.

Wipe skillet clean and add the remaining ingredients except lettuce. Bring to a boil over high heat, stirring constantly. Remove from heat. Pour over tuna mixture and toss gently to coat. To serve warm, spoon tuna mixture over lettuce; to serve chilled, cover and refrigerate the tuna mixture separately from the lettuce. Before serving, toss tuna mixture and spoon over lettuce.

COOK'S TIP ON GREEN BEANS: When choosing green beans, avoid those that are bulging or leathery or that have brown spots.

Scallops in Wine Sauce

Coquilles Saint-Jacques

This creamy scallop dish is a classic along the French coastline, where shellfish are abundant. It is typically served in individual coquille shells, which are available at some gourmet shops. Or simply serve it in au gratin dishes or custard cups.

1 pound bay or sea scallops
Vegetable oil spray
1 teaspoon acceptable margarine
1 cup chopped chanterelle, shiitake, porcini, oyster, or button mushrooms or a combination (about 3 ounces)
1 medium leek, top removed, leaving about 1 inch of green, rinsed well and sliced
2 cloves garlic, minced
1 tablespoon all-purpose flour
5-ounce can evaporated skim milk
3 tablespoons dry white wine or nonalcoholic white wine
1 teaspoon chopped fresh herbs (thyme, tarragon, oregano, or a combination) or $1/4$ teaspoon dried, crumbled
$1/2$ cup plain soft bread crumbs (about 2 slices)
Paprika

Serves 4; $1/2$ cup per serving

Nutrient Analysis (per serving)

Calories 247
Protein 31 g
Carbohydrate 22 g
Cholesterol 38 mg
Sodium 478 mg
Total fat 3 g
 Saturated 1 g
 Polyunsaturated 1 g
 Monounsaturated 1 g

Place scallops in a colander and rinse to remove any grit. If using sea scallops, cut into $1/2$-inch pieces. Place scallops in a medium saucepan of boiling water. Return to boiling; reduce heat. Simmer, covered, for 1 to 2 minutes, or until scallops turn opaque. Drain and set aside.

Spray a large skillet with vegetable oil spray and place over medium heat. Melt margarine. Cook mushrooms, leek, and garlic in skillet for 5 to 7 minutes, or until tender, stirring occasionally. Stir in flour.

Preheat oven to 400° F.

Add milk to mushroom mixture. Cook over medium heat for about 5 minutes, or until thickened and bubbly, stirring occasionally. Cook and stir for 1 minute. Stir in scallops, wine, and herbs. Remove from heat.

Spoon scallop mixture into 4 coquille shells, au gratin dishes, or 6-ounce custard cups. Sprinkle bread crumbs over scallop mixture. Sprinkle with paprika. Place containers in a shallow baking pan.

Bake, uncovered, for 7 to 9 minutes, or until crumbs brown. Serve warm.

COOK'S TIP ON SOFT BREAD CRUMBS: It's easy to make soft bread crumbs. Tear the bread, with or without crusts, into bite-size pieces and place in a blender or the work bowl of a food processor fitted with a metal blade. Process until pulverized into crumbs.

A handy way to keep from wasting leftover bread is to freeze extra crumbs in an airtight plastic bag. Use crumbs straight from the freezer.

Chicken with Tarragon Sauce

Fricassée de Poulet

When you cook chicken and make a creamy sauce from the cooking liquid, you've made a fricassée. The French like to use whole birds when making this dish. Our version uses low-fat, fast-cooking chicken breasts, yet yields rich and creamy results. Serve with cooked noodles, pasta, or rice and your favorite steamed vegetables.

4 boneless, skinless chicken breast halves (about 4 ounces each), all visible fat removed
Vegetable oil spray
10½-ounce can low-sodium chicken broth
½ cup sliced onion (about 1 small)
½ cup sliced celery (about 1 stalk)
2 slices lemon
1 bay leaf
½ teaspoon dried tarragon, crumbled
¼ teaspoon salt
⅛ teaspoon black pepper, or to taste
1 tablespoon all-purpose flour
5-ounce can evaporated skim milk
2 tablespoons chopped fresh parsley

Rinse chicken and pat dry with paper towels. Spray vegetable oil spray in a large skillet. Place over medium-high heat. Brown chicken in hot skillet for 2 minutes on each side. Remove chicken from skillet and set aside.

Add broth, onion, celery, lemon, bay leaf, tarragon, salt, and pepper to skillet. Bring to a boil over high heat. Return chicken to skillet. Reduce heat and simmer, covered, for 10 minutes, or until chicken is tender and no longer pink inside. With a slotted spoon, transfer chicken and vegetables to a warm platter. Discard lemon and bay leaf.

Measure out ¾ cup chicken broth mixture; discard the rest. Place flour in a small bowl. Add about 2 tablespoons reserved broth, stirring until

Serves 4; 1 breast half and ¼ cup sauce per serving

Nutrient Analysis (per serving)

Calories 190
Protein 29 g
Carbohydrate 9 g
Cholesterol 63 mg
Sodium 279 mg
Total fat 4 g
  Saturated 1 g
  Polyunsaturated 1 g
  Monounsaturated 1 g

smooth. Whisk in the milk. Return mixture to skillet. Cook over medium heat until thickened and bubbly, about 6 to 9 minutes. Stir in parsley.

Return chicken and vegetables to skillet and spoon sauce over until well coated. Heat over low heat for 1 minute and serve.

Chicken with 40 Cloves of Garlic

Poulet aux Quarante Gousses d'Ail

Don't worry! As the chicken cooks, so does the garlic, rendering a sweet flavor and soft texture. Be sure to save the garlic to spread on crusty bread, which makes a nice accompaniment to the chicken.

3 pounds chicken pieces (breasts, thighs, and drumsticks), skinned, all visible fat removed
40 cloves garlic, separated from head and unpeeled (3 to 4 heads)
Vegetable oil spray
$\frac{1}{2}$ cup dry white wine or low-sodium chicken broth
$1\frac{1}{2}$ teaspoons chopped fresh thyme or $\frac{1}{2}$ teaspoon dried thyme, crumbled
About $\frac{1}{3}$ cup low-sodium chicken broth, if needed
$\frac{1}{4}$ cup low-sodium chicken broth or water
2 tablespoons all-purpose flour

Serves 6

Nutrient
Analysis*
(per serving)

Calories 234
Protein 34 g
Carbohydrate 9 g
Cholesterol 87 mg
Sodium 89 mg
Total fat 6 g
  Saturated 2 g
  Polyunsaturated 1 g
  Monounsaturated 2 g
Assuming no extra chicken broth was added

Rinse chicken pieces and pat dry with paper towels. Set aside.

Place cloves of garlic in a medium saucepan. Add enough water to cover garlic. Bring to a boil over high heat. Reduce heat and simmer, covered, for 10 minutes; drain. Set aside.

Preheat oven to 325° F.

Spray a Dutch oven with vegetable oil spray. Place over medium-high heat. Add chicken to hot Dutch oven and brown on all sides, turning chicken as necessary. This should take about 7 to 10 minutes.

Add wine, thyme, and garlic to Dutch oven. Bring to a boil over high heat. Bake, covered, for 40 to 45 minutes, or until chicken is tender and no longer pink on the inside.

Transfer chicken and garlic to a serving platter and keep warm. Measure cooking liquid. Add enough chicken broth, if necessary, to measure 1 cup. Return liquid to Dutch oven, bring to a boil over high heat, and reduce heat to medium. Stir together $\frac{1}{4}$ cup broth and the flour. Add to liquid in Dutch oven. Cook and stir constantly until thickened and bubbly, about 3 to 5 minutes. Cook and stir 1 minute more. Spoon over chicken.

COOK'S TIP: Although the classic French dish uses 40 cloves of garlic, you may prefer to use only 1 or 2 heads. Less garlic won't significantly alter the flavor of the recipe.

Beef Burgundy

Boeuf Bourguignonne

This rich, hearty stew is one of Burgundy's most famous dishes. Now that wild mushrooms are more readily available, give them a try. Their exotic flavors add that extra touch of sophistication.

3 slices turkey bacon, chopped (optional)
1 pound round steak, all visible fat removed, cut into ½-inch cubes
1 cup chopped onion (about 2 medium)
4 large cloves garlic, peeled and left whole
1 tablespoon acceptable margarine
2 tablespoons all-purpose flour
½ cup water
1½ cups dry red wine or nonalcoholic red wine
1 cup low-sodium beef broth, plus more if needed
1 cup coarsely chopped carrots (about 1½ medium)
1 cup frozen pearl onions (about 4 ounces)
8 ounces chanterelle, shiitake, or button mushrooms, or a combination (coarsely chop any large mushrooms)
¼ cup Cognac or brandy (optional)
1 tablespoon dark brown sugar
1 tablespoon no-salt-added tomato paste
1 teaspoon dried rosemary, crushed using mortar and pestle
4 teaspoons chopped fresh thyme (optional)

Preheat oven to 350° F.

In an ovenproof Dutch oven, cook bacon over medium heat for 5 minutes, stirring occasionally. Remove from Dutch oven and set aside.

Increase heat to medium-high. Brown beef in Dutch oven, half at a time, until brown on all sides, about 5 to 7 minutes per batch. Remove meat from Dutch oven and set aside. Reduce heat to medium and add onion, garlic, and margarine. Cook for 5 minutes, stirring often. Stir in flour.

Serves 4; 1 cup per serving

Nutrient Analysis (per serving)

Calories 269
Protein 26 g
Carbohydrate 21 g
Cholesterol 60 mg
Sodium 126 mg
Total fat 7 g
  Saturated 2 g
  Polyunsaturated 1 g
  Monounsaturated 3 g

Add turkey bacon, browned beef, and remaining ingredients except thyme. Bring to a boil over high heat. Remove from heat. Bake, covered, about $1\frac{1}{2}$ hours, or until meat is tender, stirring occasionally and adding more beef broth, if necessary. Garnish each serving with chopped thyme, if desired.

COOK'S TIP ON TOMATO PASTE: What do you do when you need only a small amount of tomato paste and don't want to waste what remains in the can? Freeze the rest in tablespoon-size batches on waxed paper or in the compartments of an ice tray. Then store them in a freezer bag for up to 4 months. Any time you need more, just reach into your freezer.

Veal and Bell Pepper Stew

Soupe de Veau et Poivrons

I n France, this veal stew would be made with spicy espelette peppers, which are grown along the Spanish border. This version uses colorful bell peppers and cayenne to simulate their flavor.

Vegetable oil spray
1 small red bell pepper, chopped
1 small yellow bell pepper, chopped
$1/2$ cup chopped onion (about 1 medium)
2 cloves garlic, minced
1 pound veal or pork tenderloin, all visible fat
    removed, cut into $1/2$-inch cubes
1 tablespoon all-purpose flour
2 $10^1/2$-ounce cans low-sodium chicken broth
1 teaspoon grated orange zest
$1/2$ teaspoon ground coriander
$1/2$ teaspoon salt
$1/8$ to $1/4$ teaspoon cayenne

Serves 4; $1\frac{1}{4}$ cups per serving

Nutrient Analysis (per serving)

Calories 147
Protein 20 g
Carbohydrate 6 g
Cholesterol 72 mg
Sodium 386 mg
Total fat 5 g
    Saturated 2 g
    Polyunsaturated 0 g
    Monounsaturated 2 g

Spray a Dutch oven with vegetable oil spray. Cook bell peppers, onion, and garlic over medium heat for 10 minutes, or until tender, stirring occasionally. Remove from Dutch oven.

Increase heat to medium-high. Brown the veal, half at a time, stirring occasionally. Each batch will take about 5 minutes. Return all veal to Dutch oven and stir in flour.

Stir cooked vegetables and remaining ingredients into veal mixture. Bring to a boil over high heat. Reduce heat and simmer, covered, for 20 minutes, or until veal is tender.

COOK'S TIP ON FREEZING BELL PEP-PERS: You can freeze bell peppers for 6 to 8 months. Seed and chop the peppers (you do not need to blanch them) and place them in an airtight plastic bag. They are best used in cooked dishes, since they tend to lose their crispness when frozen.

Normandy Pork with Calvados Cream Sauce

Porc à la Normande

Pork tenderloin and evaporated skim milk cut down on the fat but leave the flavor in this dish.

Serves 4; 3 ounces pork and 2 tablespoons sauce per serving

1 pound pork tenderloin, all visible fat removed, cut into 1-inch-thick slices
Vegetable oil spray
2 teaspoons acceptable margarine
¹/₃ cup sliced green onions (about 4)
2 cloves garlic, crushed or minced
¹/₄ cup Calvados, other apple brandy, or unsweetened apple juice
¹/₄ teaspoon salt
¹/₈ teaspoon black pepper
5 ounces evaporated skim milk
1 teaspoon chopped fresh thyme or ¹/₄ teaspoon dried thyme, crumbled
Fresh thyme for garnish (optional)

Nutrient Analysis (per serving)

Calories 245
Protein 29 g
Carbohydrate 11 g
Cholesterol 73 mg
Sodium 271 mg
Total fat 6 g
  Saturated 2 g
  Polyunsaturated 1 g
  Monounsaturated 3 g

Place pork between 2 sheets of plastic wrap. Use a meat mallet to pound pork to ¹/₄-inch thickness.

Spray a large skillet with vegetable oil spray and place over medium-high heat. Add pork in a single layer to hot skillet and cook for about 2 minutes on each side, or until tender. Transfer to a serving plate and keep warm.

In the same skillet, melt margarine. Add green onions and cook over medium heat for 1 minute, stirring constantly. Add garlic and cook for 1 minute, continuing to stir. Remove skillet from heat. Stir in Calvados, salt, and pepper. Return skillet to heat. Cook and stir over medium heat, scraping up browned bits. Stir in milk and thyme. Simmer, uncovered, for 2 minutes, or until slightly thickened, stirring often.

To serve, spoon sauce over pork. Garnish with fresh thyme, if desired.

Vegetable Quiche in Brown Rice Crust

A classic French quiche is a rich cheese custard tart that originated in Alsace and Lorraine. This lightened version is brimming with vegetables and herbs, making it a perfect one-dish meal for brunch, lunch, or dinner. A low-fat feature: its nutty-tasting brown rice crust.

1½ cups water
¾ cup brown rice
1 small or ½ medium yellow summer squash
2 medium Italian plum tomatoes
1 large green onion
2 cloves garlic or 1 teaspoon prepared minced garlic
Vegetable oil spray
1 egg white
¼ teaspoon salt
Egg substitute equivalent to 2 eggs, or 2 eggs
1 cup evaporated skim milk
¼ teaspoon salt
⅛ teaspoon black pepper
2 tablespoons chopped fresh basil or dill, or 1 teaspoon dried basil, crumbled, or dried dill weed
2 tablespoons grated or shredded Parmesan cheese

Serves 6; 1 wedge per serving

Nutrient Analysis (per serving)

Calories 155
Protein 9 g
Carbohydrate 27 g
Cholesterol 3 mg
Sodium 319 mg
Total fat 2 g
  Saturated 1 g
  Polyunsaturated 0 g
  Monounsaturated 0 g

Place water in a small saucepan and bring to a boil over high heat. Add rice and stir. Return to boiling. Reduce heat and simmer, covered, for 35 to 40 minutes, or until rice is tender and liquid is absorbed.

Meanwhile, chop or slice squash. Cut tomatoes in half, scoop out juice and seeds with a spoon, then chop. Slice green onion and mince garlic. (You should have about ½ cup squash, ½ cup tomatoes, 2 tablespoons green onion, and 1 teaspoon garlic.) Set tomatoes aside.

Preheat oven to 450° F.

Spray a medium skillet and a 9-inch quiche dish or pie pan with vegetable oil spray. Sauté squash, green onion, and garlic in skillet over medium-low heat for 5 minutes, or until crisp-tender, stirring occasionally.

In a small mixing bowl, stir together cooked rice, egg white, and ¼ teaspoon salt. Press mixture onto the bottom and up the sides of quiche dish. Bake, uncovered, for 5 minutes. Remove from oven and reduce oven temperature to 325° F.

In a medium mixing bowl, stir together egg substitute, milk, ¼ teaspoon salt, and pepper. Stir in cooked vegetable mixture, tomatoes, and basil.

Pour egg mixture into hot rice crust. Sprinkle with Parmesan cheese. Bake for 35 to 40 minutes, or until a knife inserted near the center comes out clean. Let stand 10 minutes before cutting. To serve, cut into 6 wedges.

COOK'S TIP ON STORING FRESH HERBS: To store leftover fresh basil, place sprigs in a small vase or jar with water and keep at room temperature for several days. To store other fresh herbs, such as chives, tarragon, or mint, wrap in damp paper towels, place in a plastic bag, and refrigerate, tightly sealed, for 2 to 3 days.

Watercress–Cheese Soufflé

Cresson du Fromage Soufflé

The soufflé is probably the most famous creation to emerge from French cooking. It is light and airy and makes a stunning addition to any meal. This main-dish soufflé is made with nonfat egg substitute and gets its richness from evaporated skim milk and low-fat cheese. Watercress, a staple in French cooking, adds a peppery tang and pretty flecks of green color to the soufflé.

3 tablespoons acceptable margarine
¼ cup all-purpose flour
12-ounce can evaporated skim milk
1 cup shredded low-fat sharp Cheddar cheese
¼ cup coarsely chopped watercress, cilantro, or parsley
Egg substitute equivalent to 3 eggs
6 egg whites

Preheat oven to 350° F.

In a small saucepan, melt margarine over medium heat. Stir in flour. Add milk all at once. Cook and stir until thickened and bubbly, about 10 minutes. Remove from heat.

Add cheese and stir until melted. Stir in watercress. Place egg substitute in a medium mixing bowl. Slowly add cheese sauce to egg substitute, stirring constantly. Let cool slightly, about 5 minutes.

Place egg whites in a separate medium mixing bowl and beat with an electric mixer until stiff peaks form (tips stand straight). Using a rubber spatula, gently fold about 2 cups of the beaten egg whites into the cheese sauce.

Gradually pour cheese sauce over remaining beaten egg whites, gently folding to combine. Pour into an ungreased 2-quart soufflé dish. Bake for about 50 minutes, or until a knife inserted near the center comes out clean. Serve immediately.

Serves 6; 1 cup per serving

Nutrient Analysis (per serving)

Calories 202
Protein 17 g
Carbohydrate 13 g
Cholesterol 12 mg
Sodium 347 mg
Total fat 9 g
    Saturated 3 g
    Polyunsaturated 2 g
    Monounsaturated 3 g

COOK'S TIP: Do not substitute nonfat cheese for the low-fat cheese in this soufflé. Nonfat cheese will not melt satisfactorily when added to the thickened sauce.

COOK'S TIP ON SOUFFLÉ DISHES: You can use a 1½-quart soufflé dish for this recipe, but be sure to place a foil collar around the outside of the dish. To do this, measure enough foil to wrap around the dish with a few inches to spare. The foil needs to extend 2 inches above the top when folded into thirds lengthwise. Lightly spray one side of foil with vegetable oil spray. With oiled side in, position foil around dish, letting it extend above the top. Fasten with tape. After removing baked soufflé from oven, gently peel off foil.

Meatless Cassoulet

Cassoulet

A typical French cassoulet, named after an earthenware pot called a cassole, is a stew of white beans and meat. There are as many versions of this stew as there are cooks who make it. This unique version preserves the superb flavor of the stew yet omits the high-fat meats that are commonly used.

8 ounces dried Great Northern beans or other dried white beans
8 ounces dried black beans
6 cups water
Vegetable oil spray
1½ cups chopped carrots (about 2 medium)
1½ cups chopped celery (about 3 stalks)
1 large green bell pepper, chopped
1 large onion, chopped
4 cloves garlic, crushed or minced
2 8-ounce cans no-salt-added tomato sauce
10½-ounce can low-sodium chicken broth
½ cup dry white wine or nonalcoholic white wine
¼ cup molasses
2 bay leaves
1½ teaspoons dried fennel seeds, crushed using a mortar and pestle
½ to ¾ teaspoon crushed red pepper flakes
½ teaspoon salt
½ teaspoon dried thyme, crumbled

Rinse the beans. In a Dutch oven, combine the beans and the water. Bring to a boil over high heat. Reduce heat to low and simmer, uncovered, for 2 minutes. Remove from heat. Cover and let stand 1 hour. Or place beans and water in a large mixing bowl, cover, and let stand for 6 to 8 hours or overnight. Drain beans in a colander and rinse. Set aside.

Dry Dutch oven and spray with vegetable oil

Serves 8; 1 cup per serving

Nutrient Analysis (per serving)

Calories 271
Protein 15 g
Carbohydrate 53 g
Cholesterol 0 mg
Sodium 212 mg
Total fat 1 g
  Saturated 0 g
  Polyunsaturated 0 g
  Monounsaturated 0 g

spray. Add carrots, celery, bell pepper, onion, and garlic. Cook over medium heat for 20 minutes, or until tender, stirring occasionally. Stir in beans and remaining ingredients.

Bring to a boil over high heat. Reduce heat and simmer, covered, for $2\frac{1}{2}$ to 3 hours, or until beans are tender, adding water if necessary and stirring occasionally. Discard bay leaves.

COOK'S TIP: This hearty bean entrée gets even better when it is made ahead, allowing the flavors to blend. If desired, the recipe can be halved.

Roasted Asparagus with Dijon Vinaigrette

Rôti Asperges aux Dijon Vinaigrette

*T*he Loire Valley is called the garden of France, thanks to its abundance of fresh vegetables and fruit. Even the prized white asparagus grows there. This easy side dish is equally delicious with green asparagus (which is much easier to find). It goes nicely with roasted poultry and red potatoes.

24 fresh asparagus spears
Vegetable oil spray
¼ teaspoon grated lemon zest
1 tablespoon fresh lemon juice
1 tablespoon low-sodium chicken broth
¾ teaspoon Dijon mustard
½ teaspoon olive oil
Dash of black pepper
2 large lettuce leaves

Serves 4; 6 spears per serving

Nutrient Analysis (per serving)

Calories 32
Protein 3 g
Carbohydrate 5 g
Cholesterol 0 mg
Sodium 17 mg
Total fat 1 g
    Saturated 0 g
    Polyunsaturated 0 g
    Monounsaturated 0 g

Preheat oven to 500° F.

Snap off and discard woody bases of asparagus spears. Arrange asparagus in a single layer on a baking sheet. Spray asparagus with vegetable oil spray. Bake asparagus for 10 minutes, or until crisp-tender and lightly browned. Remove from oven.

Meanwhile, combine remaining ingredients except lettuce in a screw-top jar. Cover and shake until well combined.

To serve, place asparagus on a lettuce-lined serving plate. Drizzle vinaigrette over asparagus and toss gently to coat. Serve at once, let cool, or chill.

Young Minted Peas with Radicchio

Petit Pois à la Française

A combination of peas and lettuce is a common side dish in France. This version uses radicchio instead of the usual shredded Boston lettuce to lend a pleasant bitterness to the tender, sweet peas.

1 teaspoon acceptable margarine
¼ cup chopped onion (about ½ medium)
16-ounce package frozen, no-salt-added tiny peas
  or regular peas
⅓ cup water
1 bay leaf
¼ cup shredded radicchio or lettuce
1 tablespoon chopped fresh mint

In a medium saucepan, melt margarine over medium heat. Add onion and cook until tender, about 5 minutes, stirring occasionally. Add peas, water, and bay leaf. Increase heat to high and bring to a boil. Reduce heat and simmer, covered, for 4 to 6 minutes for tiny peas or according to package directions for regular peas. When peas are just tender, drain the mixture. Discard bay leaf. Add radicchio and mint and toss gently until well combined.

6 servings; ½ cup per serving

Nutrient Analysis (per serving)

Calories 60
Protein 4 g
Carbohydrate 10 g
Cholesterol 0 mg
Sodium 67 mg
Total fat 1 g
  Saturated 0 g
  Polyunsaturated 0 g
  Monounsaturated 0 g

Crêpes Suzette with Raspberries

The combination of orange, butter, sugar, and spirits provides a wonderful sauce for the thin French pancakes known as crêpes. This healthful version has less fat in the sauce than the original, intensifying its lovely orange flavor. The colorful raspberries add a new dimension to this classic.

Crepes

1¼ cups skim milk
¾ cup all-purpose flour
Egg substitute equivalent to 2 eggs, or 2 eggs
2 tablespoons sugar
1 teaspoon acceptable vegetable oil
Vegetable oil spray

Sauce

¼ cup acceptable margarine
1 teaspoon grated orange zest
½ cup fresh orange juice (about 2 oranges)
⅓ cup sugar
¼ cup orange liqueur or no-sugar-added orange juice
1 cup fresh or no-sugar-added frozen raspberries, thawed
¼ cup brandy (optional)

Serves 8; 2 crepes and 2 tablespoons sauce per serving

Nutrient Analysis (per serving)

Calories 197
Protein 4 g
Carbohydrate 28 g
Cholesterol 1 mg
Sodium 117 mg
Total fat 7 g
Saturated 1 g
Polyunsaturated 3 g
Monounsaturated 2 g

For crepes, combine milk, flour, egg substitute, sugar, and oil in a blender or the work bowl of a food processor fitted with a metal blade. Cover and process until well combined. Or combine ingredients in a medium mixing bowl and beat with an electric mixer until well combined.

Spray a 6-inch skillet with vegetable oil spray. Place over medium heat. When skillet is hot, remove from heat and spoon in 2 tablespoons crepe batter. Lift and tilt the skillet to spread batter. Return to heat; brown on one side only, about 1½ minutes. Invert skillet over paper towels, allowing crepe to fall out. Repeat with remaining batter, lightly spraying skillet with vegetable oil spray if necessary. You should have 16 to 18 crepes.

Fold each crepe in half, browned side out. Fold in half again, forming a triangle. Set aside.

For sauce, in a large skillet combine margarine, orange zest, orange juice, sugar, and liqueur. Bring to a boil over medium-high heat. Reduce heat and simmer, uncovered, stirring occasionally, for about 5 minutes, or until slightly thickened.

Arrange folded crepes in sauce. Sprinkle raspberries over crepes. Simmer for 3 to 5 minutes, or until just heated through, spooning sauce over crepes and berries occasionally.

Meanwhile, in a small saucepan, heat the brandy, if desired, until it almost simmers. Carefully ignite brandy and pour over crepes. When flames subside, swirl skillet to evenly distribute the brandy. Serve warm.

COOK'S TIP ON STORING CREPES: You can make the crepes in advance and store them in an airtight plastic bag for up to 2 days in the refrigerator or for several weeks in the freezer. Either way, place waxed paper between the crepes. You can prepare the sauce a day or two in advance. Simply reheat it over low heat, then add the crepes and follow instructions above.

Chocolate–Strawberry Meringue Shells

Vacherin au Chocolat et aux Fraises

A French vacherin is simply a meringue case that can hold a multitude of delicious fillings. In this version, the fat-free chocolate meringue cradles a stunning mixture of fresh strawberries and frozen yogurt drizzled with chocolate syrup. You'll definitely think you're eating something with more than 1 gram of fat per serving!

Shells

2 egg whites
½ teaspoon vanilla
¼ teaspoon cream of tartar
½ cup sugar
1 tablespoon unsweetened cocoa powder

Filling

1 tablespoon strawberry spreadable fruit
1 tablespoon no-sugar-added orange or apple juice
1 cup nonfat or low-fat vanilla frozen yogurt, or other flavor of your choice
2 cups sliced fresh strawberries or whole raspberries (about 18 medium strawberries, or 8 ounces of either fruit)
¼ cup chocolate syrup

Serves 4; 1 shell, ½ cup fruit mixture, ¼ cup frozen yogurt, and 1 tablespoon chocolate syrup per serving

Nutrient Analysis (per serving)

Calories 239
Protein 4 g
Carbohydrate 58 g
Cholesterol 1 mg
Sodium 72 mg
Total fat 1 g
  Saturated 0 g
  Polyunsaturated 0 g
  Monounsaturated 0 g

Preheat oven to 300° F. Line a baking sheet with baking parchment, plain brown paper, or aluminum foil. Draw four 4-inch circles on the paper. Set baking sheet aside.

In a large mixing bowl, beat egg whites, vanilla, and cream of tartar with an electric mixer on medium speed until soft peaks form. Gradually add sugar, 1 tablespoon at a time, beating on high speed for about 7 minutes, or until very stiff peaks form and sugar is almost dissolved. Add cocoa powder and beat until well combined.

Using a spoon, spatula, or pastry tube, spread or pipe meringue mixture over the circles on the prepared baking sheet. If using a spoon or spatula, form shells by smoothing the center and building up the sides. Or if using a pastry tube, make the base of the shells, then build up the sides.

Bake for 30 minutes. Turn off oven. Let shells dry in oven with door closed for 1 hour (do not open door). Remove from oven and peel shells from paper.

For the filling, in a medium mixing bowl stir together fruit spread and juice. Add fruit and toss gently until well coated.

To assemble, place a scoop of frozen yogurt in each shell, spoon fruit mixture over yogurt, and drizzle with chocolate syrup. Serve immediately.

COOK'S TIP ON MERINGUE SHELLS: Meringue shells can be made ahead, cooled, and stored in a covered container at room temperature for 2 to 3 days or in the freezer for up to 2 weeks. To thaw frozen shells, uncover and let stand at room temperature about 30 minutes.

COOK'S TIP ON BEATING EGG WHITES: The key to light, fluffy beaten egg whites is to handle the eggs properly. Eggs are easier to separate when they are cold, yet reward you with more volume if beaten when they have warmed to room temperature. After you separate the cold eggs, allow 30 minutes to 1 hour for the whites to come to room temperature before beating. Make sure the bowl you beat egg whites in is absolutely dry.

GERMAN CUISINE

Mushroom Strudel
Mini Potato Pancake Canapés

Cream of Potato Soup with Chunky Vegetables

Chilled Asparagus with Lemony Garlic Dressing
German Potato Salad with Baby Carrots

Bundled Trout and Vegetables

Roasted Turkey Breast with Creamed Spinach
Turkey "Meatballs" in Squash Shells

Sauerbraten
Pork Medallions in Cream Sauce
Grilled Pork with Caraway–Horseradish Sauce

Green Beans with Tomatoes and Bacon
Sauerkraut with Apples and Dried Cherries
Tiny Chive Dumplings

Black Forest Cake

Puffed Pancake with Apple-Cranberry Sauce

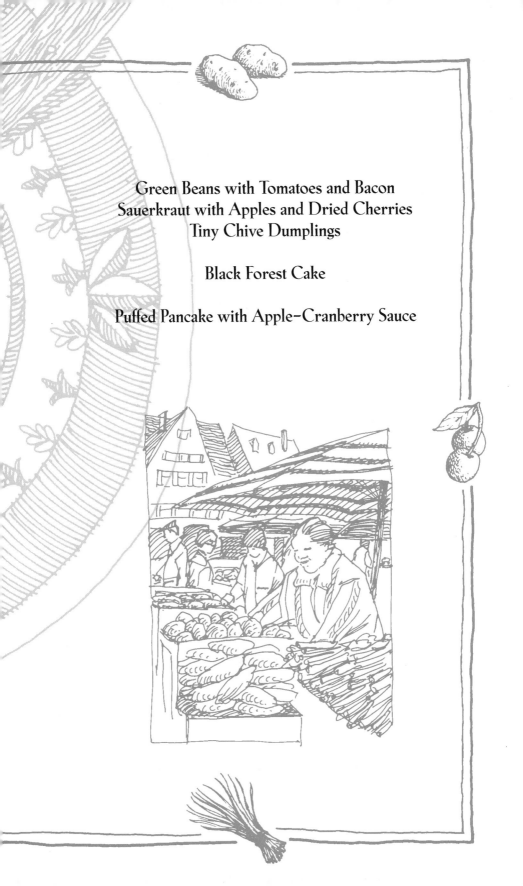

With an abundance of high-fat sausages, well-marbled roasts, high-sodium sauerkraut, thick gravies, and buttery pastries, traditional German food is hearty but not heart healthy. But today's Germany is bursting with fresh new ideas about food and cooking.

Different German regions are known for their culinary specialties. In Lüneburg, rich from the salt trade, you can find a unique breed of curly-horned sheep called Heidschnucken. In addition to the sheep farms, this area boasts apiaries and trout hatcheries. The agricultural area of Westphalia is known for its delicious smoky hams and beautiful moated castles. The Black Forest region is part woodland, where big, juicy mushrooms thrive; part vineyard; part orchard, with apples, plums, and world-famous cherries; and part small family farms that raise the prized hogs that emerge as smoky Black Forest hams. The Bodensee lake stretches across the German-Swiss border. The area around the lake is known for serving exceptionally fresh fish.

A Reason to Celebrate

Germans celebrate their history in a series of festivals. Of course, food is integral to each one. First, there are the Winzerfests, or wine festivals, of the Rhine, Moselle, and other wine-growing regions. Salatkirmes is held every spring in Schwalmstadt to celebrate the arrival of the potato. The granddaddy of all the festivals, Munich's Oktoberfest, is an annual two-week-long beer bash that begins in mid-September.

German Food Gets a Workout

Some of Germany's most celebrated ingredients include asparagus, cabbage, mushrooms, potatoes, beef, pork, poultry, wild game, fish, shellfish, and a harvest of fresh fruit. With an ample supply of these food staples, the possibilities for creative cooking are endless. The key to making the dishes healthful is choosing the right ingredients and preparing them in a way that minimizes the fat, cholesterol, and sodium. Should we throw out high-fat sauerbraten, the classic marinated beef roast served with a sweet-and-sour gravy? Never! Cut the fat instead by using a lean boneless beef rump roast. See page 82 for how to do this.

Like other people throughout the rest of the world, today's Germans are interested in fitness and healthful eating. Sauerkraut and wursts remain traditional favorites, but you'll also find cooking that is lighter and more sophisticated than in the past.

Whether it's Mushroom Strudel (page 70), Mini Potato Pancake Canapés (page 72), or Black Forest Cake (page 89), you'll find a tempting variety of both old and new styles of German cooking in this chapter. They are heartwarming—and heart healthy.

Mushroom Strudel

Pilzen Strudel

W hy wait for dessert to enjoy a good German strudel? This savory recipe allows you to serve strudel as an innovative appetizer.

Vegetable oil spray
8 ounces button mushrooms, sliced
¼ cup chopped onion (about ½ medium)
2 cloves garlic, minced
1 ounce low-fat cream cheese
1 teaspoon chopped fresh dill or ¼ teaspoon dried dill weed
⅛ teaspoon salt
Pinch of black pepper
Pinch of ground nutmeg
6 sheets frozen phyllo dough, thawed according to package directions
Vegetable oil spray

Spray a large skillet with vegetable oil spray. Heat skillet over medium heat. Cook mushrooms, onion, and garlic for 10 minutes, or until mushrooms are tender and liquid has evaporated. Stir in cream cheese, dill, salt, pepper, and nutmeg. Remove from heat.

Preheat oven to 375° F.

Working as quickly as possible so it won't dry out, stack phyllo dough on a clean dish towel. Leaving ½-inch edge, slightly mound mushroom filling at one of the short sides of phyllo dough. Fold in sides and roll up phyllo and filling jelly-roll style, using the towel to help you roll.

Spray a baking sheet lightly with vegetable oil spray. Place strudel on baking sheet, seam side down. Spray strudel lightly with vegetable oil spray. Bake, uncovered, for 30 minutes, or until phyllo is golden brown and mushroom filling is heated through.

Serves 8; 1 slice per serving

Nutrient Analysis (per serving)

Calories 64
Protein 2 g
Carbohydrate 12 g
Cholesterol 1 mg
Sodium 112 mg
Total fat 1 g
 Saturated 0 g
 Polyunsaturated 0 g
 Monounsaturated 0 g

Transfer warm strudel to a cutting board. Cut into 8 slices. Serve warm or at room temperature.

COOK'S TIP: Don't use nonfat cream cheese for this recipe. It won't provide the creamy texture you'll want in this dish.

The mushroom-and-cream-cheese mixture can be prepared ahead and refrigerated for as long as 24 hours.

Mini Potato Pancake Canapés

Kleine Kartoffelpuffer

M̲ost potato pancakes rely on eggs to hold them together. These crispy brown cakes hold up well without a bit of egg.

1 medium baking potato, peeled and shredded
2 tablespoons all-purpose flour
2 tablespoons finely chopped green onion
1 teaspoon chopped fresh thyme or ¼ teaspoon dried thyme, crumbled
1 teaspoon fresh rosemary or ½ teaspoon dried rosemary, crushed using mortar and pestle
¼ teaspoon salt
Vegetable oil spray
3 tablespoons nonfat or low-fat sour cream
Black pepper (optional)
Fresh thyme or rosemary (optional)

Serves 4; 2 pancakes per serving

Nutrient Analysis (per serving)

Calories 45
Protein 2 g
Carbohydrate 9 g
Cholesterol 0 mg
Sodium 156 mg
Total fat 0 g
    Saturated 0 g
    Polyunsaturated 0 g
    Monounsaturated 0 g

In a medium mixing bowl, combine potato, flour, green onion, thyme, rosemary, and salt. Stir with a fork until well combined.

Spray a large skillet with vegetable oil spray. Place skillet over medium-high heat until hot. Spoon potato mixture into hot skillet, forming 8 pancakes of about 1 heaping tablespoon each. Flatten with a metal spatula. Cook for 3 to 5 minutes, or until light brown. Turn and cook for 3 to 5 more minutes, or until light brown and crisp.

To serve, dollop each potato pancake with sour cream. Sprinkle with pepper and garnish with thyme or rosemary, if desired.

COOK'S TIP: Potato pancakes are typically served as a side dish to meat. For 2 side-dish servings, simply make 4 pancakes instead of 8 and increase the cooking time slightly.

Cream of Potato Soup with Chunky Vegetables

Kartoffelcremesuppe mit Gemüse

This soup gets its creaminess without a drop of cream. Instead, it comes from the pureed potato mixture. Salad and German rye bread are perfect complements.

2 medium potatoes, peeled and quartered
1 medium parsnip, peeled and cut into 1-inch
 pieces
2 cups low-sodium chicken broth
¼ teaspoon salt
Vegetable oil spray
1 medium red, yellow, or green bell pepper,
 chopped
⅓ cup sliced green onion (about 4)
⅓ cup sliced carrot (about ½ medium)
⅓ cup chopped celery (about 1 small stalk)
¼ cup diced low-fat, low-sodium boiled ham

Serves 4; 1 cup per serving

Nutrient Analysis (per serving)

Calories 111
Protein 5 g
Carbohydrate 22 g
Cholesterol 4 mg
Sodium 269 mg
Total fat 1 g
 Saturated 0 g
 Polyunsaturated 0 g
 Monounsaturated 0 g

In a medium saucepan, combine potatoes, parsnip, chicken broth, and salt. Bring to a boil over high heat. Reduce heat and simmer, covered, for 20 to 30 minutes, or until potatoes and parsnip are very tender. Do not drain.

Meanwhile, spray a large saucepan with vegetable oil spray. Add remaining ingredients except ham. Cook over medium heat for 10 minutes, or until tender, stirring occasionally. Stir in ham.

Place cooked potato mixture and liquid in a blender or the work bowl of a food processor fitted with a metal blade. Cover and process until smooth. Stir into vegetable mixture in saucepan and heat through over medium heat.

Chilled Asparagus
with Lemony Garlic Dressing

Spargel mit Knoblauchsauce

Germans love asparagus almost as much as they love their beer! This recipe features chilled asparagus tossed with a creamy low-fat dressing.

Dressing

2 tablespoons nonfat or low-fat sour cream
1 tablespoon low-fat buttermilk or skim milk
1 clove garlic, minced
1 teaspoon grated lemon zest

24 fresh asparagus spears, woody bases snapped off and discarded

Poppy seeds (optional)

In a small mixing bowl, stir together sour cream, buttermilk, garlic, and lemon zest. Cover and chill until serving time.

Cook asparagus in a large saucepan or skillet in boiling water for 5 minutes, or until crisp-tender. Drain. Rinse with cold water and drain again. Cover and chill until serving time.

To serve, gently toss asparagus spears with dressing. Sprinkle lightly with poppy seeds, if desired.

Serves 4; 6 spears and 2¼ teaspoons dressing per serving

Nutrient Analysis (per serving)

Calories 32
Protein 3 g
Carbohydrate 5 g
Cholesterol 0 mg
Sodium 14 mg
Total fat 0 g
   Saturated 0 g
   Polyunsaturated 0 g
   Monounsaturated 0 g

German Potato Salad with Baby Carrots

Kartoffelsalat mit Karotten

This classic warm German potato salad is flavored with a low-fat combination of vinegar, turkey bacon, onion, broth, and seasonings. The recipe can easily be halved.

2 pounds red potatoes, scrubbed
1 cup baby carrots (about 4 ounces)
3 tablespoons balsamic or cider vinegar
¼ teaspoon salt
⅛ to ¼ teaspoon black pepper

Dressing
Vegetable oil spray
4 slices turkey bacon, chopped
1 medium onion, chopped
½ cup low-sodium chicken broth
2 tablespoons balsamic or cider vinegar
2 tablespoons chopped fresh parsley

Place potatoes and carrots in a large saucepan, cover with water, and bring to a boil over high heat. Reduce heat and simmer, covered, until tender, 25 to 30 minutes for medium potatoes, 15 to 20 minutes for tiny potatoes. Drain. When cool enough to handle but still warm (about 7 minutes), cut potatoes into ¼-inch-thick slices. (Leave baby carrots whole.)

In a medium mixing bowl, layer warm potato slices and carrots, sprinkling the 3 tablespoons vinegar, the salt, and the pepper between layers. Let stand at room temperature while preparing dressing.

For dressing, spray a medium skillet with vegetable oil spray. Cook turkey bacon over medium heat for 3 to 5 minutes, stirring constantly. Add onion. Cook, stirring constantly, for 5 minutes, or until onion is tender.

Serves 8; 1 cup per serving

Nutrient Analysis (per serving)

Calories 133
Protein 4 g
Carbohydrate 27 g
Cholesterol 6 mg
Sodium 203 mg
Total fat 1 g
  Saturated 0 g
  Polyunsaturated 0 g
  Monounsaturated 1 g

Add chicken broth and 2 tablespoons vinegar to skillet and bring to a boil over high heat. Remove from heat and pour over potato mixture. Add parsley and toss gently to coat. Serve warm.

Bundled Trout and Vegetables

Forelle und Gemüse

Trout is served quite often in Bavaria, where ice-cold streams provide an ample supply of this tasty fish. This version is seasoned with basil and oregano, nontraditional German herbs. Serve with cooked rice or noodles.

1 cup small broccoli florets (about 6 ounces)
1 medium carrot, cut into matchstick-size strips
¹⁄₂ cup yellow summer squash, thinly sliced or cut
   into matchstick-size strips
2-pound rainbow trout, sea trout, or pike
¹⁄₂ teaspoon dried basil, crumbled
¹⁄₂ teaspoon dried oregano, crumbled
¹⁄₄ teaspoon salt
¹⁄₈ teaspoon black pepper

Preheat oven to 350° F.

Cook broccoli, carrots, and squash in a saucepan in a small amount of boiling water over high heat for 1 minute. Drain and set aside.

Rinse fish and pat dry with paper towels. To assemble fish bundle, tear off 1 or 2 pieces of foil large enough to encase the fish. Place fish in the middle of the foil.

In a small bowl, combine basil, oregano, salt, and pepper. Sprinkle half the herb mixture inside the cavity of the fish. Arrange vegetables inside and around the fish. Sprinkle with remaining herb mixture.

Bring foil up and around fish and seal tightly. Place fish bundle on a baking sheet. Bake about 40 minutes, or until fish flakes easily when tested with a fork.

To serve, unwrap fish, place it on a serving platter, and arrange vegetables around fish.

Serves 5; about 3 ounces fish and ¹⁄₃ cup vegetables per serving

Nutrient Analysis (per serving)

Calories 271
Protein 39 g
Carbohydrate 3 g
Cholesterol 119 mg
Sodium 237 mg
Total fat 10 g
   Saturated 3 g
   Polyunsaturated 3 g
   Monounsaturated 4 g

Roasted Turkey Breast with Creamed Spinach

Truthahnbrust mit Spinat

This dish uses creamed spinach as a fluffy bed for roasted turkey breast.

2½- to 3-pound turkey breast half with bone
2 10-ounce packages no-salt-added chopped frozen spinach
1 small onion
2 cloves garlic
Vegetable oil spray
1 teaspoon acceptable margarine
1 tablespoon cornstarch
12-ounce can evaporated skim milk
¼ teaspoon salt
⅛ teaspoon black pepper
Dash of ground cloves

Serves 8; 3 ounces cooked turkey and ⅓ cup spinach mixture per serving

Nutrient Analysis (per serving)

Calories 220
Protein 34 g
Carbohydrate 10 g
Cholesterol 75 mg
Sodium 242 mg
Total fat 4 g
  Saturated 1 g
  Polyunsaturated 1 g
  Monounsaturated 1 g

Preheat oven to 325° F.

Rinse turkey and pat dry with paper towels. Place turkey, breast side up, on a rack in a shallow roasting pan. Insert a meat thermometer into the thickest part of the breast. Cover turkey loosely with foil.

Roast turkey for 2 to 3 hours, or until the thermometer registers 165° F and turkey is no longer pink when cut with a sharp knife near the bone. Remove foil the last 30 minutes of roasting. Remove and discard skin from turkey.

During the final 15 minutes of roasting, prepare creamed spinach. Cook spinach according to package directions. Put spinach in a colander and drain well. Press out as much liquid as possible with the back of a large spoon. Set aside.

Finely chop onion and mince garlic. Spray a medium saucepan with vegetable oil spray. Add margarine and melt over medium heat. Cook onion and garlic in saucepan for about 5 minutes, or until onion is tender, stirring occasionally.

Stir cornstarch into onion mixture. Add skim milk, salt, pepper, and cloves. Cook over medium heat for about 5 minutes, or until thickened and bubbly, stirring often. Continue to cook and stir for 2 minutes. Stir in spinach, combining well.

To serve, spoon creamed spinach onto a platter. Slice turkey and arrange over spinach.

Turkey "Meatballs" in Squash Shells

Königsberger Klops

Named after the German city of Königsberg, this dish has a slightly tart flavor, which is common in German cooking.

2 small acorn squashes (about 1 pound each)
2 tablespoons water (if microwaving squash)
1 cup plain soft bread crumbs (about 2 slices bread)
¼ cup finely chopped onion
Egg substitute equivalent to 1 egg, or 1 egg
½ teaspoon anchovy paste
⅛ teaspoon salt
⅛ teaspoon black pepper
1 pound ground skinless turkey or chicken breast
1½ cups dry white wine or nonalcoholic dry white wine
½ cup water
4 black peppercorns
3 whole cloves
1 bay leaf
Low-sodium chicken broth or water
2 tablespoons all-purpose flour
2 teaspoons capers, rinsed and drained
Chopped fresh parsley

Serves 4;
6 meatballs, 3 tablespoons sauce, and ½ acorn squash per serving

Nutrient Analysis* (per serving)

Calories 373
Protein 31 g
Carbohydrate 39 g
Cholesterol 70 mg
Sodium 419 mg
Total fat 8 g
 Saturated 2 g
 Polyunsaturated 2 g
 Monounsaturated 2 g
*Assuming that no extra chicken broth was added after straining liquid from skillet

To cook squashes, cut them in half and remove seeds and strings. If using a microwave, place the squash halves, cut side down, in a microwave-safe baking dish. Prick skin several times with a fork. Add 2 tablespoons water. Cook, covered, on 100% power (high) for 15 to 20 minutes, or until squashes can be easily pierced with a sharp knife. Give dish a half-turn twice during cooking. Drain. To bake squashes, preheat oven to 350° F. Place halves, cut side down, in a baking dish. Bake, uncovered, for 30 minutes. Turn cut side up and bake for 20 minutes more, or until tender.

Roast Chicken with Artichokes and Tomatoes

Mini Potato Pancake Canapés

Gyros

GAZPACHO

BUNDLED TROUT AND VEGETABLES

FOREST MUSHROOM SOUP

WARM TUNA SALAD WITH DRIED TOMATOES

COUSCOUS WITH LAMB STEW

MEATLESS CASSOULET

VEGETABLE QUICHE IN BROWN RICE CRUST

Tomato-Mozzarella Salad

Dried Fruit Compote with Vanilla Yogurt

Meanwhile, in a medium mixing bowl, combine bread crumbs, onion, egg substitute, anchovy paste, salt, and pepper. Add ground turkey and mix well. Shape into 24 balls.

In a large skillet, combine wine, $\frac{1}{2}$ cup water, peppercorns, cloves, and bay leaf. Bring to a boil over high heat, then reduce heat to low. Add turkey meatballs. Simmer, covered, for 10 minutes. Remove meatballs and set aside.

Strain liquid from skillet into a 1-cup measuring cup. Add enough chicken broth or water to equal 1 cup. In a small bowl, stir about $\frac{1}{4}$ cup liquid into flour until smooth. Return remaining liquid and flour mixture to skillet. Stir to mix well. Cook over medium heat for about 5 minutes, or until thickened and bubbly, stirring often. Add capers. Continue to cook and stir for 1 minute. Return meatballs to skillet with sauce. Spoon sauce over meatballs. Cook over low heat for about 2 minutes, or until meatballs are heated through. To serve, spoon meatballs with sauce into squash halves. Sprinkle with parsley.

Sauerbraten

Be sure to plan ahead for this popular main dish since the meat marinates for 48 to 72 hours before cooking. We've added roasted red peppers for a 1990s twist.

3-pound boneless beef rump roast, all visible fat
  removed
1½ cups dry red wine or nonalcoholic red wine
1½ cups red wine vinegar
1 cup water
2 medium carrots, sliced
1 medium onion, sliced
6 whole cloves
4 black peppercorns, crushed using a mortar
  and pestle
2 bay leaves
½ teaspoon caraway seeds
¼ teaspoon ground coriander
Vegetable oil spray
½ cup crushed gingersnaps (about 7)
7-ounce jar roasted red peppers, drained and
  chopped (about ⅔ cup)

Serves 10; 3½ ounces cooked meat per serving

Nutrient Analysis (per serving)

Calories 197
Protein 28 g
Carbohydrate 8 g
Cholesterol 72 mg
Sodium 88 mg
Total fat 5 g
  Saturated 2 g
  Polyunsaturated 0 g
  Monounsaturated 2 g

Prick beef thoroughly with a fork. Place beef in a large airtight plastic bag, then put bag in a bowl or baking dish. Set aside.

In a medium saucepan, combine wine, vinegar, water, carrots, onion, cloves, peppercorns, bay leaves, caraway seeds, and coriander. Bring to a boil over high heat. Reduce heat and simmer, uncovered, for 5 minutes. Cool.

Pour marinade over roast in bag. Seal bag and marinate in the refrigerator (in bowl or baking dish) for 48 to 72 hours, turning bag occasionally to distribute marinade.

Drain roast, reserving marinade. Pat meat dry with paper towels. Spray a Dutch oven with vegetable oil spray. Place over medium-high heat.

Add meat to hot pan and brown on all sides, about 10 minutes.

Add reserved marinade to Dutch oven. Bring to a boil over high heat. Reduce heat and simmer, covered, for 2 hours, or until meat is tender. Slice roast, transfer it to a platter, and keep it warm.

Strain cooking liquid through a sieve or colander placed over a bowl. Discard solids. Skim off fat and return liquid to Dutch oven. Stir gingersnaps and roasted peppers into cooking liquid. Cook and stir over medium heat until bubbly, about 10 minutes. Serve with roast.

COOK'S TIP ON ROASTING BELL PEPPERS: Instead of buying jars of roasted peppers, you can easily make your own. Preheat broiler. Spray a broiler pan with vegetable oil spray. Halve or quarter fresh bell peppers and remove stems, membranes, and seeds. Place peppers, cut side down, on broiler pan. Broil 3 to 4 inches from the heat for 2 to 10 minutes, or until the skins are blackened. Place peppers in a plastic bag and seal bag. Let sit for at least 15 minutes, or until cool enough to handle. Using your fingers, paper towels, or a knife, remove the charred skins from bell peppers.

Pork Medallions in Cream Sauce

Schweinemedaillons

The apple-studded cream sauce served with this pork dish is reminiscent of those served at some of Germany's finest restaurants, but this sauce is low in fat.

1 pound pork tenderloin, all visible fat removed, cut into 1-inch-thick slices
Vegetable oil spray
2 teaspoons acceptable margarine
1 small onion, chopped
1 cooking apple, such as Granny Smith, peeled, cored, and chopped
2 cloves garlic, minced
5-ounce can evaporated skim milk
⅛ teaspoon salt
Pinch of white pepper
Pinch of ground nutmeg
2 tablespoons chopped fresh parsley

Serves 4; 3 ounces pork and ¼ cup sauce per serving

Nutrient Analysis (per serving)

Calories 225
Protein 29 g
Carbohydrate 11 g
Cholesterol 73 mg
Sodium 197 mg
Total fat 7 g
  Saturated 2 g
  Polyunsaturated 1 g
  Monounsaturated 3 g

Flatten each pork slice on a hard surface with the palm of your hand. Using the flat side of a meat mallet, pound pork slices to ¼-inch thickness.

Spray a large skillet with vegetable oil spray and place over medium-high heat. Add pork in a single layer. Cook for about 2 minutes on each side, or until tender and no longer pink inside. Remove from skillet. Reduce heat to medium.

In same skillet, melt margarine. Add onion and apple. Cook over medium heat for 5 minutes, or until onion is tender, stirring constantly. Add garlic and cook for 2 minutes. Stir in remaining ingredients except parsley. Simmer, uncovered, for 1 minute, stirring constantly. Stir in parsley.

Return pork to skillet. Spoon sauce over pork. Cook over low heat for 1 minute, or until heated through.

Grilled Pork with Caraway–Horseradish Sauce

Schweinefleisch mit Meerrettichsauce

This creamy, characteristically German sauce is also good with lean grilled beef or lamb. Round out the meal with steamed wedges of green cabbage and red potatoes.

1 pound pork tenderloin, all visible fat removed, cut into 4 slices
1 teaspoon acceptable margarine
2 teaspoons cornstarch
5 ounces canned evaporated skim milk
1 tablespoon prepared horseradish, drained
¼ teaspoon caraway seeds
¼ teaspoon sugar
⅛ teaspoon black pepper

Serves 4; 1 slice pork and 2 tablespoons sauce per serving

Nutrient Analysis (per serving)

Calories 196
Protein 29 g
Carbohydrate 6 g
Cholesterol 73 mg
Sodium 113 mg
Total fat 5 g
　Saturated 2 g
　Polyunsaturated 1 g
　Monounsaturated 2 g

Prepare grill. Grill pork directly over medium-hot coals for 5 minutes. Turn and grill for 4 to 6 minutes more, or until pork is light pink in the center and the juices run clear when the meat is pierced. Or preheat broiler and broil meat 4 inches from the heat for 4 to 6 minutes. Turn and broil for 4 to 6 minutes more, or until pork reaches desired doneness.

Meanwhile, in a small saucepan, melt margarine over medium heat. Stir in cornstarch. Add remaining ingredients and stir well to combine. Cook for about 5 minutes, or until thickened and bubbly, stirring often. Continue to cook and stir for 1 minute. Serve with meat.

Green Beans with Tomatoes and Bacon

Grune Bohnen mit Tomaten und Speck

This pretty green bean side dish is made by cooking green beans on a bed of seasoned tomatoes.

Vegetable oil spray
3 slices turkey bacon, coarsely chopped
1 cup chopped onion
14½-ounce can low-sodium stewed tomatoes
1 teaspoon dried thyme, crumbled
⅛ teaspoon black pepper
1 pound fresh green beans, trimmed and cut into bite-size pieces

Serves 6; ¾ cup per serving

Nutrient Analysis (per serving)

Calories 57
Protein 3 g
Carbohydrate 9 g
Cholesterol 6 mg
Sodium 119 mg
Total fat 2 g
　Saturated 0 g
　Polyunsaturated 0 g
　Monounsaturated 1 g

Spray a large skillet with vegetable oil spray. Add bacon and cook over medium heat until bacon is just crisp, about 5 to 8 minutes, stirring occasionally. Remove bacon from skillet. Set aside.

Wipe skillet with a paper towel. Add onion to skillet and cook over medium heat until tender, about 5 to 7 minutes, stirring occasionally. Add undrained tomatoes, thyme, and pepper. Bring to a boil. Place green beans on top of tomato mixture. Reduce heat to low and simmer, covered, until beans are crisp-tender, about 15 minutes.

Before serving, sprinkle bean mixture with bacon and toss gently. Serve warm. Makes 6 servings.

COOK'S TIP: To save a step, you can leave crisp-cooked bacon in skillet and add onions as directed in recipe. The flavor will be the same, but the bacon will not remain crisp.

Sauerkraut with Apples and Dried Cherries

Sauerkraut mit Äpfel und Kirschen

The sauerkraut that we know in the United States is much coarser and milder tasting than its German counterpart. Try this attractive sweet-and-sour version the next time you serve low-fat sausage, beef, or pork.

Vegetable oil spray
1 small red onion, sliced
16-ounce can sauerkraut, rinsed, drained, and squeezed
1 medium sweet potato, peeled and shredded
1 medium apple, peeled, cored, and chopped
1/2 cup dried cherries, raisins, or currants
1/2 cup low-sodium chicken broth
1 tablespoon brown sugar
1/2 teaspoon caraway seeds

Spray a large saucepan with vegetable oil spray. Sauté onion in saucepan over medium heat for 10 minutes, or until tender, stirring often. Add remaining ingredients.

Bring to a boil over high heat. Reduce heat and simmer, covered, for 15 minutes. Serve warm.

Serves 8; 1/2 cup per serving

Nutrient Analysis (per serving)

Calories 77
Protein 1 g
Carbohydrate 19 g
Cholesterol 0 mg
Sodium 174 mg
Total fat 0 g
  Saturated 0 g
  Polyunsaturated 0 g
  Monounsaturated 0 g

Tiny Chive Dumplings

Spaetzle

Spaetzle *is a cross between a noodle and a dumpling. The small, puffy morsels are a traditional German accompaniment to goulash and all types of roasts, especially Sauerbraten (page 82).*

1 cup all-purpose flour
⅛ teaspoon salt
⅛ teaspoon black pepper
⅓ cup skim milk
Egg substitute equivalent to 1 egg, or 1 egg
2 tablespoons finely chopped chives

In a Dutch oven, bring a large amount of water to a boil over high heat. Meanwhile, in a medium mixing bowl, stir together flour, salt, and pepper. Make a well in the center.

In a small bowl, stir together milk and egg substitute. Add to flour mixture. Add chives. Stir until well combined.

Hold a colander with large holes over the boiling water. Pour batter into the colander. Using a long-handled spoon, press batter through holes in colander so streams of batter fall into the water. Cook for 5 minutes, stirring occasionally. Drain well.

COOK'S TIP: If you make spaetzle frequently, you may want to invest in a spaetzle maker, available at some gourmet shops or through mail-order catalogues.

Serves 4; ½ cup per serving

Nutrient Analysis (per serving)

Calories 130
Protein 5 g
Carbohydrate 26 g
Cholesterol 0 mg
Sodium 105 mg
Total fat 0 g
  Saturated 0 g
  Polyunsaturated 0 g
  Monounsaturated 0 g

Black Forest Cake

Schwarzwälder Gebäck

This luscious chocolate dessert comes from the Black Forest region in southern Germany. Although the recipe involves several steps, it is relatively easy to make and can be assembled, except for the garnish, up to 24 hours in advance.

Filling

16-ounce can water-packed tart red cherries
¼ cup sugar
2 tablespoons cornstarch
2 tablespoons cherry or orange liqueur (optional)

Cake

Vegetable oil spray
2 tablespoons all-purpose flour
½ cup unsweetened cocoa powder
1 cup water
½ cup acceptable vegetable oil
2 teaspoons vanilla
1¼ cups all-purpose flour
1 cup sugar
½ teaspoon baking soda
½ teaspoon baking powder
⅛ teaspoon salt
3 egg whites
¼ teaspoon cream of tartar
3 tablespoons sugar

Garnish

1 cup frozen light whipped topping, thawed
Unsweetened cocoa powder (optional)
Maraschino cherries (optional)

Serves 16; 1 slice per serving

Nutrient Analysis (per serving)

Calories 198
Protein 2 g
Carbohydrate 31 g
Cholesterol 0 mg
Sodium 86 mg
Total fat 8 g
  Saturated 2 g
  Polyunsaturated 4 g
  Monounsaturated 2 g

To make the filling, combine undrained cherries, ¼ cup sugar, and cornstarch in a medium saucepan. Cook over medium heat until thickened and bubbly, about 5 minutes, stirring often. Continue to cook and stir for 2 minutes. Stir in liqueur, if desired. Let cool. Cover and chill thoroughly without stirring.

Preheat oven to 350° F. Spray two 8-inch round baking pans with vegetable oil spray. Dust pans with 2 tablespoons flour; tap out excess. Set aside.

Place cocoa powder in a medium mixing bowl. Whisk in water until smooth. Stir in oil and vanilla.

In a large mixing bowl, combine $1\frac{1}{4}$ cups flour, 1 cup sugar, baking soda, baking powder, and salt. Add cocoa mixture and stir until well combined.

Beat egg whites in a medium mixing bowl with an electric mixer until foamy. Add cream of tartar and beat until soft peaks form. Gradually add 3 tablespoons sugar, beating on high speed until stiff peaks form.

Fold egg white mixture into chocolate mixture. Divide batter evenly between pans. Bake for 20 to 25 minutes, or until a toothpick inserted near the center comes out clean. Let pans cool on wire racks for 10 minutes. Invert cakes onto racks and let cool completely.

To assemble, halve cakes horizontally. Place one layer on a serving plate. Spread $\frac{1}{3}$ of the filling (about $\frac{2}{3}$ cup) on first layer. Place second cake layer on top. Spread with $\frac{1}{3}$ of the filling. Place third cake layer on top. Spread with remaining filling. Top with last cake layer. Cover with plastic wrap and store in the refrigerator until serving time.

At serving time, cut cake into 16 wedges. Dollop each serving with whipped topping. Sprinkle lightly with cocoa powder and garnish with cherries, if desired.

COOK'S TIP: This cake cuts so easily you can get 18 slices—or even 24—if you're really watching your fat and calorie intake.

Puffed Pancake with Apple–Cranberry Sauce

Pfannkuchen Grundrezept mit Apfelsauce

L*ike French soufflés, German pancakes should be served as soon as they are removed from the oven because they won't stay puffed for very long. This dish would make an impressive addition to your next brunch menu.*

Serves 6; 1 pan-cake wedge and ¼ cup sauce per serving

Nutrient Analysis (per serving)

Calories 166
Protein 5 g
Carbohydrate 34 g
Cholesterol 0 mg
Sodium 119 mg
Total fat 2 g
  Saturated 0 g
  Polyunsaturated 1 g
  Monounsaturated 1 g

Vegetable oil spray
2 teaspoons acceptable margarine
Egg substitute equivalent to 3 eggs
½ cup all-purpose flour
½ cup skim milk
⅛ teaspoon salt
2 large cooking apples, peeled, cored, and thinly
**   sliced**
¾ cup no-sugar-added apple juice
½ cup fresh or frozen cranberries or fresh
**   or frozen no-sugar-added blackberries**
**   (about 2 ounces)**
¼ cup sugar
¼ teaspoon ground cinnamon
1 tablespoon cornstarch
2 tablespoons no-sugar-added apple juice
**   or water**
Sifted powdered sugar

Preheat oven to 400° F.

Spray a 10-inch ovenproof skillet with vegetable oil spray. Add margarine. Place skillet in oven for 3 minutes, or until margarine melts.

In a medium mixing bowl, combine egg substitute, flour, milk, and salt. Beat with an electric mixer or wire whisk until smooth. Immediately pour egg mixture into hot skillet. Bake, uncovered, for about 25 minutes, or until puffed and well browned.

Meanwhile, in a medium skillet, combine apples, ¾ cup juice, berries, sugar, and cinnamon. Bring to a boil over high heat. Reduce heat and simmer, covered, for about 10 minutes, or until fruit is tender, stirring occasionally. Place cornstarch in a small bowl. Stir in apple juice. Add cornstarch-juice mixture to apple mixture. Cook for about 2 minutes, until thickened and bubbly, stirring often.

To serve, sprinkle pancake with powdered sugar. Cut into wedges and spoon warm sauce over each serving.

COOK'S TIP: The apple-cranberry sauce can be made ahead and reheated in a small saucepan over low heat, stirring occasionally. Or place sauce in a microwave-safe cup or bowl, cover loosely with plastic wrap or waxed paper, and reheat on 100% power (high) for 1 to 2 minutes, stirring twice.

COOK'S TIP ON COOKING APPLES: Among the best cooking apples are Rome Beauty, Golden Delicious, Granny Smith, Jonathan, and Winesap.

Greek
Cuisine

Light Lemon Soup

Marinated Tomato Salad

Fish Sautéed with Tomatoes and Cinnamon
Aegean Baked Fish
Fish Wrapped in Grape Leaves

Roast Chicken with Artichokes and Tomatoes
Savory Chicken Patties

Herbed Braised Beef with Tomatoes
Gyros
Stuffed Cabbage Rolls

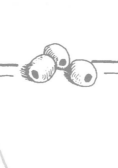

Very Versatile Mushrooms and Artichokes
Sautéed Summer Squash
Rice with Grape Leaves
Garlic Potatoes

Dried Fruit Compote with Vanilla Yogurt

G reece, the cradle of philosophy, is the gem of the Aegean. The magnificent, mountainous terrain of Greece demands that lamb—not beef—must be the primary source of meat for the country.

Unfortunately, many Americans think lamb is a tough, strong, gamy meat and avoid any recipe that features it. If you haven't had lamb in years, you're in for a pleasant surprise! Through selective breeding and modified grazing, the lamb available in today's supermarket is tender and mild. It's also lower in fat than some beef. And usually lambs are given fewer of the hormones and antibiotics that have worried health-conscious consumers lately.

For those of you who still have misgivings, we modified some of the recipes in this chapter. But for authentic Greek food, try at least a half-and-half combination of beef and lamb, as in the recipe for Gyros on page 110.

Greeks also favor chicken, as well as seafood from the clear, blue waters surrounding the islands.

Greek Gifts

The Greeks have adored olives, and their oil, for millennia. Socrates is supposed to have found olives so sustaining during those heavy philosophy sessions with his students that he always kept a handful tucked in a fold of his clothes for impromptu snacking.

The oil pressed from the olives was used not only for cooking but also for cleansing. Liberally rubbed into the skin and then scraped off with a bone or wooden spatulalike instrument called a strigil, it left the skin cleaned and softened. Modern Greek cooks still spread olive oil in a dish or pan with their fingers instead of the often-suggested paper towel or pastry brush. Then they may rub the remainder into their hands to keep them soft. Greek cooks are supremely practical, and little is wasted.

From a heart-healthy standpoint, olive oil deserves its glorified status. A monounsaturated oil, it has the same values for fat and calories as any other oil. Unlike the rest, however, it lowers blood cholesterol when eaten in a diet low in saturated fat. Greeks consider olive oil a health food.

For cooking purposes, stick with extra-virgin olive oil, which comes from the first press of the olives. Its low acidity also makes it the most stable of the grades and the slowest to become rancid once opened and exposed to air. Extra-virgin oil costs the most, but a little goes a long way in adding flavor and richness to a dish.

Virgin oil frequently has a sharp edge to its aroma and flavor. Once opened, it will spoil within two or three months. Pure olive oil, the lowest grade of all, is pure olive, all right, but it doesn't have the flavor or the shelf life of the others. Many people who claim to dislike olive oil probably tasted a salad dressing or other food made with pure oil that had already turned. If you still have a bottle of the pure stuff in a cupboard, you might want to try softening your hands with it. But for the sake of your recipes, please don't eat it!

Rigani: The Herb That Launches a Thousand Dishes

Of the seasonings, oregano is the herb most frequently associated with Greek cookery. Actually, rigani, a type of wild marjoram, is really what's used in an authentic Greek recipe. Since fresh rigani is next to impossible to find in the United States, good-quality dried oregano will do. Just make sure to crush it with your fingertips to release the remaining oils before adding it to a dish. If you don't detect a strong burst of aroma during the crushing, your herbs are too old. Toss them and buy new herbs. Don't give up on locating some dried rigani. Check at any ethnic grocers you can find. Other herbs you'll encounter in Greek cookery are rosemary, basil, flat-leaf parsley, bay leaf, and mint.

Greeks consider tomatoes, lemons, and cinnamon essential as well. (Some recipes, such as Fish Sautéed with Tomatoes and Cinnamon, page 101, and Stuffed Cabbage Rolls, page 112, combine all three.) Lemons reign supreme in Greek cooking. Their juice manages to find its way into almost every type of recipe. The tomato came to Greece from the New World via Spain, and cinnamon came from the Middle East. The Greeks accepted these newcomers enthusiastically and often combine the two. Many Greek cooks practice a little culinary trick you might choose to adopt. They automatically add a pinch of cinnamon to any recipe containing tomato in any form. It's similar to the way we tend to add pepper to just about anything to jazz it up a bit.

To Life!

A typical Greek meal is served family style, with everything put on the table at once. Diners choose from a salad, a main course, a vegetable dish or two, and bread for soaking up the flavorful sauces. Feta cheese, made from sheep's milk, is usually offered on its own or crumbled into the salad. Drinks range from mineral water or fruit juice to beer or retsina, a white wine that has been flavored with pine resin.

A Greek kitchen is quite westernized, so no special equipment or serving utensils are required for cooking or to set a Greek-style table. Whether your meal is served on a fine tablecloth set with silver, china, and crystal or outdoors with grass, stoneware, and jelly glasses, Greek food, like its cooks, is practical and adaptable. Just relax and enjoy!

Light Lemon Soup

Soupa Avgolemono

A lighter version of the rich original, and much easier to make.

6 cups low-sodium chicken broth
1 to 2 teaspoons dried dill weed, to taste
½ cup orzo or rice
2 tablespoons fresh lemon juice

Place broth, dill weed, and orzo in a large saucepan. Simmer, uncovered, until orzo is tender, about 20 minutes. Stir in the lemon juice and serve.

Serves 6; 1 cup per serving

Nutrient Analysis (per serving)

Calories 68
Protein 4 g
Carbohydrate 10 g
Cholesterol 0 mg
Sodium 58 mg
Total fat 1 g
　Saturated 0 g
　Polyunsaturated 0 g
　Monounsaturated 0 g

Marinated Tomato Salad

Tomatosalata

The longer it marinates, the better this salad tastes, though it seems to look proportionately less attractive. Balsamic vinegar gives it a special taste, but you can substitute red wine vinegar with acceptable results.

6 to 8 medium Italian plum tomatoes, sliced
8 kalamata olives, pitted and chopped
1 tablespoon grated onion
1 tablespoon balsamic vinegar or red wine vinegar
1 tablespoon honey
½ teaspoon salt
¼ teaspoon black pepper, or more to taste
½ teaspoon ground cinnamon, or to taste
1 large clove garlic, crushed or minced
1 tablespoon extra-virgin olive oil
2 tablespoons nonfat or low-fat yogurt
Chopped fresh parsley, for garnish
Kalamata olives, for garnish (optional)

Serves 6; ½ cup per serving

Nutrient Analysis (per serving)

Calories 65
Protein 1 g
Carbohydrate 9 g
Cholesterol 0 mg
Sodium 254 mg
Total fat 3 g
  Saturated 0 g
  Polyunsaturated 0 g
  Monounsaturated 2 g

Arrange the sliced tomatoes and chopped olives attractively on a serving platter. Place onion, vinegar, honey, salt, pepper, cinnamon, and garlic in a jar with a tight-fitting lid. Cover the jar and shake. Don't worry if ingredients don't blend thoroughly. Taste for balance, adding honey or vinegar as desired. Add the oil and shake again.

Drizzle the dressing over the tomato platter and chill for at least 30 minutes.

Just before serving, stir the yogurt and thin with a little water if it won't drizzle off the end of the spoon. Drizzle the yogurt over the tomatoes; garnish with chopped parsley and with kalamata olives, if desired.

Fish Sautéed with Tomatoes and Cinnamon

Psari Kapama

This versatile recipe adapts well to just about any fish, so feel free to experiment with what's freshest and most appealing to you.

3 tablespoons extra-virgin olive oil
2 stalks celery, chopped
1 medium onion, chopped
4 large cloves garlic, crushed or minced
1 pound Italian plum tomatoes, chopped
1 medium carrot, sliced thinly
1 bay leaf
$\frac{1}{2}$ teaspoon black pepper
$\frac{1}{4}$ teaspoon salt
$\frac{1}{4}$ teaspoon ground cinnamon
6 small fish fillets (about $1\frac{1}{2}$ pounds), rinsed and patted dry
2 to 3 tablespoons fresh lemon juice, to taste
Chopped parsley, for garnish

Serves 6; 1 fillet per serving

Nutrient Analysis (per serving)

Calories 186
Protein 20 g
Carbohydrate 8 g
Cholesterol 53 mg
Sodium 206 mg
Total fat 8 g
  Saturated 1 g
  Polyunsaturated 1 g
  Monounsaturated 5 g

Heat the oil in a large skillet over medium heat. Add celery, onion, and garlic to skillet. Sauté for about 2 minutes, stirring constantly, adjusting heat if necessary so mixture doesn't brown.

Add tomatoes, carrot, bay leaf, pepper, salt, and cinnamon and cook for 5 minutes. Adjust pepper and cinnamon, if desired. Make 6 depressions in the mixture; place fish in depressions. Spoon hot vegetables over fish to cover. Cook over medium heat for 3 to 5 minutes, or until fish is opaque all the way through.

Sprinkle the lemon juice over all, cover the skillet, and remove from heat. Let the skillet sit for about 5 minutes before serving so the flavors can permeate the fish. Remove bay leaf and garnish with parsley.

COOK'S TIP: Good fish fillet choices for this recipe include sole, flounder, haddock, cod, orange roughy, and catfish. A combination of fish is also tasty.

Aegean Baked Fish

Psari Plaki

Greek cooks traditionally present a whole fish at the table. If you prefer, you can use several smaller fish or even fish steaks. Any mild white fish works well with this treatment. If you don't have a favorite fish or just want to try something different, let freshness, availability, and your budget be your guides.

Vegetable oil spray
3-pound fish, such as catfish
1 small onion, grated
1 tablespoon extra-virgin olive oil
1 tablespoon fresh lemon juice
1 tablespoon dried oregano, crumbled
¼ teaspoon salt
¼ teaspoon black pepper

Serves 6; 3 ounces per serving

Nutrient
Analysis
(per serving)

Calories 236
Protein 44 g
Carbohydrate 1 g
Cholesterol 122 mg
Sodium 286 mg
Total fat 5 g
  Saturated 1 g
  Polyunsaturated 1 g
  Monounsaturated 2 g

Using vegetable oil spray, lightly spray a pan or a nest of aluminum foil just large enough to hold the fish. Rinse fish and pat dry with paper towels. Place fish in pan.

Combine remaining ingredients in a small bowl. Rub mixture on the fish, inside and out. Pour any remaining mixture over the fish. Refrigerate fish for about 15 minutes. Meanwhile, preheat oven to 400° F.

Bake the fish for about 30 minutes, or until it flakes easily with a fork and is opaque inside.

COOK'S TIP: For fish steaks, plan on about 4 ounces raw fish per serving. Proceed as directed above but adjust baking time according to the size of the steaks. The rule of thumb is to measure the fish where it's thickest and cook for about 10 minutes per inch. Fish is done when it becomes opaque, begins to flake easily when tested with a fork, and comes away from the bone readily.

Fish Wrapped in Grape Leaves

Psari Dolmatia

G rape leaves add a subtle flavor to this dish and help prevent the fish from drying out while cooking.

Vegetable oil spray
10-ounce jar grape leaves

Seasoning Mixture
2 tablespoons finely chopped fresh parsley
2 tablespoons raisins
2 tablespoons red wine vinegar
2 bay leaves
1 teaspoon dried oregano, crumbled
1 teaspoon dried thyme, crumbled
1 small clove garlic, crushed or minced
$1/4$ teaspoon dried rosemary, crushed using mortar and pestle
$1/4$ teaspoon salt
$1/4$ teaspoon black pepper
Dash of ground cinnamon, or to taste

3-pound fish, such as snapper, rockfish, or orange roughy

Preheat oven to 350° F.

Lay out a sheet of aluminum foil large enough to enclose the fish completely. Spray the foil with vegetable oil spray.

Rinse and drain 10 to 12 grape leaves. Place some of the grape leaves on foil, overlapping leaves so no foil shows through.

Combine the seasoning mixture ingredients, mashing with a fork.

Rinse fish and pat dry with paper towels. Place the fish on the grape leaves and spoon the seasoning mixture into the body cavity. If there is any remaining liquid from the seasoning mixture, drizzle it over the fish. Use the foil to help you wrap

Serves 6

Nutrient
Analysis
(per serving)

Calories 199
Protein 38 g
Carbohydrate 5 g
Cholesterol 105 mg
Sodium 367 mg
Total fat 3 g
 Saturated 1 g
 Polyunsaturated 1 g
 Monounsaturated 0 g

the grape leaves over the fish, adding more rinsed and drained leaves, if needed, to enclose the fish. Wrap tightly in the foil and bake for 40 minutes. Let the cooked fish rest for about 10 minutes before unwrapping and serving.

COOK'S TIP: Because everything is tightly wrapped in foil, this dish is ideal for grilling. Prepare the grill. When coals have a thin coating of white ash, place the foil packet 3 to 4 inches from coals. Grill 5 to 7 minutes on each side. When the packet puffs up, the fish is probably done.

Roast Chicken with Artichokes and Tomatoes

Kotopoulo

A simple roast chicken can be served at any time, for any occasion. This one suggests the warm, sunny flavors of Greece.

1/4 **cup kalamata olives**
9- or 10-ounce package frozen artichoke hearts, thawed
6 medium Italian plum tomatoes, quartered
8 large shallots, peeled
1 head garlic, cloves separated, unpeeled
2 teaspoons extra-virgin olive oil
3 tablespoons fresh lemon juice
2 tablespoons chopped fresh rosemary or 2 teaspoons dried, crushed using mortar and pestle
2 tablespoons chopped fresh thyme or 2 teaspoons dried, crumbled
1/4 **teaspoon salt**
Black pepper to taste
1 cup low-sodium chicken broth
2 1/2**- to 3-pound whole chicken**

Preheat oven to 350° F.

Slightly crush olives with the back of a spoon to release flavor. Place olives in a large roasting pan. Add artichoke hearts, tomatoes, shallots, and garlic. Add oil and lemon juice, tossing to coat evenly. Sprinkle with rosemary, thyme, salt, and pepper. Pour the chicken broth into roasting pan. Bake, covered, for 20 minutes.

Meanwhile, rinse chicken and pat dry with paper towels. Season chicken inside and out with pepper. Truss chicken, if desired.

Place chicken in the roasting pan. Bake, covered, for 1 hour. Baste chicken and vegetables occasionally with pan juices, adding a little water if broth evaporates.

Serves 4

Nutrient Analysis (per serving)

Calories 330
Protein 37 g
Carbohydrate 21 g
Cholesterol 90 mg
Sodium 401 mg
Total fat 12 g
　Saturated 3 g
　Polyunsaturated 3 g
　Monounsaturated 5 g

Increase oven temperature to 450° F. Roast, uncovered, for about 20 minutes, until chicken is brown and crisp and juices run clear when thigh is pierced with a sharp knife.

Transfer the chicken to a serving platter. With a slotted spoon, transfer artichoke hearts, tomatoes, shallots, olives, and all but 8 garlic cloves to the platter and arrange around the chicken. Cover with foil or the top of the roaster to keep warm.

To prepare sauce, squeeze reserved garlic cloves into a blender or the work bowl of a food processor fitted with a metal blade. Skim any fat from pan juices. Add pan juices to work bowl; process sauce until smooth. Taste the sauce; dilute with a little water, if necessary. Transfer to a sauceboat or small pitcher and serve with the chicken and vegetables. Don't forget to remove the skin from the chicken before eating!

COOK'S TIP: Diners who wants to add some extra zip to the taste can use a fork to squeeze the skin off the remaining garlic cloves and eat them with the chicken.

Savory Chicken Patties

Keftedes

Throughout the Mediterranean, seasoned ground meat patties are served as appetizers, main courses, and snacks. Street carts appear at lunchtime, their charcoal burners creating a trail of mouthwatering scents through the streets and alleys. Made from any variety of meat, this variation, using chicken, can be prepared ahead and reheated when needed.

Yogurt Sauce

1 cup nonfat or low-fat plain yogurt
1 tablespoon chopped fresh cilantro
Generous pinch of dried dill weed
Black pepper (optional)

Patties

2 slices firm white bread
³/₄ pound ground skinless chicken breast
2 tablespoons egg substitute
1 teaspoon dried dill weed
¹/₂ teaspoon ground cumin
¹/₄ teaspoon salt
Black pepper to taste
Pinch of ground anise (optional)
Water, if needed
¹/₂ cup all-purpose flour
Vegetable oil spray
1 tablespoon extra-virgin olive oil

To prepare sauce, combine yogurt, cilantro, and pinch of dill weed in a small bowl; season, if desired, with pepper. Cover bowl and refrigerate sauce.

Trim off and discard bread crusts. Crumble bread into a large bowl. Add ground chicken, egg substitute, 1 teaspoon dill weed, cumin, salt, and pepper, and anise, if desired. Mix thoroughly. Add a little water if the mixture is too dry. Roll into a log and cut into 16 equal portions. Form each into a

Serves 8; 2 patties per person

Nutrient Analysis (per serving)

Calories 129
Protein 13 g
Carbohydrate 12 g
Cholesterol 24 mg
Sodium 157 mg
Total fat 3 g
 Saturated 1 g
 Polyunsaturated 1 g
 Monounsaturated 2 g

patty. Sprinkle some of the flour on a platter. Set patties on platter. Sprinkle more flour on tops of patties. Lightly spray a large skillet with vegetable oil spray and drizzle with a few drops of olive oil. Fry the patties over medium heat for about 3 minutes on each side or until a quick-read thermometer inserted in the center of a patty registers 165° F.

Remove patties from skillet. To serve, drizzle each patty with yogurt sauce. Serve with your choice of side dishes or tucked into fresh pita bread and eaten as a sandwich.

Herbed Braised Beef with Tomatoes

Brazoles

Y ou don't need to buy expensive steak for this recipe. It's an excellent budget dish that isn't frugal on taste.

1½ **pounds lean steak of choice, such as round steak**
1 **tablespoon ground coriander**
2 **teaspoons dried oregano, or to taste, crumbled**
1 **teaspoon dried sage**
½ **to 1 teaspoon black pepper, to taste**
½ **teaspoon garlic powder**
¼ **teaspoon ground cinnamon**
¼ **teaspoon salt**
6 **medium Italian plum tomatoes**
1 **teaspoon sugar**
½ **cup low-sodium beef broth**
Chopped fresh parsley or cilantro (optional)

Serves 6; 1 steak per serving

Nutrient Analysis (per serving)

Calories 161
Protein 24 g
Carbohydrate 7 g
Cholesterol 60 mg
Sodium 155 mg
Total fat 4 g
    Saturated 1 g
    Polyunsaturated 0 g
    Monounsaturated 2 g

Preheat oven to 350° F.

Trim all visible fat from the steak. Cut steak across the grain into 6 equal portions. Set aside.

In a small bowl, mix coriander, oregano, sage, pepper, garlic powder, cinnamon, and salt; rub some of the seasoning mixture into steaks. Set aside remaining seasoning mixture. Place steaks in a baking dish just large enough to hold them.

Slit tomatoes lengthwise, cutting only about halfway through. Pinch to open them slightly so flavors can penetrate. Nestle them between the steaks. Add sugar to remaining seasoning mixture and sprinkle on the slit tomatoes. Pour broth into the dish, being careful not to wash off the seasoning mixture.

Bake, uncovered, for 30 minutes. Baste. Bake for 30 minutes more, or until meat is tender, basting occasionally. Sprinkle with chopped parsley or cilantro, if desired.

COOK'S TIP: Lean pork chops are a good substitute for beef in this recipe.

Gyros

Gyros are as common to the streets of Athens as the bean pot is to the streets of Cairo. Towers of meat sizzle next to charcoal ricks, and thin strips are sliced off for each sandwich as it's ordered. At lunchtime, the tantalizing aromas draw hungry patrons like lemmings. Although you can make a quite passable facsimile in your oven, the flavor improves dramatically if the loaf is at least seared on a grill. If you don't like the flavor of lamb, use beef in its place.

Serves 10; 1 sandwich per serving

Nutrient Analysis (per serving)

Calories 319
Protein 24 g
Carbohydrate 31 g
Cholesterol 58 mg
Sodium 483 mg
Total fat 10 g
  Saturated 4 g
  Polyunsaturated 1 g
  Monounsaturated 4 g

Tzatziki Yogurt Sauce

1 cup plain nonfat or low-fat yogurt
¼ cup grated cucumber, peeled or unpeeled (about 2 ounces)
¼ cup grated onion (about 1 small)
¼ teaspoon garlic powder, or to taste

Gyro Loaf

1 pound lean beef, finely ground
1 pound lean lamb, finely ground
1 small onion, grated
1 tablespoon black pepper
3 to 4 cloves garlic, crushed or minced
2 teaspoons dried oregano, crumbled
1 teaspoon dried marjoram
1 teaspoon dried thyme, crumbled
¾ teaspoon salt

Pita bread, Greek style, not pocket style
2 medium tomatoes, sliced or chopped, or to taste
1 medium onion, thinly sliced, or to taste
Lettuce leaves (optional)

Combine the sauce ingredients in a medium mixing bowl and set aside.

Preheat broiler or prepare grill.

In a large mixing bowl, thoroughly combine gyro loaf ingredients. Shape into a flattened loaf about 2 inches thick.

To broil, place on broiler pan and broil 4 inches from heat, turning occasionally, for 5 to 10 minutes per side, or until a meat thermometer inserted in the center registers at least 155° F. Remove pan from broiler. Let loaf rest for 10 minutes, then slice as thinly as possible.

To grill, prepare loaf as directed above. When coals are ready (they'll be lightly coated with a layer of ash), place loaf about 4 inches above coals. Cooking takes about 5 to 10 minutes per side, depending on your grill and your preference.

Assemble each sandwich by placing a few slices of meat in a pita and adding some tomato, a few onion rings, and lettuce, if using. Drizzle on some of the sauce. Fold up and fasten each sandwich with a toothpick. Serve with plenty of napkins.

Stuffed Cabbage Rolls

Lakano Yemista

This dish looks as if it takes more work than it really does, mainly because it can be based on leftovers. That gives you a chance to serve something different, as well as to clean out the refrigerator. You can even use a leftover vegetable, such as sautéed summer squash, as a substitute for the beef.

1 head cabbage
¼ pound ground round
1 teaspoon extra-virgin olive oil
1 medium onion, chopped
¼ cup dried mint
2 tablespoons minced fresh parsley
2 tablespoons fresh lemon juice
1 tablespoon pine nuts
1 tablespoon raisins
½ teaspoon ground cinnamon
½ teaspoon black pepper, or to taste
¼ teaspoon salt
1½ cups cooked rice (about ¾ cup uncooked)
1½ cups nonfat or low-fat marinara sauce
1 teaspoon extra-virgin olive oil
Chopped fresh parsley for garnish (optional)

Serves 4; 1 cabbage roll per serving

Nutrient Analysis (per serving)

Calories 224
Protein 11 g
Carbohydrate 35 g
Cholesterol 16 mg
Sodium 428 mg
Total fat 6 g
  Saturated 1 g
  Polyunsaturated 1 g
  Monounsaturated 3 g

Use a sharp paring knife to cut out the core of the cabbage. Bring a large stockpot of water to a boil over high heat. Carefully immerse the cabbage, turning to ensure that the boiling water gets into the leaves around the core area. Boil for 10 minutes. Remove cabbage from water and drain. Set aside to cool.

In a large skillet, cook the ground round over medium heat for about 5 minutes, or until no longer pink. Place in a colander, rinse under hot water, and drain. Wipe skillet with paper towels, place over medium heat, and heat 1 teaspoon oil. Sauté onion in hot oil until soft but not browned, about 3 minutes. Add the meat and cook until browned, stirring occasionally, about 2 minutes. Add mint, parsley, lemon juice, pine nuts, raisins, cinnamon, pepper, and salt; mix thoroughly. Add rice and mix thoroughly. Set mixture aside.

Preheat the oven to 350° F.

Pull about 24 leaves off the cabbage. Arrange them in 4 equal groups, overlapping the leaves within each group so none of the work surface shows through. Place a quarter of the filling on each group of leaves. Then fold in the sides. Trying to keep the cabbage rolls fairly tight, roll up from the end nearest you.

Transfer rolls, seam side down, to a baking dish just large enough to hold them snugly. Pour marinara sauce over the rolls. Peel off enough of the remaining cabbage leaves to cover the baking dish, tucking them in slightly to enclose the rolls and sauce. Brush with 1 teaspoon oil. Bake for 1 hour.

To serve, remove the cabbage leaves that covered the dish and place them on a serving platter. Arrange cabbage rolls on the leaves. Garnish with chopped parsley, if desired. Serve hot or warm.

Very Versatile Mushrooms and Artichokes

Manitaria Me Aginares

Trying to classify this dish is really difficult. Is it a pickle, appetizer, or vegetable side dish? Actually, it's all of the above and then some. It's great served alongside a mild-flavored dish, because it can wake up the other food.

Serves 6; 1 cup per serving

Nutrient Analysis (per serving)

Calories 44
Protein 3 g
Carbohydrate 9 g
Cholesterol 0 mg
Sodium 333 mg
Total fat 1 g
  Saturated 0 g
  Polyunsaturated 0 g
  Monounsaturated 0 g

8-ounce jar marinated or pickled artichoke hearts, quartered
2 pounds button mushrooms, stems trimmed
$\frac{1}{2}$ cup dry white wine (optional)
1 tablespoon fresh lemon juice, or to taste
3 bay leaves
1 teaspoon coriander seeds
1 teaspoon dried oregano, crumbled
1 teaspoon black pepper, or to taste
$\frac{1}{2}$ teaspoon fennel seeds
Chopped fresh parsley

Empty the jar of artichokes and their brine into a large mixing bowl. Add remaining ingredients and stir.

Refrigerate, stirring occasionally, for several hours or overnight, depending on how strong you want the taste of the mushrooms to be.

Preheat oven to 350° F.

Transfer mixture to a 2-quart casserole dish. Bake, uncovered, for 1 hour. Remove the bay leaves. Garnish with chopped parsley and serve hot, warm, or cold.

COOK'S TIP ON COOKING WITH WINE: A good rule of thumb is: Don't cook with any wine you wouldn't drink.

Sautéed Summer Squash

Briami

This quick-and-easy method of cooking squash brings out its best flavor without using a lot of other ingredients to mask its natural goodness.

1 pound zucchini, yellow crookneck squash, or a combination
1 tablespoon extra-virgin olive oil
¼ teaspoon salt
⅛ teaspoon black pepper, or to taste
1 to 3 tablespoons fresh lemon juice, to taste

Trim the ends of the squash. Cut squash into matchstick-size strips. Heat a large skillet over medium heat until quite hot. Add the oil, followed immediately by the squash. Stir continuously until the sizzling slows down somewhat. Season squash mixture with salt and pepper. When the squash is just barely tender, about 2 minutes, add the lemon juice. Taste for seasoning. Cook for 1 to 2 minutes, or until squash is crisp-tender. Serve hot or cold.

COOK'S TIP: For a zippy change of pace, add a tablespoon of rinsed capers when you add the lemon juice to the squash. If you're on a sodium-restricted diet, however, be aware that capers contain about 100 milligrams of sodium per teaspoon.

Serves 6; ¾ cup per serving

Nutrient Analysis (per serving)

Calories 31
Protein 0 g
Carbohydrate 3 g
Cholesterol 0 mg
Sodium 100 mg
Total fat 2 g
  Saturated 0 g
  Polyunsaturated 0 g
  Monounsaturated 2 g

Rice with Grape Leaves

Pilaf Dolmatia

Dolmas, stuffed grape leaves, are common throughout the Mediterranean. The trouble with them is the amount of work that goes into wrapping all the tiny bundles. If you want the flavor of rice-stuffed dolmas without all the fuss, try this recipe.

3¹/₂ cups water
2 cups rice
Grape leaves (about ¹/₃ of 10-ounce jar)
¹/₂ cup raisins or currants (about 3 ounces)
¹/₄ cup lightly toasted pine nuts (about 1 ounce)
¹/₄ cup finely chopped fresh parsley
3 tablespoons finely chopped onion
1 tablespoon fresh lemon juice
¹/₂ teaspoon salt
¹/₄ teaspoon ground coriander
¹/₄ teaspoon black pepper
1 tablespoon extra-virgin olive oil

Serves 8; ¾ cup per serving

Nutrient Analysis (per serving)

Calories 257
Protein 5 g
Carbohydrate 50 g
Cholesterol 0 mg
Sodium 233 mg
Total fat 5 g
  Saturated 1 g
  Polyunsaturated 1 g
  Monounsaturated 2 g

In a large saucepan over high heat, bring water to a boil and add rice. Stir. When water returns to a boil, immediately reduce heat and simmer, covered, for 10 minutes. Remove the pan from the heat and set aside, still covered.

Preheat oven to 350° F.

Meanwhile, rinse and drain the grape leaves. Place some on the bottom of a 2-quart casserole, allowing them to overlap the sides of the dish.

Uncover the rice and mix in the remaining ingredients except oil. The mixture will be wet. Pour all the rice mixture, including the liquid, into the casserole, being careful not to pack it down; the ingredients must be fluffy. Gently overlap the grape leaves, adding more to completely cover the contents. Brush grape leaves with oil and bake, covered, for 30 minutes.

Let the casserole rest for 5 minutes before

serving. To serve, cut straight down into portions with a sharp knife and remove with a spatula.

COOK'S TIP: Some people choose not to eat the aromatic grape leaves. If you're one of them, simply slit open the top of the casserole with a sharp knife and peel back the leaves to display the contents.

Refrigerate any leftover grape leaves for use in another recipe, such as Fish Wrapped in Grape Leaves (page 103).

Garlic Potatoes

Patates Skortou

This country-style recipe, flavored with garlic, makes a fine accompaniment to many types of entrée. Depending on whether you use boiling (waxy) potatoes or baking potatoes, your results will be creamier or fluffier, respectively. Don't be tempted to make this in a food processor—this is one recipe that should be homey and have lots of texture.

2 pounds boiling or baking potatoes
6 large cloves garlic
1 tablespoon extra-virgin olive oil
2 teaspoons fresh lemon juice
1 teaspoon balsamic vinegar (optional)
¹⁄₂ teaspoon chopped fresh rosemary
¹⁄₂ teaspoon chopped fresh oregano
¹⁄₄ teaspoon salt
¹⁄₄ teaspoon black or white pepper

Serves 6; ¾ cup per serving

Nutrient Analysis (per serving)

Calories 156
Protein 3 g
Carbohydrate 32 g
Cholesterol 0 mg
Sodium 108 mg
Total fat 2 g
  Saturated 0 g
  Polyunsaturated 0 g
  Monounsaturated 2 g

Bring a large stockpot of water to a boil.

Meanwhile, scrub potatoes and cut in half. Peel garlic. Place potatoes and whole garlic in the boiling water. There should be enough water to cover them. Boil for about 30 minutes, or until potatoes are soft all the way through when tested with a knife.

Using a slotted spoon, transfer the potatoes to a large mixing bowl and remove garlic. Set the potato water aside. Press or mash the garlic cloves, add to the potatoes, and combine lightly with a potato masher or large fork.

Stir in the remaining ingredients, adding a little hot potato water to adjust consistency, if necessary.

COOK'S TIP: For a taste change, substitute other fresh herbs for the rosemary and/or oregano. Parsley and sage are just two possibilities.

Dried Fruit Compote with Vanilla Yogurt

Kochafia

If you're lucky enough to have any of this refreshing fruit compote left over, it makes a delightful breakfast dish. Make lots, because it just gets better every day as the cinnamon continues to spice the fruit.

4 cups dried fruit, any combination of figs, prunes, apricots, raisins, apples, pears, and peaches
1 large lemon, cut into paper-thin slices, seeds removed
3 tablespoons fresh lemon juice
½ cup honey
¼ cup pine nuts (about 1 ounce)
3 cinnamon sticks, broken in half
10 coriander seeds
3 whole cloves
¾ cup vanilla-flavored nonfat or low-fat yogurt
2 tablespoons pine nuts

Serves 6; 1 cup per serving

Nutrient Analysis (per serving)

Calories 360
Protein 4 g
Carbohydrate 88 g
Cholesterol 1 mg
Sodium 36 mg
Total fat 4 g
    Saturated 1 g
    Polyunsaturated 1 g
    Monounsaturated 1 g

Put all the dried fruit in a large saucepan with enough water to cover. Simmer, covered, for about 15 minutes over medium heat, or until fruits are just tender. Add the lemon and juice, honey, ¼ cup pine nuts, cinnamon sticks, coriander seeds, and cloves. Simmer, covered, for 5 minutes, or until the syrup reaches the desired thickness. Remove from the heat and let the covered pot stand for 1 hour. This compote can be refrigerated and reheated if desired. Serve, warm or cold, in small bowls. Top with a dollop of yogurt and a sprinkle of pine nuts. Make sure you include the lemon slices, which are completely edible.

COOK'S TIP: You can puree the compote in a blender or food processor to make fruit soup. Garnish with a swirl of yogurt and a few pine nuts.

MIDDLE EASTERN CUISINE

Red Lentil Soup

Lemony Cucumber with Yogurt Salad
Any-Bean Salad

Grilled Fish with Cumin-Lemon Rub

Lemon Chicken
Herb-Crusted Chicken Breasts

Sizzling Flank Steak
Couscous with Lamb Stew

Beans Egyptian-Style
Stuffed Zucchini
Cinnamon Rice

Pita Bread

Lemon Cream
Walnut-Semolina Cake

I n the Middle East, just as in America, dietary boundaries are feathered with a culinary airbrush. The flavors and variations change slightly from village to village, town to town, region to region, in a gentle flow that defies hard lines.

Despite the similarities, though, the cuisines of the region vary according to each Middle Eastern country's access to the sea, religious convictions and holidays, history, and availability of pastureland for raising livestock, herbs, and spices.

Land of the Pharaohs

Egypt is for many the heart of the Middle East. Today, the peoples of the Middle East enjoy the same foods as the Egyptian pharaohs. Legumes are still a staple protein, and the Red Lentil Soup recipe found on page 125 is virtually identical to one written down about 3,500 years ago.

Onions are the most common vegetable in Middle Eastern recipes. Garlic is very popular in some areas but relatively ignored in others. The tomato, a relatively recent addition to the diet, has been adopted enthusiastically.

Feta Cheese: A Fortunate Accident

Bedouin traders are credited with discovering the miracle of cheese. Supposedly, some extra camel milk was stored in a cleaned animal stomach, a common container used by nomads because it wouldn't spill or break during transport. The natural enzymes, or rennet, in the skin of the container interacted with the milk proteins. A brave soul sampled the resulting curds and extolled their fine flavor. The accident became tradition when people noticed that the curded milk took far longer to spoil than did the fresh product. Feta cheese and its variants are modern equivalents of this type of cheese. An animal stomach is no longer used, so you need not be squeamish about trying it.

Birds of many kinds find their way into Middle Eastern cooking pots, but chicken is by far the most popular. Most are free-range, and all that exercise makes them leaner and sometimes a bit stringy. The cook compensates by adding broth and cooking the chicken longer. If you can find free-range chickens at your market or health-food store, give them a try. They're harvested younger so the meat is still tender. The notable absence of fat pockets under the skin makes for a more heart-healthy bird, and the flavor is more concentrated than in the mass-produced variety.

Beef is popular but expensive. Pork is available, though Muslims and Jews shun it for religious reasons.

Medieval Imports

Fruit is popular in all its forms, and many of our favorites were first cultivated in the Middle East. The semimythical "golden apple" referred to in the chronicles of the Middle Ages is actually the lowly orange, introduced in Europe by Crusaders returning from the Holy Land. Like pepper, another exotic wonder, it was once literally worth its weight in gold. The next time you peel an orange or drink a glass of its juice, imagine that you're about to taste it for the very first time and that it just cost you a hundred dollars!

Roses were another medieval import from the Crusades. In the Middle East, the flowers are valued for more than their beauty and aroma. Rose water, an extract from the petals, has been manufactured for thousands of years. It is still sprinkled on visitors' feet in Yemen and flavors numerous sweets and beverages throughout the Middle East. Those uses are a surprise to most Westerners, who aren't accustomed to having their food perfumed! Try the Walnut-Semolina Cake on page 141 to find out whether you prefer to eat or wear your perfume.

Food is prepared with the freshest possible ingredients. Despite cultural conceptions, it's not unusual to find that the cook is the man of the house. Preparing food is considered an honor. Recipes are seldom written down. More often, they're passed along by word or example. Each cook adds touches to his version, depending on seasonal availability or personal whim. Don't be afraid to do the same. Dishes can be served in courses or placed all at once on the table or the rug-covered floor. Some diners use their fingers, some use Western utensils. All eat bread, which is reverently broken and shared. After the meal, it's time to talk and to drink tea or coffee. A little later, perhaps there will be a sweet, such as Lemon Cream (page 140), to enjoy.

Coffee is a favorite beverage throughout the Middle East. Whether it's Egyptian, Syrian, Arabic, or Turkish, it's always very, very strong. The desserts are usually rich with butter and highly sweetened with sugar or dripping with honey. Cloying on their own, the flavors offset the coffee's strength and bitterness.

Eating in Peace

Mealtimes vary in their hour and complexity, but the act of coming together over food is always a serious matter. From the first nomads, encountering one another with veiled suspicion on the scorching pan of the desert, the agreement to sit down and share a meal held a tacit promise to set aside their personal differences until they once again parted company. This tradition threads its way into the present, when the host answers the door with the words "*Echlen wesechlen*" ("Welcome, enter") and the guest replies, "*Salaam alaikum*" ("Peace to you").

Welcome, enter, and delight in the history and flavor of the exotic Middle East!

Red Lentil Soup

Shurbit Ahdz

THROUGHOUT THE MIDDLE EAST

This soup uses the red lentil, which is more common to the Middle East than the brown lentil we're accustomed to in the United States. Available at most health-food stores as well as Middle Eastern and Indian groceries, the red lentil actually looks orange and turns yellow when cooked. The red variety has a delicate flavor and lovely color and takes only a fraction of the time that most other lentils require to cook.

6 cups low-sodium chicken broth
1½ cups red lentils, rinsed and picked over for
    small stones and shriveled lentils
1 small onion, grated
¼ teaspoon ground cumin
Generous sprinkling of cayenne, to taste
Chopped fresh parsley (optional)
Croutons (optional)

Serves 6; ¾ cup per serving

Nutrient Analysis (per serving)

Calories 190
Protein 15 g
Carbohydrate 30 g
Cholesterol 0 mg
Sodium 59 mg
Total fat 1 g
    Saturated 0 g
    Polyunsaturated 0 g
    Monounsaturated 0 g

Place the broth, red lentils, onion, cumin, and cayenne in a medium saucepan and simmer, partially covered, until lentils are soft, about 30 minutes. Pour the soup into a blender or the work bowl of a food processor fitted with a metal blade and process until smooth (you may have to do this in batches). Return soup to the pan and simmer until it is the desired thickness, stirring frequently. (Some people like this soup almost spreadable, but be careful not to let it burn.) Garnish with chopped fresh parsley and/or croutons, if desired.

COOK'S TIP: If you have a hand-held immersion blender, you can puree the soup right in the pot while it cooks.

Lemony Cucumber with Yogurt Salad

Hijarah Salata

EGYPT

Cucumber salads are widespread throughout the Middle East and into India. Serve this one by itself as a cool refresher or alongside any spicy entrée to tame the heat.

3 to 4 medium cucumbers, cut into pieces or thickly sliced
3 cups plain nonfat or low-fat yogurt
2 tablespoons fresh lemon juice
2 large cloves garlic, minced
2 teaspoons chopped fresh parsley
1 teaspoon chopped fresh mint (optional)
Black pepper (optional)

Combine all ingredients in a medium bowl and serve. Can be made a day ahead and chilled in a nonmetallic bowl until ready to serve.

COOK'S TIP: If you refrigerate this dish for long, the cucumbers will exude some liquid. The result will be a thin liquid layer on top. Mix it in or pour it off. The flavor won't be affected.

Serves 4; ⅔ cup per serving

Nutrient Analysis (per serving)

Calories 132
Protein 12 g
Carbohydrate 20 g
Cholesterol 3 mg
Sodium 147 mg
Total fat 1 g
 Saturated 0 g
 Polyunsaturated 0 g
 Monounsaturated 0 g

Any-Bean Salad

Fasoolya Beyda Barda

EGYPT

B eans are a favorite form of protein in the hot
summer months, when spoilage can be a problem
with dishes that include meat. According to folk
wisdom, this recipe is supposed to help cool the body,
so it's a terrific recipe for picnics and pool parties.

**¹/₂ pound dried beans, any kind, or a mixture,
    rinsed and picked over for stones and shriveled
    beans**
3 tablespoons fat-free Italian salad dressing
¹/₄ teaspoon salt
Black pepper to taste
2 medium red onions
3 Italian plum tomatoes
1 tablespoon chopped fresh flat-leaf parsley
1 teaspoon dried oregano, crumbled (optional)

In a medium saucepan, soak the beans overnight in
cold water to cover. Change the water several times,
if possible. Drain the beans, return them to the pot,
and cover with fresh water. Bring to a boil over
medium-high heat. Reduce heat and simmer,
uncovered, until tender, about 20 to 40 minutes,
depending on the beans you choose. Drain the
beans and spread them out on a platter to cool.

Meanwhile, using a whisk, combine salad dressing, salt, and pepper in a small bowl. Set aside.

Slice the onions very thinly, then chop coarsely.
Place onions in a large mixing bowl and add the
cooled beans. Dice the tomatoes and add them
along with any juice. Add the dressing and parsley,
and oregano, if using. Toss gently and serve, or let
marinate several hours or overnight before serving.

Serves 4; 1 cup
per person

Nutrient
Analysis
(per serving)

Calories 219
Protein 13 g
Carbohydrate 41 g
Cholesterol 0 mg
Sodium 269 mg
Total fat 1 g
  Saturated 0 g
  Polyunsaturated 1 g
  Monounsaturated 0 g

Grilled Fish with Cumin–Lemon Rub

Samakh

SAUDI ARABIA

Most fish in the Middle East is prepared simply, grilled and dressed with a little lemon juice. For this recipe, you can vary the rub seasoning according to your instincts and preferences.

2 teaspoons ground cumin, or to taste
1 small onion, pureed
1 tablespoon fresh lemon juice
1 teaspoon olive oil
1 small mild-flavored fish or 4-ounce fillet, such as flounder, orange roughy, catfish, or grouper
Lemon wedges

Serves 1

Nutrient Analysis (per serving)

Calories 181
Protein 21 g
Carbohydrate 9 g
Cholesterol 56 mg
Sodium 98 mg
Total fat 7 g
   Saturated 1 g
   Polyunsaturated 1 g
   Monounsaturated 4 g

Prepare grill. Soak two or three 8-inch wooden skewers in water for 10 minutes.

In a small bowl or cup, mix cumin with onion puree and a little of the lemon juice to make a paste. Add more juice if needed. Stir in oil.

Rinse fish and pat dry with paper towels. If using whole fish, cut a few deep slashes in the sides to allow the seasonings in and to speed cooking. Rub a little of the seasoning mixture on the whole fish, inside and out, or on both sides of fillet.

Thread fish on skewers (use an in-and-out "basting stitch") and grill over hot coals for about 5 minutes on each side, or until fish flakes easily when tested with a fork. The fish should still be moist. Serve hot with lemon wedges.

COOK'S TIP: Some fish, particularly thin fillets, may be too fragile to stay on the skewer. If in doubt, use a grill basket, available in most kitchenware shops, to hold the fish fillets. Be careful not to overgrill—the fish will continue to cook a little after it's off the heat.

Lemon Chicken

Farrough Limuna

YEMEN

A Yemenite tang of lemon brings out the taste of chicken in this simple recipe. To cut the strength of the lemon, you can omit the grated lemon peel.

2 lemons
3 to 4 cloves garlic, crushed or minced
2 teaspoons hot paprika
Black pepper to taste
3-pound whole chicken
Vegetable oil spray

Preheat oven to 350° F.

Grate the lemons. Juice the lemons and save what's left of the rinds. Set aside.

In a small bowl, combine grated zest, garlic, paprika, black pepper, and enough lemon juice to make a paste. Set aside.

Add the remaining lemon juice to a bowl of cool water and use the lemon water to rinse the chicken, inside and out. Pat dry with paper towels. Use your fingers to work under the skin and gently separate it from the breast meat of the chicken, being careful not to tear through. If you're careful, you can even work down the thighs and back of the bird. Rub the seasoning paste under the skin, directly onto the meat. Pat the skin back into place.

Lightly spray a roasting pan with vegetable oil spray. Put the chicken in the pan and place the reserved lemon rinds inside the cavity of the chicken. Roast for about 1½ hours, or until a thermometer in the thigh registers 165° F. Remove pan from the oven and let the chicken rest for about 10 minutes. Cut the chicken into 4 portions. Remove and discard the skin and all visible fat. Serve chicken hot with the pan juices.

Serves 4; ¼ chicken per serving

Nutrient Analysis (per serving)

Calories 230
Protein 35 g
Carbohydrate 4 g
Cholesterol 98 mg
Sodium 94 mg
Total fat 8 g
  Saturated 2 g
  Polyunsaturated 2 g
  Monounsaturated 2 g

Herb-Crusted Chicken Breasts

THROUGHOUT THE MIDDLE EAST

M ost people think of marinating as immersing a food in a seasoned liquid, but this marinade is rubbed on, for a more intense flavor. If your favorite seasonings aren't included among the ingredients here, you can add them. Some worth a try are basil, tarragon, and parsley.

Serves 6; 1 breast half per serving

Nutrient Analysis (per serving)

Calories 134
Protein 25 g
Carbohydrate 0 g
Cholesterol 62 mg
Sodium 57 mg
Total fat 3 g
 Saturated 1 g
 Polyunsaturated 1 g
 Monounsaturated 1 g

Vegetable oil spray
6 boneless, skinless chicken breast halves
 (about 4 ounces each), all visible fat removed
1 tablespoon fresh lemon juice
1 teaspoon dried rosemary, crushed
1 teaspoon dried oregano, crumbled
1 teaspoon dried sage, crumbled
¼ teaspoon cracked black pepper

Using vegetable oil spray, lightly spray a small roasting pan or a casserole dish just large enough to hold breasts. Rinse chicken and pat dry with paper towels. Arrange chicken in pan.

Combine remaining ingredients except pepper and rub well on each breast. Sprinkle with pepper. Refrigerate, covered, for at least 1 hour. For even more flavor, marinate the chicken overnight.

Preheat oven to 350° F.

Bake the chicken, uncovered, for 35 to 40 minutes, or until juices run clear when breasts are pierced with a knife. Serve with any pan juices.

Sizzling Flank Steak

Kostoh

THROUGHOUT THE MIDDLE EAST

This is a great summer dish but can also be made in the winter under the broiler. Just be sure to plan ahead—the meat marinates overnight. Serve it with the Cinnamon Rice on page 137.

Marinade

1 medium onion, grated

5 tablespoons fresh lemon juice (about 2 medium lemons)

1 tablespoon olive oil

2 tablespoons chopped fresh parsley

2 tablespoons grated fresh gingerroot (about 1½ ounces)

2 tablespoons light soy sauce

1 tablespoon ground cumin

1 tablespoon chili powder

2 large cloves garlic, crushed or minced

2 teaspoons dry sherry (optional)

1 teaspoon turmeric

1 teaspoon dried oregano, crumbled

1 teaspoon black pepper

2 pounds flank steak, all visible fat removed
Fresh cilantro sprigs

Mix all the marinade ingredients in a shallow baking dish. Add the meat, turning to coat. Cover and refrigerate overnight, turning the meat occasionally.

Prepare the grill. The coals are ready when they are no longer flaming and are covered with a thin, gray layer of ash.

Remove the meat from the marinade, reserving marinade. Grill the meat to desired doneness, about 5 minutes per side for medium. Transfer the meat to a platter and let it stand for about 5 minutes to stabilize the juices.

Serves 9;
3 ounces steak per serving

Nutrient Analysis (per serving)

Calories 181
Protein 22 g
Carbohydrate 2 g
Cholesterol 57 mg
Sodium 197 mg
Total fat 9 g
  Saturated 3 g
  Polyunsaturated 0 g
  Monounsaturated 4 g

Meanwhile, strain marinade into a small saucepan and discard the solids. Bring the marinade to a boil over high heat, 3 to 5 minutes. Cook for 1 to 2 minutes.

Cut the meat diagonally into thin slices and arrange on a platter. To serve, pour marinade over the meat and garnish with cilantro sprigs.

COOK'S TIP FOR MARINATING: Try using an airtight plastic bag for marinating. When it's time to turn the food, all you have to do is flip the bag.

Couscous with Lamb Stew

THROUGHOUT THE MIDDLE EAST

Couscous, steamed semolina native to the Middle East, is served as a side dish with a variety of stewed or braised entrées. In this recipe, it's cooked along with a savory stew that delicately flavors the grain. Couscous is usually made in a special two-part pot called a couscousière, but a large pot with a steamer insert works equally well. In a pinch, you can improvise with an oriental bamboo steamer basket set over your stockpot. Although lamb is traditionally used in this recipe, feel free to substitute beef cubes in its place.

Serves 8; 1 to 1¼ cups per serving

Nutrient Analysis (per serving)*

Calories 466
Protein 23 g
Carbohydrate 77 g
Cholesterol 31 mg
Sodium 265 mg
Total fat 8 g
   Saturated 2 g
   Polyunsaturated 2 g
   Monounsaturated 3 g
* Using lamb stew meat

1 tablespoon olive oil
1 tablespoon acceptable margarine
1 pound boneless lamb, lean cut, cut into bite-size cubes, all visible fat removed
2 large onions, sliced
2 teaspoons black pepper
1 teaspoon ground ginger
1 teaspoon turmeric
Pinch of saffron threads (optional)
16 ounces dry couscous
2 cups water
¼ cup raisins (optional)
¼ cup pine nuts (about 1 ounce) (optional)
6 medium carrots, quartered
3 medium potatoes, peeled and quartered
3 medium turnips, peeled and quartered
4 medium zucchini, sliced
15-ounce can chick-peas, rinsed and drained
¼ teaspoon salt, if needed
Cayenne (optional)

Over medium-high heat, heat oil and margarine in the bottom of a couscousière or in a large stockpot. Sear the lamb until lightly browned on all sides, about 5 minutes. Add onions, pepper, ginger, and turmeric, and saffron, if using. Stir. Add enough water to cover 2 inches above ingredients. Bring to a simmer, covered, over low heat.

Meanwhile, put the couscous in a large mixing bowl and moisten with about 2 cups water, a little at a time, rubbing the couscous between your hands to remove all lumps and to thoroughly moisten all the grains. (Do not get the grains soaking wet.)

Mix in the raisins and pine nuts, if desired.

Line the top of the couscousière or a steamer with dampened cheesecloth or a dampened dish towel. Place the couscous in the cheesecloth or towel; do not pack the couscous. Place the container holding the couscous inside the stockpot (the simmering lamb remains in the bottom). Simmer and steam, covered, for 1 hour. Gently stir the mixture every 10 minutes or so to circulate the grains. This keeps the couscous fluffy during cooking so that the steam can cook the grains.

At the end of the hour, remove the steamer and set aside. Add the carrots, potatoes, and turnips to the lamb stew in the bottom of the stockpot and cook for 20 minutes. Add a little boiling water if the stew looks too dry. Add the zucchini and chickpeas and cook for 20 minutes. Taste the stew and add the salt if needed.

To serve, mound the couscous in the center of a large platter and arrange the meat and vegetables around it. Serve the remaining broth in a gravy boat. If you like spicy food, mix a little cayenne into a spoonful of the broth and drizzle that over your couscous.

Beans Egyptian–Style

Ful Mudammes

EGYPT

Beans of many kinds have been a dietary staple in Egypt since the pharaohs ruled. A favorite is fava beans, cooked down into a thick, savory stew. Street vendors appear early in the morning with charcoal-burning pushcarts and three or four huge pots of fava beans, or ful (the pronunciation is halfway between "fool" and "full"). For about 20 cents, you can buy two thick, warm, homemade pita breads overflowing with the rich brown beans.

2 cups dried fava beans or other dark beans, rinsed and picked over for stones and shriveled beans
5 cloves garlic, minced
1 tablespoon ground cumin
2 tablespoons olive oil
1 small bunch flat-leaf parsley
1 tablespoon fresh lemon juice
¼ teaspoon salt

In a medium saucepan with a lid, soak the beans in cold water to cover and set aside, covered, for about 8 hours. Change the water several times, if possible. Drain the beans, return them to the pan, and cover with fresh water. Add the garlic, cumin, and oil. Simmer, covered, until tender, about 45 minutes.

Meanwhile, chop the parsley.

When beans are tender, add parsley, lemon juice, and salt to the pot. Simmer for about 30 minutes, or until some of the beans begin to break down, forming a creamy base for the rest. Serve as a pita filling or in bowls with pita alongside.

COOK'S TIP: Any leftovers can be reheated—again and again and again. . . .

Serves 6; ¾ cup per serving

Nutrient Analysis (per serving)

Calories 180
Protein 8 g
Carbohydrate 26 g
Cholesterol 0 mg
Sodium 171 mg
Total fat 5 g
  Saturated 1 g
  Polyunsaturated 1 g
  Monounsaturated 3 g

Stuffed Zucchini

THROUGHOUT THE MIDDLE EAST

Zucchini is an ancient vegetable that stands alone or serves well as a backdrop for other flavors. In this case, the flavors come from a savory stuffing that doesn't overpower the zucchini's own delicate aroma and flavor.

3 large zucchini (about 10 ounces each)
1 cup plain dry bread crumbs
1 teaspoon dried oregano, crumbled
¼ teaspoon black pepper
3 large Italian plum tomatoes, chopped
2 tablespoons fresh lemon juice
2 tablespoons grated Romano or Parmesan cheese
⅓ cup low-sodium chicken broth

Serves 6; ½ stuffed zucchini per serving

Nutrient Analysis (per serving)

Calories 111
Protein 4 g
Carbohydrate 21 g
Cholesterol 1 mg
Sodium 198 mg
Total fat 2 g
  Saturated 1 g
  Polyunsaturated 0 g
  Monounsaturated 1 g

Preheat oven to 350° F.

Cut zucchini in half lengthwise. Using a spoon or melon baller, scoop out a hollow down the length of the zucchini and discard that pulp.

Place bread crumbs, oregano, pepper, tomatoes, and lemon juice in a medium mixing bowl; squeeze with your hands to moisten the mixture thoroughly. Divide the mixture evenly among the zucchini halves. Sprinkle with the cheese. Transfer to a casserole just large enough to hold the zucchini; pour the chicken broth around the zucchini, being careful not to pour on top.

Bake, uncovered, for about 40 minutes, or until a knife inserted into the center goes in easily and the zucchini are tender. Serve hot, warm, or cold.

COOK'S TIP: If a casserole or baking dish of the right size is unavailable, you can improvise by molding aluminum foil around the zucchini, then placing the container on a baking sheet.

Cinnamon Rice

Ros

THROUGHOUT THE MIDDLE EAST

I n the Middle East, many people eat rice with every meal, sometimes even with sugar and raisins for breakfast. Basmati rice, available at most supermarkets, approximates the flavor preferred throughout the Middle East. Rinsing the rice before cooking is a critical step. It not only helps prevent stickiness but also helps prevent a burned layer from forming on the bottom of the pot.

1¾ **cups water**
1-inch piece cinnamon stick
1 cardamom pod
⅛ **teaspoon salt**
1 whole clove
Several saffron threads (optional)
1 cup basmati rice, rinsed well and drained

In a medium saucepan, bring water, cinnamon stick, cardamom pod, salt, and clove, and saffron, if using, to a boil over high heat. Add the rice and stir well. Return the water to a boil, reduce heat, and simmer, covered, for 15 minutes, or until all the water has been absorbed. Remove the pan from heat, stir with a fork to fluff up the rice, cover again, and let sit for 5 minutes. Remove cinnamon stick, cardamom pod, and clove before serving rice.

Serves 4; ½ cup per serving

Nutrient Analysis (per serving)

Calories 184
Protein 4 g
Carbohydrate 40 g
Cholesterol 0 mg
Sodium 74 mg
Total fat 0 g
  Saturated 0 g
  Polyunsaturated 0 g
  Monounsaturated 0 g

Pita Bread

THROUGHOUT THE MIDDLE EAST

Traditional among Middle Eastern peoples, this bread tastes wonderful fresh from the oven but will keep for days and reheats well. Although you can substitute dried yeast, the fresh yeast has more flavor. This pita will be softer and thicker than commercial pita, making it ideal for accompanying Beans Egyptian-Style (page 135) and for Gyros (page 110).

2 cakes yeast
2 cups warm water (105° F)
8 cups unbleached white flour
2 cups whole-wheat flour
¼ teaspoon salt
Unbleached white flour

Serves 12; 1 small pita loaf per serving

Nutrient Analysis (per serving)

Calories 379
Protein 12 g
Carbohydrate 79 g
Cholesterol 0 mg
Sodium 53 mg
Total fat 1 g
    Saturated 0 g
    Polyunsaturated 1 g
    Monounsaturated 0 g

In a small bowl, dissolve the yeast in the water. Combine the flours in a large mixing bowl. Mix in the salt. Pour in the yeast mixture, and, if necessary, add a little more water. The dough should be very stiff. Turn the dough out onto a lightly floured surface and knead until smooth, about 10 minutes. Cover with a clean dish towel and let rise in a warm place until doubled, about 1 hour. Punch down, then divide the dough into 12 equal pieces.

Roll each piece between your palms until it is smooth. Flatten dough into disks. Place on a lightly floured surface, cover loosely with plastic wrap, and allow to rise for about 1 hour.

Place an overturned baking sheet or baking stones in the center of the oven and preheat the oven to 525° F.

On a floured board, roll out one disk of dough into a pancakelike circle 8 to 9 inches in diameter. Carefully place one loaf on the baking sheet in the hot oven. (A flat wooden tool called a baker's peel makes this operation easier.) Bake for about 4 minutes. Keep an eye on the oven, because each loaf takes only a few minutes to bake. Very light brown spots will form on the loaf, and it will puff up quite a bit. Remove it from the oven and transfer to a basket lined with a dish towel. Cover with another towel and stack the loaves as they come from the oven. Eat pita loaves while warm or cover them until cool so they don't dry out.

While each loaf is baking, roll out the next and repeat the procedure.

COOK'S TIP: Make sure your oven is nice and clean before baking the pita, or the high temperature will create a lot of smoke.

Lemon Cream

Ulum Limuna

THROUGHOUT THE MIDDLE EAST

Many Middle Eastern desserts are soaked in butter. Not this tangy pudding, though it is typical of the region. It works equally well if you substitute oranges for the lemons.

2 large lemons or 2 small oranges
¾ cup sugar
5 tablespoons cornstarch
3½ cups water
1 tablespoon finely chopped pistachios or almonds

Grate the lemons. Stop when you reach the bitter white pith. Place grated zest in a medium saucepan. Mix in the sugar, pressing with the back of a spoon so the sugar absorbs the lemon oil. Squeeze the lemons into a small bowl, strain out any seeds, and pour the juice into the saucepan. Place cornstarch in a small bowl. Stir in water. Add cornstarch-water mixture to saucepan. Bring to a boil over high heat, stirring constantly, about 5 minutes. When thickened, pour the pudding into small dessert dishes. Sprinkle each serving with ½ teaspoon chopped nuts. Serve warm or let it thicken a little while cooling, then chill it.

Serves 6; ½ cup per serving

Nutrient Analysis (per serving)

Calories 130
Protein 0 g
Carbohydrate 34 g
Cholesterol 0 mg
Sodium 2 mg
Total fat 0 g
   Saturated 0 g
   Polyunsaturated 0 g
   Monounsaturated 0 g

Walnut–Semolina Cake

Haliba

EGYPT

Many home-style Middle Eastern desserts are sweetened grain puddings perfumed with either rose water or orange water. This one can be made ahead of time and served warm or cold. You might even want to try the leftovers for breakfast.

3 cups dry ready-to-cook wheat or rice cereal (farina) or semolina
1 cup sugar
4 cups skim milk
1 teaspoon rose water
$^1/_4$ cup ground walnuts (about $1^1/_4$ ounces)

Mix the cereal, sugar, and milk in a large saucepan and bring to a slow boil over medium heat, stirring constantly. After about 5 minutes, when the cereal has begun to thicken, stir in the rose water. Quickly pour the dessert into a 1-quart casserole dish and spread out evenly with a wet spatula. Sprinkle with the ground nuts and allow to cool. Once the dessert has set, cut into diamonds and serve. You can refrigerate the leftovers, tightly covered, for 7 to 10 days. They can be lightly toasted, if desired.

COOK'S TIP: This recipe makes a thick cake. For a softer texture, add 1 cup of water along with the milk.

Serves 8; 1 slice per serving

Nutrient Analysis (per serving)

Calories 397
Protein 11 g
Carbohydrate 81 g
Cholesterol 2 mg
Sodium 69 mg
Total fat 3 g
  Saturated 0 g
  Polyunsaturated 1 g
  Monounsaturated 0 g

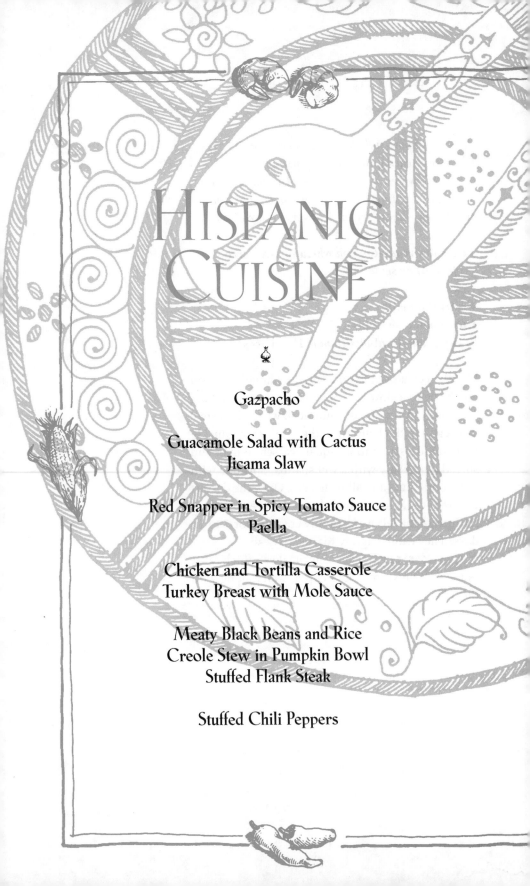

Hispanic Cuisine

Gazpacho

Guacamole Salad with Cactus
Jicama Slaw

Red Snapper in Spicy Tomato Sauce
Paella

Chicken and Tortilla Casserole
Turkey Breast with Mole Sauce

Meaty Black Beans and Rice
Creole Stew in Pumpkin Bowl
Stuffed Flank Steak

Stuffed Chili Peppers

Vegetable Pancakes
Corn, Zucchini, and Tomatoes

Flan
Orange Almond Cake

Sangría
Cinnamon-Nutmeg Hot Chocolate
Coffee Cooler

Mix equal parts of Spain's fragrant olive oil and garlic and Mexico's corn. Add South America's hearty meat dishes and rich coffee. Throw in a dash of fiestas and family fun, and you have a tasty recipe for success known as Hispanic cuisine. The food is exciting, and the added benefit of a good siesta after feasting awaits you.

Old World Spain was at its peak between the sixteenth and nineteenth centuries and had great influence over the regions whose foods make up Hispanic cuisine. An excellent climate helped provide this lush, green country with a variety of crops and a great wealth of food. From grains, fruits, and vegetables to meats and seafood, Spaniards enjoyed fresh ingredients as a flavorful base for their cooking. Olive oil and garlic are the main seasoning staples in a Spanish kitchen. Because they're easy to prepare and clean up, one-dish meals are favored. A meal can be as simple as beans and potatoes, accompanied by fruit, olives, and bread. Bread is a Spanish essential at each meal. Many Spanish meals end simply with cheese. A late supper, probably after nine o'clock, is usually very simple, often featuring light, healthful fare, such as gazpacho, a chilled tomato-base soup. (See page 147 for a novel serving idea.) Another essential is wine, served with every meal except breakfast.

Paella Cookoff

One of Spain's best-known dishes is paella. This popular rice and vegetable creation boasts a variety of seafood, as well as meats, such as chicken, pork, and chorizo sausage. Spanish chorizo sausage is seasoned ground pork that's stuffed into casings and smoked. It's difficult to find in the United States. On the other hand, you can find Mexican chorizo in most supermarkets, but instead of being smoked, it's sold fresh. Unfortunately, it's swimming in fat, so substitute a reduced-fat smoked sausage, as we do on page 154.

Paella gets its trademark bright yellow-orange color from saffron. If you get sticker shock when you see the price of saffron, keep in mind that the spice is used sparingly. What makes saffron cost so much? It comes from a purple crocus plant that bears only three stigmas. These stigmas are handpicked and dried. It takes thousands of stigmas to yield one ounce of saffron. But when added to your cooking liquid, a tiny bit of saffron releases its bright color and unique flavor. Paella is traditionally cooked outdoors.

Like the participants in our famous chili cookoffs, Spanish cooks compete with great pride to see whose paella is the tastiest.

Midafternoon and late evening are times for tapas. These delightful appetizers range from a simple slice of salami to an elaborate Spanish omelet known as a tortilla. Tapas are served alongside a favorite cocktail or glass of sherry. Tapas bars are common social gathering spots in Spain. People go there not only to get a bit of nourishment but also to catch up on the news of the day.

Mexican Fiesta

The native Indians of Mexico relied on the modest local vegetation. Meat was only a small part of their diet. But when the Spanish conquistadors arrived, they shared herbs and spices, rice, beans, chickens, cattle, sheep, and pigs. Mexico thus became rich with foodstuffs. After Mexico revolted against Spain, the Spanish influence was still strong, and Spanish was the principal language spoken.

The main staple of Mexican cuisine is corn. It's used in every form imaginable to create dishes from comforting soups to crisp tortillas. Even the husks are used for tamales. The Mexicans season many of their dishes with both fresh and dried chilies. Sweet pastries are favored for breakfast, and egg custards, such as flan (page 173), are a popular dessert.

One of the most interesting tools in the Mexican kitchen is the molcajete. A large mortar and pestle carved from stone, it is used for mashing garlic, making pastes, or grinding herbs and spices. It is fun to use and can sometimes be found in gourmet shops, specialty stores, or grocery stores that carry Hispanic ingredients.

The people of Mexico love a good fiesta. These outdoor celebrations are filled with colorful Mexican costumes, music, dancing, and, of course, good food. One widely celebrated festival is Cinco de Mayo, Mexican independence day. It celebrates Mexico's freedom from French rule, won on May 5, 1862. Every year, on the fifth of May, the remembrance of this victory lives on in the hearts of Mexicans. Many North Americans, especially in the southwestern states bordering Mexico, join in the festivities.

Eating to a Latin Beat

The cuisine of South America is as hearty and vast as this large continent. The terrain is varied, with plains, rain forests, deserts, and mountains. Each area dictates the food served. Brazil and the surrounding areas enjoy meat dishes because of abundant grazing lands. A typical Saturday includes a feijoada feast (page 160), which is a large spread of cooked meats, rice, black beans, and edible garnishes. It's easy to overeat at a feijoada dinner, so it's a good idea to go easy on portions. The northwestern part of South America features dishes overflowing with rice, noodles, potatoes, and corn. Coffee is a trademark of Colombia, one of the world's biggest suppliers.

When cooking Hispanic meals, remember that although olive oils are much lower in saturated fat than some other oils, they should be used in moderation. Steer clear of Mexican dishes with lard or bacon drippings— substitute small amounts of vegetable oil and use a bit of smoke-flavored liquid seasoning to make up for any lost flavor. Use lean cuts of meat, carefully trimming away any visible fat. If a recipe calls for lots of cheese, cut back on the amount and try nonfat or reduced-fat cheeses. Also, add vegetables to put more balance in your diet. Avoid deep-fried corn or flour tortilla shells and chips—baked tortilla chips are becoming more readily available in groceries and are quite good.

Hispanic cooking is more than just hot and spicy food. True, many Mexican and Latin dishes use hot chili peppers, but those dishes are just a small part of the total variety of tastes offered from Spain to Mexico to South America. When you're preparing recipes from these countries, add the spices you like in the amount to suit your taste. After all, creativity is an old Hispanic tradition!

Gazpacho

*A*lthough most Spaniards would enjoy this soup accompanied by sandwiches, fruit, and cheese for a late-evening supper, you can enjoy this cold vegetable soup anytime. Traditional gazpacho uses ripe red tomatoes, but for a different twist, this recipe calls for vivid yellow tomatoes and a sweet yellow bell pepper. You can substitute red tomatoes and/or any color of bell pepper that you prefer. If you have a green thumb and grow your own vegetables, you will enjoy experimenting with this soup.

Soup

4 medium yellow tomatoes, coarsely chopped
1 medium cucumber, peeled, seeded, and chopped
1 medium yellow bell pepper, coarsely chopped
2 shallots, chopped
1 clove garlic, minced
2 tablespoons white wine vinegar
$1/4$ teaspoon salt
$1/8$ teaspoon black pepper

4 green bell peppers (optional)
1 carrot (optional)
1 stalk celery (optional)
$1/4$ cup toasted croutons (optional)

Serves 4; 1 cup per serving

Nutrient Analysis (per serving)

Calories 60
Protein 2 g
Carbohydrate 13 g
Cholesterol 0 mg
Sodium 188 mg
Total fat 1 g
    Saturated 0 g
    Polyunsaturated 0 g
    Monounsaturated 0 g

Put all the soup ingredients in a blender or the work bowl of a food processor fitted with a metal blade (you may need to do this in batches) and process until mixture is slightly chunky. Pour into a bowl, cover, and refrigerate 4 to 6 hours before serving.

Meanwhile, if using green bell peppers, slice off stem ends, leaving peppers whole. Remove membranes and seeds. Make sure not to pierce the shell. Peel carrot, if using, and cut it and optional celery into 4 sticks each.

Serve cold soup in hollowed-out bell peppers with a carrot stick and celery stick in each, garnished with croutons, if desired. Or ladle soup into bowls and serve.

COOK'S TIP: Add 1 or 2 chopped canned jalapeños to this recipe and it becomes a wonderful salsa to serve with baked tortilla strips or poached fish or to spoon on salads.

Guacamole Salad with Cactus

Ensalada de Guacamole con Nopales

CENTRAL AMERICA/MEXICO

T*he love of avocados is widespread throughout the Hispanic culture. Some parts of Central America and Mexico also enjoy the mellow flavor of nopales (cactus pads) and have found many delicious uses for them. This fresh salad can accompany almost any Hispanic meal, or serve it with tortillas or baked tortilla chips for a snack.*

Dressing
2 tablespoons fresh lime juice (about 2 medium limes)
1 teaspoon acceptable vegetable oil
1 clove garlic, minced
¼ teaspoon chili powder
⅛ teaspoon ground cumin
⅛ teaspoon black pepper
Dash of cayenne

2 small cactus pads
1 medium avocado, peeled, seeded, and diced
2 Italian plum tomatoes, diced
½ small red onion, chopped
4 cups shredded iceberg lettuce (about ½ head)

In a small bowl, combine the dressing ingredients. Set aside.

With a vegetable peeler, shave off any stickers or eyes on the cactus pads. Use the peeler to remove any fibrous or dry parts of the pads. Thoroughly rinse cactus pads under cold water.

Place whole cactus pads in a pan that is fitted with a steamer rack and filled with water to just below the rack. Bring the water to a simmer. Steam cactus pads, covered, over medium-low heat for 3 to 5 minutes, or until they reach the desired tenderness (crisp-tender is preferred for this recipe). Plunge the pads into ice-cold water to set

Serves 4; ½ cup guacamole and 1 cup lettuce per serving

Nutrient Analysis (per serving)

Calories 106
Protein 2 g
Carbohydrate 9 g
Cholesterol 0 mg
Sodium 20 mg
Total fat 8 g
    Saturated 1 g
    Polyunsaturated 2 g
    Monounsaturated 4 g

the color and stop the cooking. With a sharp knife, cut the pads into matchstick-size strips.

In a large mixing bowl, combine the cactus pads, avocado, tomatoes, and red onion. Place shredded lettuce on four plates, divide the avocado mixture among the plates, and top with the reserved dressing.

COOK'S TIP ON AVOCADOS: The common Hass avocado is ripe when the pebbly skin is dark and the fruit yields to gentle pressure near the stem end. To ripen them quickly, place avocados in a paper bag for 1 or 2 days. Once ripened, they will keep in the refrigerator for up to 10 days. It is important to remove the small stem before cutting the avocado open so it doesn't get scooped out with the green flesh. Cutting the avocado into quarters lengthwise makes it easy to remove the pit. If the avocado is ripe, you can easily peel the skin from the flesh.

Jicama Slaw

Ensalada de Jicama

MEXICO

A refreshing blend of citrus combines with the crunch of the juicy white flesh of the jicama to produce a salad that is a great palate cleanser. A native of Mexico, the brown-skinned, round root vegetable known as jicama can be briefly stir-fried, added to soups or peeled, sliced, and served raw as a snack.

1 small jicama (about ½ pound)
¼ medium red bell pepper
1 green onion (green and white parts)
2 sprigs fresh cilantro

Dressing
¼ teaspoon grated lemon zest
¼ teaspoon grated lime zest
¼ teaspoon grated orange zest
1 tablespoon fresh lemon juice
1 tablespoon fresh lime juice
1 tablespoon fresh orange juice
1 teaspoon acceptable vegetable oil
1 teaspoon honey
¼ teaspoon chili powder
¼ teaspoon salt
⅛ teaspoon white pepper

Serves 4; ½ cup per serving

Nutrient Analysis (per serving)

Calories 57
Protein 1 g
Carbohydrate 11 g
Cholesterol 0 mg
Sodium 153 mg
Total fat 1 g
  Saturated 0 g
  Polyunsaturated 1 g
  Monounsaturated 0 g

With a sharp knife, peel the brown skin off the jicama. Rinse jicama and pat dry with paper towels.

Cut jicama in half, then into thin slices, and finally into matchstick-size strips. Place jicama in a large mixing bowl.

Cut red bell pepper into ¼-inch dice; add to bowl with jicama. Cut green onion crosswise into 3 pieces. Cut into thin strips and add to bowl. Coarsely chop cilantro (leaves and stems) and add to bowl.

Combine the dressing ingredients in a separate bowl and pour over the salad, tossing to coat.

Red Snapper in Spicy Tomato Sauce

Salsa Huachinango

MEXICO

In Mexico, the word salsa means "sauce" and applies to fresh, as well as cooked, combinations of vegetables and/or fruits. This zesty salsa goes well with the delicate flavor of the red snapper for a taste combination that's a winner.

1 teaspoon acceptable vegetable oil
1 medium onion, chopped
1 clove garlic, minced
14.5-ounce can no-salt-added tomatoes, diced, with juice reserved
1 fresh jalapeño pepper, seeded and chopped* (about 1 tablespoon)
¼ teaspoon sugar
¼ teaspoon ground cumin
⅛ teaspoon black pepper
1 pound red snapper fillets (about 4 small fillets)
1 teaspoon grated lime zest
2 tablespoons fresh lime juice (about 2 medium limes)
¼ cup sliced black olives
2 tablespoons chopped fresh cilantro

Serves 4; 1 fillet per serving

Nutrient Analysis (per serving)

Calories 163
Protein 23 g
Carbohydrate 10 g
Cholesterol 60 mg
Sodium 184 mg
Total fat 4 g
  Saturated 1 g
  Polyunsaturated 1 g
  Monounsaturated 1 g

In a large skillet, heat oil over medium-low heat and sauté onion and garlic until tender, about 2 to 3 minutes. Add the tomatoes with their juice and the jalapeño, sugar, cumin, and black pepper and simmer, partially covered, for 10 minutes. You can add 2 to 3 tablespoons water if mixture gets dry.

Meanwhile, rinse the snapper fillets and pat dry with paper towels. Add snapper and the remaining ingredients except cilantro to the skillet and simmer, covered, over medium-low heat for 10 to 13 minutes, or until fish flakes when tested with a fork.

Remove fillets from pan and place on a serving platter. Stir cilantro into sauce, then immediately pour sauce over fillets. Serve warm.

COOK'S TIP ON STORING CILANTRO:
One of the best ways to store cilantro is to place it, stems down, in a glass of cold water. Wrap the leaves with plastic or place a plastic bag over them. Cilantro will keep in the refrigerator for about 7 days. It is best to change the water every 2 to 3 days. Add small amounts of chopped cilantro to soups, salads, and sauces to enhance the flavor.

*Wear rubber gloves when handling hot peppers or wash hands thoroughly after handling. Skin, especially around the eyes, is very sensitive to the oil from peppers.

Paella

SPAIN

*T*his national dish of Spain is full of surprises.
You'll discover tender chunks of chicken and
pork, as well as sausage, vegetables, and seafood, in
the bright saffron-flavored rice. Paella takes its name
from the large, two-handled pan it's traditionally
cooked in. This ideal one-dish meal is great for
casual dinner parties.

**2 boneless, skinless chicken breast halves (about
4 ounces each), all visible fat removed**

**$\frac{1}{2}$ pound boneless pork loin chops (about 2 to 3
pork chops), all visible fat removed**

1 tablespoon extra-virgin olive oil

1 medium onion, chopped

1 clove garlic, minced

4 cups hot water

**$\frac{1}{2}$ teaspoon saffron threads, crushed using a
mortar and pestle**

$\frac{1}{8}$ teaspoon black pepper

2 cups uncooked rice

**$\frac{1}{4}$ pound light smoked sausage, cut into $\frac{1}{2}$-inch
slices**

1 medium red bell pepper, chopped

**14-ounce can water-packed artichoke hearts,
rinsed, drained, and quartered**

**$\frac{1}{2}$ pound large shrimp, peeled, deveined, and
rinsed**

1 cup frozen peas (about 4 ounces)

1 cup water

8 fresh clams, scrubbed

8 fresh mussels, scrubbed and debearded

2 medium limes, cut into wedges

Rinse the chicken and pat dry with paper towels.
Cut chicken and pork into cubes. In a paella pan or
stockpot, heat the oil over medium-low heat. Add
the chicken and pork cubes and cook over medium

Serves 8

Nutrient
Analysis
(per serving)

Calories 392
Protein 30 g
Carbohydrate 49 g
Cholesterol 94 mg
Sodium 298 mg
Total fat 7 g
  Saturated 2 g
  Polyunsaturated 1 g
  Monounsaturated 2 g

heat until meats are almost cooked through, about 5 to 6 minutes. Add the onion and garlic and cook for 2 minutes.

Meanwhile, combine 4 cups hot water with the saffron and black pepper in a medium saucepan and heat over medium-low heat for 2 minutes. When onions are tender, add the water mixture to the stockpot, along with the rice, sausage, and red bell pepper. Cook, covered, over low heat for 20 minutes, or until rice is done. Add the artichoke hearts, shrimp, and peas to the stockpot and cook, covered, for 5 minutes, or until shrimp is done.

While shrimp is cooking, heat 1 cup water in a large saucepan. Add the clams and mussels and cook, covered, over medium-low heat until they are fully opened, about 3 to 4 minutes; do not overcook. Discard any unopened clams or mussels. Garnish the top of the paella with the clams, mussels, and lime wedges and serve hot. This dish reheats wonderfully in the microwave.

COOK'S TIP ON MUSSELS AND CLAMS: When picking mussels and clams, they should not have an offensive odor and should be tightly closed. They may open and close periodically before being cooked, though. They are alive if the shell closes when tapped. When you cook them, discard any that do not open (they were dead, and therefore no good, before they were cooked).

Chicken and Tortilla Casserole

Chilaquiles

MEXICO

This layered casserole was invented as a handy way to use leftovers. It tastes somewhat like chicken enchiladas but is prepared without all the fuss. The green tomatillo sauce (or salsa verde) in this recipe can be used over enchiladas, chicken, or fish, or even as a dip for baked tortilla chips.

10 corn tortillas
1 teaspoon acceptable vegetable oil
1 medium onion, chopped
2 cloves garlic, minced
14.5-ounce can no-salt-added tomatillos, drained
** (or substitute tomatoes, if desired)**
2 cups low-sodium chicken broth
1 fresh jalapeño pepper, seeded and diced*
** (about 1 tablespoon)**
⅛ teaspoon black pepper
Vegetable oil spray
2 pounds boneless, skinless chicken breasts,
** cooked and cubed**
1 cup shredded low-fat Monterey Jack cheese
** (about 8 ounces)**
½ cup nonfat sour cream

Serves 8; 1 slice per serving

Nutrient Analysis (per serving)

Calories 320
Protein 37 g
Carbohydrate 24 g
Cholesterol 80 mg
Sodium 246 mg
Total fat 8 g
  Saturated 3 g
  Polyunsaturated 2 g
  Monounsaturated 2 g

Preheat oven to 350° F.

Cut the tortillas into quarters and place them in a single layer on an ungreased baking sheet. Bake for 10 minutes, or until they are crisp. Set aside. (Baking helps to deepen the flavor of the tortilla.)

In a large skillet, heat the vegetable oil over medium heat and sauté the onion and garlic for 2 to 3 minutes, or until tender.

Place the tomatillos, broth, jalapeño, and black pepper in a blender. Blend until smooth. Add this mixture to the onion mixture and simmer, uncovered, for 15 minutes over medium heat. Set aside.

Spray a 9 × 13-inch baking dish lightly with vegetable oil spray. Place half the tortilla quarters on the bottom of the dish, followed by half the chicken, half the tomatillo mixture, and half the cheese. Repeat layers.

Bake, uncovered, for 40 minutes. Remove from oven and spread sour cream on top. Serve warm.

COOK'S TIP: This recipe leaves plenty of room for your own touches. If you have leftover chicken, turkey, or even lean roast beef, about $2\frac{1}{4}$ cups of any of these, give them a try as a substitute for the chicken breasts. Have an extra piece of bell pepper or leftover vegetables in your refrigerator? Toss them in as well. You can add more cheese, but cut back on the poultry or meat if you do.

*Wear rubber gloves when handling hot peppers or wash hands thoroughly after handling. Skin, especially around the eyes, is very sensitive to the oil from peppers.

Turkey Breast with Mole Sauce

MEXICO

If you enjoy a good "concoction," which is what the Nahuatl word molli means, you will have fun with this dish. Many traditional dishes use mole (MOH-lay) sauce and are highlights at Mexican festivals. A wide variety of ingredients make up the rich, dark sauce. Chocolate is usually used for mole sauces, but cocoa powder is a super substitute that will still give you the unique flavor this dish is known for.

2 pounds boneless, skinless turkey breast
1 teaspoon acceptable vegetable oil
1 cup water
1 teaspoon acceptable vegetable oil
1 medium onion, chopped
1 clove garlic, minced
1 cup low-sodium chicken broth
2 tablespoons unsweetened cocoa powder
2 tablespoons sunflower seeds
2 tablespoons pumpkin seeds
1 tablespoon chili powder
1/2 teaspoon sugar
1/4 teaspoon ground cumin
1/4 teaspoon salt
1/4 teaspoon ground cinnamon
1/8 teaspoon ground cloves

Serves 8; about 3 ounces turkey per serving

Nutrient Analysis (per serving)

Calories 258
Protein 38 g
Carbohydrate 5 g
Cholesterol 90 mg
Sodium 203 mg
Total fat 9 g
  Saturated 2 g
  Polyunsaturated 4 g
  Monounsaturated 2 g

Rinse turkey and pat dry with paper towels. In a large skillet, heat 1 teaspoon vegetable oil over medium heat. Brown the turkey breast on both sides, about 2 to 3 minutes per side. Add the water and simmer, covered, over medium-low heat for 1 hour, or until turkey is no longer pink in the center. Remove turkey and place in an ungreased 1-quart baking dish; set aside. Discard cooking liquid.

Preheat oven to 350° F.

In a small skillet, heat 1 teaspoon vegetable oil over medium heat. Sauté onion and garlic for 2 to 3 minutes, or until tender. Place mixture in a blender or the work bowl of a food processor fitted with a metal blade. Add the remaining ingredients, blend until smooth, and pour over turkey. Bake, uncovered, for 30 minutes. Serve warm.

COOK'S TIP ON GRINDING DRIED CHILI PEPPERS, HERBS, AND SPICES: If you enjoy grinding your own dried chili peppers, an electric coffee grinder is the best tool for the job. If you choose this method, you will want to dedicate the coffee grinder to grinding only chili peppers—otherwise, "hot coffee" could take on a whole new meaning! Electric coffee grinders are also great for perking up your dried herbs or spices. Give them a whirl and smell the aroma!

Meaty Black Beans and Rice

Feijoada Completa

BRAZIL

Saturday is usually reserved for feijoada in Brazil, because after indulging in this national dish— with its variety of cooked meats, black beans, rice, greens, onions, and oranges—it is necessary to rest on Sunday! The leftovers keep well, so it is best not to overdo on the first day of your feijoada feast!

1 pound dry black beans, rinsed and sorted for stones or shriveled beans

8 cups water

5 cups water

2 cups low-sodium chicken broth

2 cloves garlic

1 teaspoon smoke-flavored liquid seasoning

⅛ teaspoon black pepper

1 pound corned beef, uncooked

Vegetable oil spray

2 pounds pork loin roast, all visible fat removed

1 cup water

2 teaspoons grated orange zest

3 cups rice

2½ teaspoons acceptable vegetable oil

½ teaspoon annatto (achiote seeds)

¾ cup manioc (cassava) meal or farina

2 pounds fresh collard greens

1 teaspoon extra-virgin olive oil

1 medium onion, sliced

3 medium cloves garlic, minced

2 tablespoons water

2 oranges, peeled and sliced

1 red or yellow onion, thinly sliced

In a large mixing bowl, place beans in 8 cups water and soak for 4 to 10 hours, covered. Drain water from beans. Discard the water. Place beans in a large stockpot along with 5 cups water, broth, garlic

Serves 12

Nutrient Analysis (per serving)

Calories 520
Protein 37 g
Carbohydrate 64 g
Cholesterol 71 mg
Sodium 326 mg
Total fat 12 g
  Saturated 4 g
  Polyunsaturated 2 g
  Monounsaturated 5 g

cloves, smoke-flavored liquid seasoning, and black pepper. Bring to a boil over high heat, then reduce heat to medium-low and cook, partially covered, for 2 to 3 hours, or until beans are tender. Set aside, with beans still in cooking liquid.

Meanwhile, place the corned beef in a large saucepan. Fill the pan with enough cold water to cover the meat by 3 inches. Bring to a boil over high heat, then reduce heat to medium-low and cook, partially covered, for 2 hours, or until tender. Remove beef from pan and set aside. Discard the cooking liquid.

While the corned beef cooks, spray a Dutch oven with vegetable oil spray. Place pork roast in Dutch oven and brown over medium heat for 2 to 3 minutes on each side. Add 1 cup water and cook, covered, over low heat for 2 hours, or until meat is tender. Add grated orange zest and cook for 5 minutes. Set aside.

Cook rice according to package instructions, omitting the margarine and salt, while the pork cooks.

Make annatto oil by placing $2\frac{1}{2}$ teaspoons vegetable oil and annatto in a small saucepan. Heat the mixture over medium heat for 3 to 4 minutes. Remove pan from the heat and cool, uncovered, for 30 minutes. Strain oil into a glass jar, discarding seeds. Cool thoroughly.

Meanwhile, in a medium nonstick skillet, heat the manioc meal over low heat until it is a light golden brown, about 3 to 5 minutes. Drizzle in the annatto oil and cook for 1 minute. Remove from heat and set aside.

Meanwhile, rinse collards, remove stems, cut leaves into thin strips, and dry thoroughly. In a large skillet, heat the olive oil over medium-low heat and sauté the onion and garlic for 2 to 3 minutes, or until tender. Add the collard greens and 2 tablespoons water and cook over low heat for 8 to 10 minutes, or until tender. Set aside.

To serve, place beans and cooked rice in separate serving bowls. Slice meats and arrange on a large platter, along with the collards, orange slices, and onion slices. Sprinkle manioc meal mixture on top. Serve warm.

When stored in airtight containers, the feast will keep for up to 4 days in the refrigerator or up to 4 months in the freezer. You can refrigerate and freeze the black beans, corned beef, pork roast, and manioc meal mixture. The rice, collards, orange slices, and onion slices are best when made fresh on the day you serve the feijoada. The entire meal reheats wonderfully in the microwave.

COOK'S TIP: Annatto, also known as achiote seeds, is used here to infuse vegetable oil with color and flavor. The fragrant seeds are covered with an orangey-red coating that gives the oil a similar coloring. The oil has a light, flowery taste. Look for annatto in gourmet shops or Hispanic markets. Buy the brightest-colored seeds—the darker ones are past their prime.

Creole Stew in Pumpkin Bowl

Carbonada Criolla

ARGENTINA

This classic stew from Argentina combines hearty beef, vegetables, and, for an interesting twist, fruit. It also includes pieces of corn on the cob, a common ingredient in South American dishes. This recipe can be made even more elaborate by serving it grandly from a baked pumpkin. Perfect for a fall gathering or when you need a good warm-up!

Serves 4; about 2½ cups per serving

Nutrient Analysis (per serving)

Calories 422
Protein 32 g
Carbohydrate 65 g
Cholesterol 60 mg
Sodium 253 mg
Total fat 7 g
  Saturated 2 g
  Polyunsaturated 1 g
  Monounsaturated 2 g

1 teaspoon acceptable vegetable oil
1 pound lean stew meat, all visible fat removed
2 cups low-sodium beef broth
1 cup water
1 medium tomato, peeled, seeded, and chopped
½ medium red bell pepper, chopped
2 cloves garlic, minced
1 serrano pepper, seeded and chopped*
½ teaspoon dried oregano, crumbled
¼ teaspoon dried thyme, crumbled
1 bay leaf
¼ teaspoon salt
⅛ teaspoon black pepper
1 pumpkin, preferably with a protruding stem, scrubbed and rinsed in cold water (about 5 to 6 pounds)
1 ear of corn, shucked and desilked
1 medium potato, preferably russet
1 medium sweet potato
1 medium zucchini
8 pearl onions
¼ cup dried mixed fruit, chopped (equal amounts of peaches, apricots, and apples) (about 1 ounce)

In a Dutch oven, heat the vegetable oil over medium-high heat. Add the meat and brown on all sides, 8 to 10 minutes. Add the broth, water, tomato, bell pepper, garlic, chili pepper, oregano, thyme, bay leaf, salt, and black pepper. Bring mixture to a boil over medium-high heat, then reduce heat and simmer, covered, for $1\frac{1}{2}$ hours, or until meat is tender.

Preheat oven to 350° F. While meat mixture is cooking, use a sharp knife to cut a lid from the top of the pumpkin. Using a metal spoon, scrape the seeds and fibers from the lid and inside of the pumpkin. Discard fibers and seeds. Place pumpkin on a baking sheet and put the lid on the pumpkin. Bake for $1\frac{1}{2}$ hours, or until pumpkin is tender. (It should yield to gentle pressure when pressed on the outside with a spoon. If it gets too tender, it could collapse.) Set aside.

While pumpkin is baking, prepare the remaining vegetables for the stew. Using a sharp knife or cleaver, cut the corncob into 1-inch slices. (You can use the flat side of a meat mallet as you would a hammer to aid the knife cutting through the cob.) Peel the potatoes and cut into 1-inch cubes. Cut the zucchini crosswise into $\frac{1}{2}$-inch slices, then cut each slice in half. Peel the pearl onions (see Cook's Tip, next page). Add the vegetables and dried fruit to the meat mixture and simmer, covered, for 10 to 15 minutes, or until vegetables are tender.

To serve, pour the stew into the baked pumpkin and then present it on a platter. Use a metal ladle or deep metal spoon to scoop out the stew and scrape some of the baked pumpkin from the inside. Or add scraped pumpkin to the stew and serve from a soup tureen.

When making this dish ahead, store the stew and baked pumpkin separately. Reheat stew over medium-low heat for 10 to 15 minutes on the stove or 5 to 6 minutes on 100% power (high) in the microwave (full recipe) in a covered microwave-safe dish. If using pumpkin, reheat it in a 350° F oven for 15 to 20 minutes or on a microwave-safe plate on 100% power (high) for 4 to 6 minutes, depending on the microwave. Freeze cooked pumpkin in an airtight plastic bag for up to 6 months. Freeze stew in a rigid container for up to 4 months.

COOK'S TIP ON PEARL ONIONS: To peel pearl onions easily, drop them into boiling water and boil for 1 minute. Remove onions from the water and cool. Trim ends off and remove skin.

*Wear rubber gloves when handling hot peppers or wash hands thoroughly after handling. Skin, especially around the eyes, is very sensitive to the oil from peppers.

Stuffed Flank Steak

Matambre

ARGENTINA/SOUTH AMERICA

This hearty, eye-catching beef roll, served hot or cold, is called matambre, which means "kill hunger." Marinate the beef overnight for maximum flavor.

1½-pound flank steak, all visible fat removed

Marinade

¼ cup red wine vinegar
1 tablespoon olive oil
2 cloves garlic, minced
½ teaspoon ground cumin
½ teaspoon dried thyme, crumbled
½ teaspoon coriander seeds, ground using a mortar and pestle
¼ teaspoon salt
⅛ teaspoon black pepper

Filling

2 cups spinach leaves, rinsed, stems removed (about 4 ounces)
2 medium carrots
1 small onion, thinly sliced
4 cloves garlic
½ red bell pepper, thinly sliced
1 hard-boiled egg, peeled and cut into wedges, yolk discarded
1 serrano pepper, seeded and chopped*
1 teaspoon dried oregano, crumbled
¼ teaspoon salt
⅛ teaspoon black pepper

Cooking Liquid

2 cups water
1 cup low-sodium beef broth

Serves 6; about a
1-inch slice per serving

Nutrient
Analysis
(per serving)

Calories 211
Protein 27 g
Carbohydrate 7 g
Cholesterol 65 mg
Sodium 305 mg
Total fat 8 g
  Saturated 3 g
  Polyunsaturated 0 g
  Monounsaturated 3 g

Butterfly the flank steak using a long, sharp knife (a Chinese chef's knife works well), cutting parallel to your surface and starting at the widest edge, stopping at about $\frac{1}{2}$ inch from the other edge. Open the split flank steak and remove any visible fat or gristle. Place a piece of plastic wrap on top of the steak. Pound steak with the flat side of a meat mallet to help break up the tissue. Do not pound thinner than $\frac{1}{4}$ inch.

In a nonmetallic bowl or an airtight plastic bag, combine the marinade ingredients. Add the steak, turning it a few times to completely coat it in the marinade. Chill for approximately 8 hours.

About 15 to 20 minutes before preparing the filling, gather the ingredients for it.

When ready to assemble filling, preheat oven to 375° F. Lay the opened flank steak on a cutting board or baking sheet. Evenly place the filling ingredients over steak in the order listed above.

Starting from the longest edge, roll the steak around the filling (like a jelly roll) and, using kitchen string, tie the steak at 2-inch intervals to secure it. Place steak in a Dutch oven or deep stockpot and add the cooking liquid. Bake for $1\frac{1}{2}$ hours, or until beef is tender. Remove from liquid; let stand at least 10 minutes before slicing. Serve hot or cold. When sliced crosswise, this beef roll reveals a colorful filling.

COOK'S TIP: For extra appeal, use a peeler to cut the carrots lengthwise, evenly spacing the strips. The carrot will resemble a flower when the beef roll is cut.

*Wear rubber gloves when handling hot peppers or wash hands thoroughly after handling. Skin, especially around the eyes, is very sensitive to the oil from peppers.

Stuffed Chili Peppers

Chiles Rellenos

MEXICO

Chiles rellenos *is one of the best ways to glorify the chili pepper. A roasted, peeled, and seeded poblano or Anaheim pepper is stuffed with any of a variety of fillings—cheese, beef, chicken—and coated with an egg batter. The stuffed pepper is usually deep-fried, but this version is baked or cooked on a griddle.*

Vegetable oil spray
4 Anaheim peppers (about 8 ounces)
2 ounces shredded low-fat Monterey Jack cheese
2 ounces nonfat or low-fat ricotta cheese
1/2 teaspoon chili powder
1/2 teaspoon garlic powder
1/8 teaspoon cayenne
1/8 teaspoon ground cumin
1/8 teaspoon black pepper
1/4 cup all-purpose flour
3 egg whites
Vegetable oil spray

Serves 4; 1 stuffed pepper per serving

Nutrient Analysis (per serving)

Calories 105
Protein 10 g
Carbohydrate 11 g
Cholesterol 8 mg
Sodium 173 mg
Total fat 3 g
  Saturated 2 g
  Polyunsaturated 0 g
  Monounsaturated 1 g

Preheat broiler.

Spray a broiling pan with vegetable oil spray. Using a thin, sharp knife, make a small slit near the stem of each pepper so steam will be released. Place peppers on broiling pan and broil 3 to 4 inches from the heat for 1 to 2 minutes on each side, or until the skins are blackened. Do not overcook. Place peppers in a plastic bag and seal bag. Let peppers sit for at least 15 minutes, or until cool enough to handle. Using your fingers, paper towels, or a knife, remove the charred skins from peppers. Cut the stem end off and remove membranes and seeds. Rinse peppers in cold water and pat dry with paper towels.

In a small bowl, combine Monterey Jack cheese, ricotta cheese, chili powder, garlic powder, cayenne, cumin, and black pepper. Spoon one-fourth of this mixture through the stem end of a chili pepper. Repeat with remaining filling and peppers. Lightly coat the outside of the peppers with flour and set aside.

With an electric mixer, beat the egg whites in a medium mixing bowl until stiff peaks form. Set aside.

To bake peppers, preheat oven to 350° F and lightly spray a baking sheet with vegetable oil spray. To cook peppers on the stovetop, lightly spray a nonstick griddle with vegetable oil spray. Heat the griddle over medium heat.

Coat the chili peppers with egg whites and place on the baking sheet if baking. Bake, uncovered, for 15 to 20 minutes, until tops are lightly browned. Or cook egg-coated chilies over medium heat for 2 to 3 minutes on each side, until golden brown. Serve hot. The peppers are best when served right away but can be stuffed and refrigerated up to 3 days, then dipped in flour and coated with egg just before baking.

COOK'S TIP ON SMOKED CHILI PEPPERS AND BELL PEPPERS: When you use your gas grill or have hot charcoal remaining after your barbecue, throw a few pierced chili peppers (or even bell peppers) on and singe the skins as directed above. Peel as directed, then chop or leave in one piece. Freeze the peppers in airtight plastic bags for up to 8 months. You will have a roasted and peeled pepper at a moment's notice.

Vegetable Pancakes

Tortas de Verduras

MEXICO

A wide variety of vegetables goes into these crisp-edged pancakes. Even the fussiest of vegetable eaters may go for them. Top each pancake with about a tablespoon of your favorite nonfat salsa or serve with Red Snapper in Spicy Tomato Sauce (page 152) or Turkey Breast with Mole Sauce (page 158).

Serves 4; 2 pancakes per serving

Nutrient Analysis (per serving)

Calories 73
Protein 3 g
Carbohydrate 11 g
Cholesterol 0 mg
Sodium 251 mg
Total fat 2 g
    Saturated 0 g
    Polyunsaturated 1 g
    Monounsaturated 1 g

½ cup diced broccoli florets (about 2 ounces)
½ cup diced cauliflower (about 2 ounces)
1 small cactus pad, stickers removed, diced
½ cup diced mushrooms (about 4)
½ cup diced onion (about 1 medium)
¼ cup diced red bell pepper
Egg substitute equivalent to 1 egg
¼ cup all-purpose flour
½ teaspoon baking powder
½ teaspoon chili powder
¼ teaspoon ground cumin
¼ teaspoon salt
⅛ teaspoon black pepper
1 teaspoon acceptable vegetable oil
1 teaspoon acceptable margarine

In a medium mixing bowl, combine, in order, broccoli, cauliflower, cactus pad, mushrooms, onion, bell pepper, egg substitute, flour, baking powder, chili powder, cumin, salt, and pepper.

Heat a large nonstick skillet over medium heat. Add vegetable oil and margarine. Melt margarine and swirl skillet to evenly coat the bottom with the oil-margarine mixture.

With a measuring cup, scoop up ¼ cup of the vegetable mixture. Carefully mound it in the skillet, using a spatula to press down on the mixture and flatten it slightly. Repeat with the remaining mixture, making 8 pancakes all together. Cook over medium heat for 5 to 7 minutes, or until browned.

Turn pancakes over with a spatula. Cook for 5 to 7 minutes, or until bottoms are browned. Serve pancakes warm.

To reheat, place pancakes on an ungreased baking sheet (do not thaw if frozen) and bake in a preheated 400° F oven for 5 minutes (8 minutes if frozen).

COOK'S TIP ON CACTUS PADS: Use a vegetable peeler to shave off any stickers or eyes on the cactus pads. Remove any fibrous or dry areas with the peeler.

Corn, Zucchini, and Tomatoes

Elote y Calabacitas y Tomates

MEXICO

This colorful side dish is seasoned not only with leafy green cilantro (also known as coriander or Chinese parsley) but also with the seed of the same herb. The seed is also known as coriander. When crushed or ground, coriander seeds taste lemony. They are a wonderful seasoning for meat. Fresh cilantro leaves have a completely different flavor from that of the seeds. It is almost like a cross between parsley and fresh basil.

1 tablespoon acceptable margarine
1 medium onion, sliced
2 cloves garlic, minced
2 cups fresh or frozen corn (about 8 ounces)
1 pound zucchini, thinly sliced crosswise
2 large tomatoes, peeled, seeded, and diced
¼ cup low-sodium chicken broth
¼ teaspoon salt
¼ teaspoon ground coriander seeds
⅛ teaspoon black pepper
1 tablespoon chopped fresh cilantro

Serves 6; ¾ cup per serving

Nutrient Analysis (per serving)

Calories 94
Protein 3 g
Carbohydrate 18 g
Cholesterol 0 mg
Sodium 136 mg
Total fat 2 g
    Saturated 0 g
    Polyunsaturated 1 g
    Monounsaturated 1 g

In a large skillet, melt the margarine over medium heat. Add the onion and garlic and sauté for 2 minutes, or until tender. Add the remaining ingredients except the fresh cilantro. Bring mixture to a simmer over medium-high heat. Reduce heat to low and cook, partially covered, for 4 to 5 minutes, or until vegetables are just tender; do not overcook. Stir in the cilantro and remove pan from heat. Serve warm or cold.

COOK'S TIP ON PEELING TOMATOES: To peel a tomato quickly, drop it into a small pot of boiling water for about 10 seconds, remove, and let cool. The peel will come off easily.

Flan

SPAIN/CUBA/MEXICO

*C*aramelized sugar adds rich color and intensifies the taste of the velvety-smooth egg custard known as flan. This dessert is especially satisfying after a spicy dinner. It seems to mellow the tongue and is not too heavy in taste, texture, or guilt. Top a wedge of flan with fresh fruit—such as strawberries, mango slices, or thin slices of a crisp Red Delicious apple—for a pretty garnish and terrific treat.

⅓ cup sugar
3 tablespoons water
14-ounce can low-fat sweetened condensed milk
Egg substitute equivalent to 5 eggs
1 cup skim milk
⅓ cup sugar
1 tablespoon grated lime zest (about 2 medium limes)
1 teaspoon vanilla
Fresh fruit (optional)

Serves 12; 1 slice per serving

Nutrient Analysis (per serving)

Calories 160
Protein 5 g
Carbohydrate 32 g
Cholesterol 6 mg
Sodium 85 mg
Total fat 1 g
  Saturated 1 g
  Polyunsaturated 0 g
  Monounsaturated 0 g

In a heavy, medium saucepan, combine ⅓ cup sugar and the water. Heat over low heat, stirring occasionally, until sugar dissolves, about 2 to 3 minutes. Bring mixture to a boil over medium-high heat and cook, rotating pan occasionally, until mixture is a caramel color, about 8 to 10 minutes. Do not let mixture burn.

Pour into a 1-quart round flan pan (like a pie pan) or 9-inch round cake pan. Let mixture cool.

Preheat oven to 350° F.

In a medium mixing bowl, whisk the remaining ingredients, except fruit, together. Slowly pour into pan with cooled syrup; do not stir. Place the pan in the middle of a 12×17×1-inch jelly-roll pan. Fill the jelly-roll pan half full with warm water. Or place flan pan in a baking pan and add warm water to a depth of 1 inch. Bake for 1 hour, or until a knife inserted in the center of flan comes out clean. Remove flan pan from water and let cool on a wire rack for 30 minutes. Cover with plastic wrap and chill in refrigerator for at least 8 hours. Run a knife around the sides of the pan and invert onto a serving plate with 1-inch sides. Serve chilled.

COOK'S TIP ON EGG CUSTARD: If you have had trouble with egg custards being watery, you may have overheated the mixture. Slow cooking at the proper temperature is the key. When you pour water into the jelly-roll pan surrounding the flan pan, make sure it is warm, but not boiling. Cooking custards in a water bath, or bain-marie, helps to protect the custard from the direct oven heat. Bake the custard until the center is just set; do not overcook. These tips should help you create the perfect custard.

Flan can be left in the baking pan and refrigerated for up to 2 days, then unmolded at the last minute.

Orange Almond Cake

Torta de Almendra

SPAIN

This moist, delicious cake is a great sweet ending to a paella dinner party. The terrific taste of fresh oranges is accented with almonds and coupled with delightful Cuban red bananas, which have an intense banana flavor. Orange Almond Cake is simple to put together but is certainly not short on flavor.

Vegetable oil spray
1 tablespoon all-purpose flour
1³/₄ cups cake flour
³/₄ cup sugar
1¹/₂ teaspoons baking powder
¹/₄ teaspoon baking soda
¹/₄ teaspoon salt
2 tablespoons acceptable vegetable oil
Egg substitute equivalent to 1 egg
1 tablespoon grated orange zest
1¹/₄ cups fresh orange juice (about 5 medium oranges)
2 tablespoons sliced almonds
2 cups sliced Cuban red bananas (about 4) (optional)
1 cup orange slices (optional)

Preheat oven to 350° F.

Lightly spray an 8-inch round or square cake pan or springform pan with vegetable oil spray. Sprinkle 1 tablespoon all-purpose flour in the pan, shaking to coat sides. Discard any excess flour.

In a large mixing bowl, combine the cake flour, sugar, baking powder, baking soda, and salt. In a medium mixing bowl, combine the oil, egg substitute, orange zest, and orange juice. Pour the liquid mixture into the dry mixture and beat with an electric mixer on medium speed until mixture is moistened. Scrape bowl with a rubber scraper, then beat the mixture on high speed for 2 minutes. Pour

Serves 8; 1 slice per serving

Nutrient Analysis (per serving)

Calories 220
Protein 3 g
Carbohydrate 42 g
Cholesterol 0 mg
Sodium 215 mg
Total fat 4 g
    Saturated 1 g
    Polyunsaturated 2 g
    Monounsaturated 1 g

into prepared pan and arrange almond slices on top. Bake for 40 to 45 minutes, or until a sharp knife inserted into the center of the cake comes out clean.

Let cool in pan for 10 minutes. Run a knife along the side of the pan, invert cake on a wire cooling rack, and let it cool thoroughly. Garnish with sliced Cuban bananas and/or orange slices, if desired.

CHICKEN PICCATA

Pasta Primavera

Tropical Fruit Salad with Cherimoya Dressing

Shredded Beef with Bok Choy and Carrots

BLACK FOREST CAKE

Right: LAYERED LOBSTER SALAD
STUFFED ZUCCHINI

Chocolate-Strawberry Meringue Shells

Calypso Rice

CHICKEN WITH 40 CLOVES OF GARLIC

TURKEY ROLLS WITH PROSCIUTTO AND CHEESE

Sangría

A proper way to toast an outdoor Spanish feast is with sangría, a refreshing blend of fruit juices with the bubble of club soda and some sweet, fresh fruit over ice.

48-ounce bottle no-sugar-added red grape juice, chilled
⅓ cup sugar
3 tablespoons fresh lemon juice (about 1 medium lemon)
3 tablespoons fresh lime juice (about 2 medium limes)
5 cups club soda, chilled
2 peaches or nectarines, each sliced into 6 pieces

Combine the grape juice, sugar, lemon juice, and lime juice in a large glass pitcher, stirring well. Slowly pour the club soda into the juice mixture and stir. Serve over ice in wineglasses. Place a peach or nectarine slice in each glass. Serve immediately. The fruit juice mixture will keep for up to 2 days in a covered pitcher, but for best results, pour the club soda in just before serving.

   VARIATION: Follow above recipe, substituting an equal amount of dry red wine, such as burgundy, or nonalcoholic red wine for the grape juice.

Serves 12; 8 ounces per serving

Nutrient Analysis (per serving)

With grape juice

Calories 107
Protein 1 g
Carbohydrate 27 g
Cholesterol 0 mg
Sodium 26 mg
Total fat 0 g
   Saturated 0 g
   Polyunsaturated 0 g
   Monounsaturated 0 g

Nutrient Analysis (per serving)

With wine

Calories 112
Protein 0 g
Carbohydrate 9 g
Cholesterol 0 mg
Sodium 32 mg
Total fat 0 g
   Saturated 0 g
   Polyunsaturated 0 g
   Monounsaturated 0 g

Cinnamon-Nutmeg Hot Chocolate

MEXICO

A long with an English muffin, this hot chocolate can start your day with chocolate bliss. Or end a chilly evening with this sweet Mexican beverage, which traditionally uses a large bar of Mexican chocolate for its flavor. This version substitutes more healthful ingredients but maintains the same taste. If you have one, you can use a traditional wooden Mexican molinillo to whip a cup of chocolate into a frothy delight. It may be fun the first time, but you'll soon prefer using a modern blender!

4 cups skim milk
¼ cup unsweetened cocoa powder
¼ cup sugar
¾ teaspoon ground cinnamon
¼ teaspoon ground nutmeg
⅛ teaspoon almond extract

Serves 4; 1 cup per serving

Nutrient Analysis (per serving)

Calories 149
Protein 9 g
Carbohydrate 28 g
Cholesterol 4 mg
Sodium 128 mg
Total fat 1 g
   Saturated 1 g
   Polyunsaturated 0 g
   Monounsaturated 0 g

Combine all ingredients in a medium saucepan. Heat over medium-low heat until mixture is warmed through, about 3 to 4 minutes.

Froth the mixture by using a whisk with an up-and-down motion, or pour the mixture into a blender and process for a few seconds. Pour the hot chocolate into mugs and serve warm.

Coffee Cooler

Café Temperado

BRAZIL

This frosty coffee drink is so smooth and rich that you may forget you are sipping something low fat. It is based on a spicy Brazilian coffee drink that is infused with the mellow vanilla bean and other spices, then combined with fresh cream. This more healthful version will have you singing its praises.

1¼ cups water
2½ tablespoons ground coffee (regular or decaffeinated)
½ vanilla bean, about 3 to 4 inches, split in half to expose seeds
½ teaspoon whole cloves
2 cups frozen nonfat vanilla yogurt
1 cup skim milk
½ teaspoon ground cinnamon
4 cinnamon sticks
Freshly grated nutmeg

Serves 4; about 1 cup per serving

Nutrient Analysis (per serving)

Calories 123
Protein 5 g
Carbohydrate 27 g
Cholesterol 2 mg
Sodium 83 mg
Total fat 0 g
  Saturated 0 g
  Polyunsaturated 0 g
  Monounsaturated 0 g

Pour the water into a percolator or electric drip coffeemaker and brew the coffee. When finished, pour the hot coffee into a small mixing bowl, add the vanilla bean and cloves, and cover with aluminum foil. Let steep for 1 hour. Strain mixture, discarding vanilla bean and cloves, and chill coffee for at least 1 hour.

When ready to serve, combine the coffee, frozen yogurt, skim milk, and ground cinnamon in a blender or the work bowl of a food processor fitted with a metal blade. Process until smooth. Pour into 4 clear glasses and garnish each with a cinnamon stick and freshly grated nutmeg. Mixture will keep in the refrigerator for up to 30 minutes.

COOK'S TIP: Pour ½ cup of the mixture into a paper cup, stand a wooden stick in the middle, and freeze for at least 8 hours. To serve, remove the paper and eat as a frozen cooler on a stick. The whole recipe should yield about 8 of these treats.

CARIBBEAN CUISINE

Shrimp and Crab Legs with Spicy Tomato Sauce

Spinach, Crab, and Ham Soup

Marinated Chayote and Mixed Vegetables
Tropical Fruit Salad with Cherimoya Dressing
Layered Lobster Salad

Seafood in Creole Sauce

Jerked Chicken

Skewered Steak Supper
"Old Clothes" Stew
Black-Eyed Peas and Corned Beef
Spicy Glazed Pork Cubes

Yuca Root with Tomatillo Sauce
Calypso Rice

Griddle Biscuits
Coconut Quick Bread

Honey-Rum Mango Sauce

Sweet Stuffed Cornmeal

Piña Colada Shake

V isitors to the Caribbean swear that they have arrived in paradise. Why? Because the water is crystal clear, the scenery is breathtaking, and fresh foods—such as seafood, meats, fruits, and vegetables—are abundant and lovingly prepared.

Goodbye, Columbus—Hello, Caribbean Food

In his quest to find the highly prized spices of India, Christopher Columbus stumbled across the Caribbean islands and thought at first that he had found India. Although the islands did not bear the rich spices he was looking for, they did offer a place to trade food products. One of the most important products introduced to the islands was sugarcane. Today, sugarcane is still the reason for the big Cropover festival in August. It signifies the harvest and is a time of major celebration. Participants in colorful costumes dance in the streets. Delectable food is prepared, and the competition for the tastiest dish runs high among neighbors. Another festival is the pre-Lenten celebration of Carnival. It begins early Monday morning, two days before Ash Wednesday, and continues until midnight on Tuesday. Those two days are filled with calypso music, steel-drum bands, elaborate costumes, and lots of food.

European Settlers in the Kitchen

After Columbus, buccaneers, pirates, and missionaries flooded into the Caribbean. They brought settlers (and culinary influences) from Africa, France, China, India, Great Britain, and others. Traditional European foods were blended with island spices, and a truly varied cuisine evolved.

Most traditional Caribbean food is simply prepared. Meats are usually roasted or grilled. Cooks take great care to season and garnish food with different spices, herbs, and condiments. This turns an everyday meal into something exciting. The main flavorings used in Caribbean cooking are garlic, onion, celery, chives, chili peppers, bay leaves, thyme, marjoram, cloves, and black pepper. Since the islands now cater to millions of tourists every year, many hotels and resorts keep the food simple and familiar. Roadside stands and local restaurants boast everything from *roti* (curried meat wrapped in a thin pancake, much like a crepe) to spectacular seafood, like Creole shrimp. Many dishes are rich with coconut or deep-fried, but these tastes can be adapted for the health-conscious home cook. Try our Coconut Quick Bread, page 207, for one example.

Unfortunately, coconut meat and coconut oil contain lots of saturated fat. A few drops of coconut extract offer the same taste without the fat. If the recipe calls for coconut milk, a combination of skim milk and coconut extract makes an excellent substitute. Try our Piña Colada Shake on page 213 and taste for yourself. Small amounts of shredded coconut are usually okay when you simply cannot do without the texture. Always remember, moderation is the key.

No discussion of Caribbean cooking is complete without mentioning the area's world-famous export, rum. Flavoring everything from meats to desserts to beverages, this mellow-tasting liquor is made by distilling sugar cane or molasses. Rums produced in the Caribbean range in color from clear to dark brown. Small amounts of rum add a deep flavor to Caribbean dishes. If you prefer to use a nonalcoholic ingredient, substitute small amounts of rum extract for the real stuff.

Fishing for Flavor

Surrounded by the Atlantic Ocean and the Caribbean Sea, islanders have a bounty of seafood to choose from. They routinely cook tuna, herring, salmon, cavalli, red snapper, barracuda, grouper, shark, and the popular favorite in Barbados, flying fish.

Salt fish (salted cod) is a popular imported staple. Its best-known use is in Jamaica's national dish, saltfish and ackee (a tropical fruit). Shrimp, crab, lobster, and other crustaceans and mollusks round out the seafood fare. The most prized mollusk is the conch. Its flesh is a bit tough, so it must be tenderized before cooking. The empty shell is used as a horn. During the summer months, you may be able to find fresh conch in certain fish markets or in Chinese markets. Otherwise, you might get lucky and find it canned or frozen.

When cooking Caribbean food, you must have fun, mon! How can you be serious when you're cooking traditional dishes called *callaloo* (Spinach, Crab, and Ham Soup, page 186), *jug jug* (Black-Eyed Peas and Corned Beef, page 201), and *duckanoo* (Sweet Stuffed Cornmeal, page 211)? Enliven your taste buds and your sense of humor. Decorate for a party and have your own Caribbean festival.

Shrimp and Crab Legs with Spicy Tomato Sauce

Red Ti-Malice Sauce

HAITI

*T*he perfect way to serve this outdoor treat is to
spread the table with newspapers, then get out
the paper towels, nutcrackers, and hammers and let
your guests have fun peeling, cracking, and dipping.
Festive feasting is at your fingertips!

Serves 8 as an
appetizer

Nutrient
Analysis
(per serving)

Calories 75
Protein 12 g
Carbohydrate 5 g
Cholesterol 80 mg
Sodium 150 mg
Total fat 1 g
  Saturated 0 g
  Polyunsaturated 0 g
  Monounsaturated 0 g

Sauce

1 small onion, finely chopped
4 shallots, finely chopped
¼ cup fresh lime juice (about 3 medium limes)
8-ounce can no-salt-added tomato sauce
1 jalapeño pepper, seeded and chopped*
2 cloves garlic, minced
⅛ teaspoon black pepper

Shrimp and Crab Legs

8 cups water
½ cup dry white wine or nonalcoholic white wine
2 teaspoons coriander seeds
2 bay leaves
1 teaspoon whole allspice
1 teaspoon black peppercorns
1 pound shrimp, unpeeled
1 pound snow crab legs, frozen

To prepare sauce, combine the onion, shallots, and
lime juice in a medium mixing bowl. Let sit at room
temperature for 15 minutes. Add the remaining
sauce ingredients. Stir to combine. Refrigerate until
ready to use.

   In a large stockpot, combine water, wine,
coriander, bay leaves, allspice, and peppercorns.
Bring to a boil over high heat, then lower to
medium heat and simmer, uncovered, for 10
minutes. Add the shrimp and simmer, uncovered,
for 2 to 3 minutes, or until shrimp is pink and
cooked through; do not overcook! With a slotted

spoon, place shrimp in a colander to drain; reserve liquid. Place the frozen crab legs in the simmering water and cook over medium-low heat, covered, for 20 to 30 minutes, or until crab is warmed through. Remove with slotted spoon from water and place in a colander to drain.

You can serve the seafood hot or cold. Arrange it on a large platter and accompany with the chilled sauce.

*Wear rubber gloves when handling hot peppers or wash hands thoroughly after handling. Skin, especially around the eyes, is very sensitive to the oil from peppers.

Spinach, Crab, and Ham Soup

Callaloo

BARBADOS

The large, edible leaves of the taro root are known in the Caribbean as callaloo. Since callaloo greens are difficult to find in North American markets, you can substitute spinach, turnip greens, or mustard greens in this flavorful soup. It has many variations and can include sweet potatoes, white potatoes, and cassava root (or yuca root). Also, you can substitute 3 ounces of cooked chicken for the ham.

1 tablespoon acceptable margarine
1 large onion, chopped
1 clove garlic, minced
2 cups spinach, turnip greens, or mustard greens, finely chopped (about 2 ounces)
3 cups low-sodium chicken broth
$\frac{1}{2}$ cup skim milk
$\frac{1}{8}$ teaspoon coconut extract
$\frac{1}{8}$ teaspoon white pepper
4 ounces fat-free imitation crabmeat
3 ounces low-fat, low-sodium ham, cut into thin strips or $\frac{1}{2}$-inch pieces
$\frac{1}{8}$ teaspoon red hot-pepper sauce (optional)

Serves 6; 1 cup per serving

Nutrient Analysis (per serving)

Calories 88
Protein 9 g
Carbohydrate 7 g
Cholesterol 13 mg
Sodium 374 mg
Total fat 3 g
  Saturated 1 g
  Polyunsaturated 1 g
  Monounsaturated 1 g

In a large saucepan, melt the margarine over medium-low heat. Reduce heat to low and add the onion and garlic. Cook, covered, for 3 to 4 minutes, stirring occasionally. Add the spinach and cook, uncovered, for 2 minutes. Add the broth, milk, coconut extract, and white pepper. Bring mixture to a boil over medium-high heat, then reduce heat and simmer, uncovered, for 3 to 4 minutes.

Add the crabmeat and ham, and the hot pepper sauce, if using. Cook for 2 to 3 minutes, or until meat is warmed through. Serve warm.

Marinated Chayote and Mixed Vegetables

ALL ISLANDS

The spicy condiments that adorn many a Caribbean table inspired this recipe. Good whenever a light side dish is called for, it also makes an eye-catching garnish.

4 cups water
1 small chayote squash, peeled, seed removed, and cut into $^1\!/_2$-inch cubes
1 habañero, serrano, or jalapeño chili pepper*
2 shallots
1 large carrot, cut into matchstick-size strips
1 cup chopped cauliflower ($^1\!/_2$-inch pieces)
2 tablespoons fresh lime juice (about 2 medium limes)
1 teaspoon acceptable vegetable oil
1 clove garlic, minced
$^1\!/_2$ teaspoon sugar
$^1\!/_2$ teaspoon salt
$^1\!/_8$ teaspoon black pepper

Serves 6; $^1\!/_2$ cup per serving

Nutrient Analysis (per serving)

Calories 31
Protein 1 g
Carbohydrate 6 g
Cholesterol 0 mg
Sodium 212 mg
Total fat 1 g
    Saturated 0 g
    Polyunsaturated 1 g
    Monounsaturated 0 g

Bring the water to a boil in a medium saucepan over high heat. Add the chayote squash and simmer over medium heat, uncovered, for 15 minutes, or until the squash is tender but not mushy.

Meanwhile, remove and discard seeds from habañero. Slice the habañero. Finely chop the shallots. Set aside separately.

When squash is tender, add the carrot and cauliflower and simmer for 1 minute.

Drain the vegetables and plunge them into ice cold water. Drain again and pat vegetables dry with paper towels. Place vegetables in a nonmetallic bowl, add the sliced habañero, and set aside.

In a small mixing bowl, combine the shallots, lime juice, oil, garlic, sugar, salt, and pepper. Pour mixture over vegetables, toss well to coat, and chill for at least 1 hour before serving.

COOK'S TIP ON CHILI PEPPERS: The habanero is a native Caribbean chili pepper and is one of the hottest, spiciest peppers available. It resembles a tiny green-to-orange bell pepper and is becoming more widely available. If you prefer a milder taste in this recipe, substitute a seeded jalapeño or an Anaheim chili pepper.

COOK'S TIP ON CHAYOTE: Use a vegetable peeler to remove most of the peel from the chayote. Then use a small, sharp knife to remove the hard-to-reach peel at the puckered end. Cut the chayote in half and remove the seed.

*Wear rubber gloves when handling hot peppers or wash hands thoroughly after handling. Skin, especially around the eyes, is very sensitive to the oil from peppers.

Tropical Fruit Salad with Cherimoya Dressing

ALL ISLANDS

W hen pureed, the fragrant cherimoya takes on the consistency of a creamy custard that tastes like a cross between strawberry and pineapple. If you can't find a cherimoya, however, the salad can stand alone without a dressing, or top it with nonfat or low-fat yogurt. You can serve this fruit salad as a side dish to a hearty Caribbean meal or as a light dessert.

Dressing

1 ripe cherimoya, peeled, seeded, and cut into 1-inch cubes
2 tablespoons fresh lime juice (about 2 medium limes)
1 tablespoon sugar
¼ teaspoon ground nutmeg

Salad

2 mangoes
½ small, ripe papaya, peeled and seeded
1 orange, peeled
1 ugli fruit, peeled, or ½ grapefruit, peeled and thinly sliced
1 banana
1 ripe guava, peeled and seeded
Mint sprigs for garnish

Serves 4; about 1 cup fruit plus ¼ cup dressing per serving

Nutrient Analysis (per serving)

Calories 277
Protein 3 g
Carbohydrate 71 g
Cholesterol 0 mg
Sodium 7 mg
Total fat 1 g
  Saturated 0 g
  Polyunsaturated 0 g
  Monounsaturated 0 g

In a blender or the work bowl of a food processor fitted with a metal blade, combine the ingredients for the dressing and process until mixture is smooth, about 30 to 60 seconds. Place in a non-metallic bowl and chill until ready to use. The dressing will keep up to 8 hours in the refrigerator, but it will turn pink, which does not affect the flavor (and depending on your taste, may enhance the presentation).

For the salad, place a mango on its flattest side. Using a sharp knife, slice the top part of the mango off (the large, flat pit is lodged in the center of the mango and does not "let go" of the flesh), keeping it all in one piece. Flip the mango over and slice off the other top part. This leaves two oval slices of mango and a middle section. Trim off peel around the pit and cut off any remaining flesh around the pit; place flesh in a nonmetallic bowl. Place the oval mango slices with the flesh side up on a cutting board. Using a sharp knife, make diagonal cuts, about ½ inch apart, being careful not to cut through the skin and leaving the flesh attached to the skin. Make diagonal cuts in the opposite direction, about ½ inch apart (do not cut through the skin) to form a crosshatch design (diamond shapes). With your hands, gently bend the mango half inside out so that your diagonal cuts spread out and expose the flesh—it will slightly resemble a porcupine. Repeat with remaining mango half. Set aside on a plate. Repeat entire process with the remaining mango. Set aside.

Cut remaining fruit into a variety of sizes and shapes. Add fruit to the bowl with the mango pieces and toss gently. To serve, place each mango half on a decorative plate. Spoon a heaping half cup of the fruit on one side of each mango. Spoon about ¼ cup of the dressing over the fruit and garnish with mint.

COOK'S TIP ON NONMETALLIC BOWLS: When storing foods with an acidic content, such as citrus juice, wine, or tomatoes, it's best to use a plastic, glass, china, or stainless steel container. Aluminum, carbon steel, or cast iron will react with the acid and leave your food with a metallic taste.

COOK'S TIP: If you don't have time to make the mango porcupines, remove the peel and the seed from the mangoes, chop the flesh, and add it to the other fruit instead.

Layered Lobster Salad

ALL ISLANDS

I n this succulent dish, which might be found anywhere in the Caribbean, the sweet, tender flesh of lobster shares a place on leafy greens with crisp celery and onions, vivid tomatoes, and delicately flavored hearts of palm. This classy Caribbean salad would be perfect for a sunny outdoor luncheon.

Dressing

2 tablespoons acceptable vegetable oil
2 tablespoons malt vinegar
2 cloves garlic, minced
1/4 teaspoon salt
1/4 teaspoon dried dill weed
1/8 teaspoon black pepper

Salad

2 cups torn Bibb lettuce leaves (bite-size pieces)
(about 2 ounces)
2 cups torn fresh spinach leaves (bite-size pieces)
(about 2 ounces)
1/2 medium cucumber, unpeeled and sliced
2 ounces hearts of palm, thinly sliced
2 Italian plum tomatoes, thinly sliced
3 hard-cooked eggs, whites thinly sliced and yolks discarded
2 stalks celery, thinly sliced
2 green onions, thinly sliced
1 pound lobster tails, cooked, meat removed from tails and sliced (about four 4-ounce tails), or 12 ounces fat-free imitation lobster meat, sliced

In a small bowl, whisk the dressing ingredients together and set aside.

On a large platter or four dinner plates, layer the salad ingredients in the following order: Bibb lettuce, spinach, cucumber, hearts of palm, tomatoes, egg whites, celery, and green onions. Arrange

Serves 4; 2 cups per serving

Nutrient Analysis (per serving)

Calories 137
Protein 11 g
Carbohydrate 8 g
Cholesterol 20 mg
Sodium 403 mg
Total fat 7 g
  Saturated 1 g
  Polyunsaturated 4 g
  Monounsaturated 2 g

slices of lobster meat over the top and drizzle the dressing over all. For best results, plan on serving this salad the day you make it. Undressed salad can be covered with plastic wrap and kept in the refrigerator for up to 24 hours. Add the dressing just before serving.

Seafood in Creole Sauce

DOMINICAN REPUBLIC

This popular dish, best served over fluffy rice, lends itself well to experimentation. You may want to add special touches such as fresh herbs or chili peppers. Because shrimp is high in cholesterol, we added some fat-free imitation crab.

8 ounces fresh shrimp, peeled, deveined, and rinsed (see Cook's Tip on page 194)
6 ounces imitation (fat-free) crab legs, cut into ¹/₂-inch pieces
1 tablespoon fresh lime juice
1 tablespoon acceptable margarine
1 medium onion, chopped
1 green bell pepper, chopped
1 stalk celery, chopped
14.5-ounce can no-salt-added tomatoes
2 green onions, white and green parts, chopped
1 jalapeño pepper, seeded and chopped*
2 tablespoons chopped fresh parsley
2 tablespoons dry white wine or nonalcoholic white wine
¹/₈ teaspoon black pepper
Water (optional)

Serves 4; 1 cup per serving

Nutrient Analysis (per serving)

Calories 142
Protein 14 g
Carbohydrate 13 g
Cholesterol 66 mg
Sodium 494 mg
Total fat 4 g
    Saturated 1 g
    Polyunsaturated 2 g
    Monounsaturated 1 g

Place shrimp in a nonmetallic bowl or shallow casserole. Add crab and lime juice and toss well. Marinate, covered, for 20 minutes in refrigerator.

Meanwhile, in a medium skillet, melt the margarine over medium heat. Add the onion, bell pepper, and celery and cook, stirring occasionally, for 2 to 3 minutes, or until vegetables are tender. Add the remaining ingredients, except water, and bring to a simmer over medium-high heat. Reduce heat to medium-low and cook, covered, for 15 minutes.

Drain lime juice from shrimp and crab legs, discarding juice. Add shrimp and crab to the tomato mixture. Cook, covered, over medium-low heat for 5 minutes, or until shrimp is pink and cooked through. If needed to prevent sticking, add water a tablespoon at a time. Do not overcook shrimp or it will become rubbery. Serve warm.

COOK'S TIP ON DEVEINING SHRIMP: Fresh shrimp should be shiny and firm with no black spots (a sign that the shrimp is losing its freshness). There should be no strong shrimp or fish odor. To devein peeled shrimp, slice along the top of the shrimp with a sharp knife and remove the vein. Specially designed tools make this task easier. Or use a paper towel to grasp the vein from the cut-off head end, pulling out the vein without having to cut open the back.

*Wear rubber gloves when handling hot peppers or wash hands thoroughly after handling. Skin, especially around the eyes, is very sensitive to the oil from peppers.

Jerked Chicken

JAMAICA

This spicy, flavorful dish is perfect for those who are in a chicken rut! Highlighted by the popular Jamaican "jerked" seasoning—a combination of cinnamon, nutmeg, onion, chilies, rum, and allspice—this entrée is traditionally made with pork. Our version uses chicken and less allspice, plus it has a few updated twists to create a taste sensation.

2 teaspoons whole or ground allspice
1 1/2 to 2 teaspoons light soy sauce
2 tablespoons fresh lime juice (about 2 medium limes)
1 tablespoon red wine vinegar
1 jalapeño pepper, seeded and chopped*
1 shallot, peeled and chopped
1 tablespoon rum or 1/8 teaspoon rum extract
2 cloves garlic, minced
1 tablespoon acceptable vegetable oil
1/2 teaspoon ground ginger
1/4 teaspoon dried thyme, crumbled
1/4 teaspoon salt
1/4 teaspoon ground cinnamon
1/8 teaspoon ground nutmeg
1/8 teaspoon black pepper
4 boneless, skinless chicken breast halves (about 4 ounces each), all visible fat removed

Serves 4; 1 breast half per serving

Nutrient Analysis (per serving)

Calories 133
Protein 24 g
Carbohydrate 0 g
Cholesterol 62 mg
Sodium 277 mg
Total fat 3 g
  Saturated 1 g
  Polyunsaturated 1 g
  Monounsaturated 1 g

In a small skillet over medium-low heat, dry-roast the whole allspice for 1 to 2 minutes (1 minute for ground allspice). This will help bring out the full flavor. Grind whole allspice in a mortar and pestle or coffee grinder.

Put allspice into a blender or the work bowl of a food processor fitted with a metal blade. Add the remaining ingredients except chicken. Process for 20 to 30 seconds, then pour into a shallow non-metallic bowl.

Rinse chicken and pat dry with paper towels. Place chicken breasts in mixture and let marinate for 2 to 10 hours, covered, in the refrigerator. Turn breasts twice while marinating.

When ready to cook, prepare grill or preheat broiler. Grill chicken over medium-hot coals or broil in a broiler-safe pan, 4 to 6 inches from heat, for 3 to 4 minutes on each side, or until it is cooked through.

COOK'S TIP: Cook extra breasts for "planned-overs." You can slice them and use them in a fresh green vegetable salad. They are also good sliced, wrapped in a warm low-fat flour tortilla, and topped with shredded lettuce, nonfat cheese, and fresh tomatoes for a tropical soft taco.

*Wear rubber gloves when handling hot peppers or wash hands thoroughly after handling. Skin, especially around the eyes, is very sensitive to the oil from peppers.

Skewered Steak Supper

ANGUILLA

This recipe makes a great light supper, complete with meat, vegetables, fruit, and rice. Since cherry tomatoes tend to get mushy when grilled with the steak, they are coupled with the fresh pineapple on their own skewer and used as an edible garnish. Enjoy the contrasting colors, tastes, and textures of this Caribbean shish kebab.

20-ounce can pineapple chunks, canned in fruit juice with no sugar added
1 teaspoon grated lemon zest
2 tablespoons fresh lemon juice
1 teaspoon molasses
⅛ teaspoon black pepper
1 pound sirloin steak, all visible fat removed, cut into 1-inch cubes
8 cherry tomatoes
1 star fruit, sliced crosswise into ½-inch slices
Vegetable oil spray
1 medium onion
1 medium bell pepper, any color
4 cups cooked rice (about 1⅓ cups uncooked), kept warm
4 sprigs fresh parsley

Serves 4; 1 meat skewer, 1 fruit skewer, and 1 cup rice per serving

Nutrient Analysis (per serving)

Calories 420
Protein 28 g
Carbohydrate 66 g
Cholesterol 60 mg
Sodium 52 mg
Total fat 4 g
   Saturated 1 g
   Polyunsaturated 0 g
   Monounsaturated 2 g

Drain juice from canned pineapple, reserving ¼ cup for the marinade. Pour reserved juice into a shallow nonmetallic bowl or casserole and set pineapple chunks aside. Add the lemon zest, lemon juice, molasses, and black pepper to the pineapple juice. Stir to combine. Add the steak cubes and let marinate, covered, in the refrigerator for 2 to 12 hours, stirring occasionally.

Soak four 8-inch wooden skewers in water for 10 minutes or more (these will be for skewering the steak), or use metal skewers. On four unsoaked 8-inch wooden skewers, or on metal skewers, thread the pineapple chunks, cherry tomatoes, and star fruit alternately. Cover with plastic wrap and refrigerate.

Preheat broiler. Spray a broiler pan lightly with vegetable oil spray.

Peel and quarter onion and separate into pieces. Cut bell pepper in half, remove seeds, and cut into 1-inch squares. Thread the steak cubes alternately with the onion and green pepper on the skewers. Place beef skewers on prepared broiler pan 4 to 6 inches from broiler. Broil for 3 to 4 minutes on one side, then turn and broil for 3 to 4 minutes, or until meat is cooked to desired doneness.

To assemble dish, place 1 cup cooked rice on each plate. Lay a beef skewer at one side of plate and a pineapple and tomato skewer at the other. Place a sprig of parsley in the middle for garnish. Serve warm.

COOK'S TIP: You can grill these skewers over medium-hot coals (or medium-high heat if using gas, electric, or propane grill) for 3 to 4 minutes on one side. Turn skewers over and cook an additional 3 to 4 minutes, or until food has reached desired doneness. Also, you can substitute $1/2$-inch slices of mango or papaya for the star fruit if you wish.

"Old Clothes" Stew

Ropa Vieja

CUBA

One would never guess that something that tastes so rich and is so tender would be referred to as "old clothes," but that is what *ropa vieja means.* This dish is made from an inexpensive cut of meat and cooked until very tender. When the meat is shredded, its appearance evokes the name, but don't let the name fool you. The succulent meat is usually served with Cuban black beans (which are very similar in preparation to the black beans in the Brazilian *feijoada completa, Meaty Black Beans and Rice, page 160*) or could be served wrapped in tortillas.

Serves 12; ½ cup per serving

Nutrient Analysis (per serving)

Calories 148
Protein 23 g
Carbohydrate 3 g
Cholesterol 60 mg
Sodium 97 mg
Total fat 4 g
    Saturated 1 g
    Polyunsaturated 0 g
    Monounsaturated 2 g

1 teaspoon acceptable vegetable oil
3 pounds round steak, all visible fat removed
1 cup water
1 bay leaf
¼ teaspoon salt
⅛ teaspoon black pepper
1 medium onion
1 medium green bell pepper
1 clove garlic
14.5-ounce can no-salt-added tomatoes
1 teaspoon extra-virgin olive oil
⅛ teaspoon ground cinnamon

In a Dutch oven, heat the vegetable oil over medium heat. Add beef and brown on both sides. Add the water, bay leaf, salt, and pepper and simmer, covered, over low heat for 2 to 3 hours, or until meat is very tender. Remove and discard bay leaf. Remove meat from pan and let cool. Reserve juices in pan.

Meanwhile, slice onion and bell pepper. Mince garlic. Dice tomatoes, reserving juice.

In a medium skillet, heat the olive oil over medium-low heat. Add onion, bell pepper, and garlic and sauté for 2 to 3 minutes, or until tender. Add this mixture to the reserved pan juices in the Dutch oven, along with the tomatoes, reserved tomato juice, and cinnamon.

Shred the meat with two forks, removing any fat or gristle. Add shredded meat to the Dutch oven and cook, uncovered, for 10 to 15 minutes. Serve warm with cooked black beans, rice, or tortillas.

Black-Eyed Peas and Corned Beef

Jug Jug

BARBADOS

Traditionally served at Christmastime, this hearty recipe is lower in fat than most jug jug. But it's still rich and thick and doesn't sacrifice the flavor of the higher-fat version.

1 pound dried black-eyed peas, rinsed and sorted
    for stones or shriveled peas
8 cups water
½ pound corned beef brisket, uncooked
12 cups water
4 cups low-sodium chicken broth
1 teaspoon smoke-flavored liquid seasoning
1 medium onion
1 fresh jalapeño pepper*
1 clove garlic
½ teaspoon dried thyme, crumbled
⅛ teaspoon black pepper
½ cup cornmeal
1 medium green bell pepper, chopped (optional)
¼ cup chopped fresh parsley

Serves 10; 1 cup per serving

Nutrient Analysis (per serving)

Calories 229
Protein 15 g
Carbohydrate 34 g
Cholesterol 16 mg
Sodium 212 mg
Total fat 4 g
    Saturated 1 g
    Polyunsaturated 1 g
    Monounsaturated 2 g

In a large bowl, soak the black-eyed peas in 8 cups water for 4 hours or overnight.

Meanwhile, place corned beef and 8 cups water in a large stockpot. Bring to a simmer over medium-high heat, then reduce heat to low and cook, partially covered, for 1½ to 2 hours, or until meat is tender. Remove from water, drain, and let cool. Rinse with cold water to remove excess salt. Chop into bite-size pieces and refrigerate.

Drain the black-eyed peas. Place them in a separate large stockpot. Add broth, 4 cups water, and smoke-flavored liquid seasoning. Bring to a simmer over medium-high heat, then reduce heat to low and cook, covered, for 1 hour, or until peas are tender.

Meanwhile, chop the onion, seed and chop the jalapeño, and mince the garlic. After 1 hour, add them, as well as the thyme and black pepper, to the peas. Simmer, covered, for 10 minutes.

Uncover pot and bring mixture to a simmer over medium heat. While stirring, slowly add the cornmeal. Let simmer, uncovered, for 5 minutes, stirring occasionally. Reduce heat to low, stir in the corned beef, and cook, partially covered, for 20 minutes, stirring occasionally. Sprinkle bell pepper, if desired, and parsley over the top and serve warm.

COOK'S TIP: Most corned beef briskets come in rather large sizes. If you purchase a brisket that weighs more than half a pound, freeze the remaining corned beef in small portions in freezer bags for making jug jug in the future.

*Wear rubber gloves when handling hot peppers or wash hands thoroughly after handling. Skin, especially around the eyes, is very sensitive to the oil from peppers.

Spicy Glazed Pork Cubes

Griots

HAITI

*E*nhanced by a light glaze of citrus, tempting tidbits of pork with a bite of chili pepper will satisfy hunger in a hurry. Try serving this over nut-flavored brown rice for a change of pace.

1 teaspoon acceptable vegetable oil
2 pounds boneless pork loin, all visible fat removed, cut into 1-inch cubes
1 medium onion, chopped
2 cloves garlic, minced
$1/2$ cup fresh orange juice (about 2 medium oranges)
$1/4$ cup fresh lime juice (about 3 medium limes)
1 tablespoon light brown sugar
1 habañero or jalapeño chili pepper, seeded and finely chopped*
$1/4$ teaspoon salt
$1/2$ teaspoon turmeric
$1/8$ teaspoon black pepper

Serves 8; about ½ cup per serving

Nutrient Analysis (per serving)

Calories 215
Protein 26 g
Carbohydrate 6 g
Cholesterol 72 mg
Sodium 120 mg
Total fat 9 g
   Saturated 3 g
   Polyunsaturated 1 g
   Monounsaturated 4 g

In a large skillet, heat the vegetable oil over medium heat. Brown the pork cubes for 6 to 8 minutes, stirring occasionally. Add the onion and garlic, lower the heat to medium-low, and cook for 2 minutes. Add the remaining ingredients and bring the mixture to a simmer, then cook, covered, over low heat for 40 to 50 minutes, or until pork is tender. Uncover pan and cook over medium-high heat for 5 to 10 minutes, until juices have reduced to a thick glaze. Serve warm.

  *Wear rubber gloves when handling hot peppers or wash hands thoroughly after handling. Skin, especially around the eyes, is very sensitive to the oil from peppers.

Yuca Root with Tomatillo Sauce

CUBA

I n Cuba, yuca (or cassava) dishes are considered the most important component of the meal. Here the mellow yuca root is enhanced with a spicy sauce made from the small, green tomatolike vegetables known as tomatillos.

2 pounds yuca root, peeled and quartered
½ pound tomatillos, papery skin removed, rinsed
with cold water and quartered
1 cup low-sodium chicken broth
2 teaspoons chili powder
1 clove garlic, minced
1 tablespoon chopped fresh cilantro
1 tablespoon fresh lime juice

Serves 4; ¾ cup per serving

Nutrient Analysis (per serving)

Calories 302
Protein 9 g
Carbohydrate 66 g
Cholesterol 0 mg
Sodium 38 mg
Total fat 2 g
 Saturated 0 g
 Polyunsaturated 0 g
 Monounsaturated 0 g

Place yuca in a medium saucepan. Fill pan with enough cold water to cover by 2 inches. Bring water to a boil over high heat. Reduce heat and simmer, partially covered, for 20 to 30 minutes, until yuca is tender when pierced with a knife. Drain off liquid and set yuca aside on a warm platter.

Meanwhile, in a separate medium saucepan, combine the tomatillos, broth, chili powder, and garlic. Bring mixture to a boil over high heat, then reduce heat to low and simmer for 15 minutes, or until tomatillos are tender. Stir in cilantro.

Place the mixture in a blender or the work bowl of a food processor fitted with a metal blade and process until smooth. Stir in lime juice.

Serve sauce warm or cold over the yuca or on the side. For best results, serve immediately.

COOK'S TIP: To peel yuca easily, take a sharp knife and cut the root into 3-inch sections. Make a lengthwise slit down one side of each piece. Using a paring knife, pull off the tough skin. Always cook yuca, since some varieties can be toxic if eaten raw.

Calypso Rice

TRINIDAD

The origin of calypso music lies deep in Trinidad. The improvised lyrics, based on humorous subjects, shine bright with laughter and color. Also colorful, this rice makes a perfect accompaniment to any Caribbean feast. Or serve it when you just want to add a little fun to the dinner table. Turning on a little calypso music wouldn't hurt either!

1½ cups low-sodium chicken broth
½ cup no-sugar-added pineapple juice
1 cup uncooked rice
1 medium onion, chopped
½ red bell pepper, chopped
½ green bell pepper, chopped
½ teaspoon turmeric
½ teaspoon salt
⅛ teaspoon black pepper
¼ cup chopped fresh parsley

In a medium saucepan, bring broth and pineapple juice to a boil over high heat. Stir in the remaining ingredients except parsley. Reduce heat to low and cook, covered, for 20 minutes. Remove from heat and let stand, covered, for 5 minutes, or until all liquid is absorbed. Fluff rice with a fork and serve with fresh parsley sprinkled on top.

Serves 8; ½ cup per serving

Nutrient Analysis (per serving)

Calories 114
Protein 3 g
Carbohydrate 24 g
Cholesterol 0 mg
Sodium 158 mg
Total fat 0 g
  Saturated 0 g
  Polyunsaturated 0 g
  Monounsaturated 0 g

Griddle Biscuits

Bakes

TRINIDAD

These biscuits often are deep-fried in oil. For this more healthful version, the bakes are cooked on a griddle. They are excellent with stews and one-dish meals. Spread with jam or honey, bakes are also a breakfast treat or even a quick snack.

2 cups all-purpose flour
2 teaspoons baking powder
¼ teaspoon salt
½ cup water
2 tablespoons acceptable vegetable oil
2 teaspoons sugar
Vegetable oil spray

Serves 8; 2 biscuits per serving

Nutrient Analysis (per serving)

Calories 149
Protein 3 g
Carbohydrate 25 g
Cholesterol 0 mg
Sodium 195 mg
Total fat 4 g
  Saturated 0 g
  Polyunsaturated 2 g
  Monounsaturated 1 g

In a medium mixing bowl, combine the flour, baking powder, and salt. In a small mixing bowl, combine the water, vegetable oil, and sugar. Pour this mixture into the flour mixture and mix with a spoon until just combined. Add water, small amounts at a time as needed, if mixture is too dry.

Roll out dough on a lightly floured cutting board or waxed paper to ¼-inch thickness. (If using a small board, roll out half the dough at a time.) Using a 2½-inch biscuit or cookie cutter, cut dough into circles. Bring together scraps of dough, roll out again, and cut more circles. Do not overhandle the dough. Repeat until all dough is used.

Lightly spray a nonstick griddle with vegetable oil spray and preheat over medium heat. Cook the biscuits on one side for 3 minutes, or until golden brown, then cook on the other side for 3 minutes. Remove from griddle and serve warm. Bakes will keep in an airtight container in the refrigerator for up to 4 days and in the freezer for up to 2 months. To recrisp the bakes, place them, uncovered, in a preheated 375° F oven for 5 to 10 minutes.

Coconut Quick Bread

BARBADOS

A tasty tropical treat, this quick bread is a must for coconut fans. It is good for breakfast and can also double as a dessert. Coconut bread, of course, usually contains lots of high-fat coconut. This easy-to-make version cuts back on the coconut and compensates with coconut extract, pineapple juice for flavor, and mashed banana for flavor and extra moisture.

Serves 16; 1 slice per serving

Nutrient Analysis (per serving)

Calories 135
Protein 2 g
Carbohydrate 25 g
Cholesterol 0 mg
Sodium 128 mg
Total fat 3 g
    Saturated 1 g
    Polyunsaturated 1 g
    Monounsaturated 0 g

Vegetable oil spray
1 tablespoon all-purpose flour
2 cups all-purpose flour
¾ cup sugar
¼ cup shredded coconut
1½ teaspoons baking powder
½ teaspoon baking soda
¼ teaspoon salt
¾ cup no-sugar-added pineapple juice
½ cup mashed banana (about 1 large)
2 tablespoons acceptable vegetable oil
Egg substitute equivalent to 1 egg, or 1 egg
2 teaspoons coconut extract
¼ teaspoon vanilla
1 teaspoon shredded coconut

Preheat oven to 350° F. Lightly spray a 9 × 5 × 2½-inch loaf pan with vegetable oil spray. Sprinkle 1 tablespoon flour over surface and shake pan to coat it. Shake out any excess flour.

In a medium mixing bowl, combine 2 cups flour, sugar, ¼ cup coconut, baking powder, baking soda, and salt. In a separate medium mixing bowl, combine remaining ingredients except 1 teaspoon coconut. Pour liquid mixture into flour mixture and stir until just combined. Pour batter into prepared pan, sprinkle 1 teaspoon shredded coconut over the top, and bake for 45 to 50 minutes, or until a toothpick inserted in the center of the bread comes out clean.

Allow bread to cool in pan for 10 minutes. Run a knife along the sides of pan and invert bread onto a cooling rack. Let cool at least 15 minutes before cutting. For best results, let whole loaf cool thoroughly for 1 to 2 hours. Wrap in plastic wrap and refrigerate. After about 8 hours, the moisture will have permeated the bread, making it even more delicious.

Honey–Rum Mango Sauce

ALL ISLANDS

Y ou can serve this versatile sauce warm or cold over nonfat or low-fat frozen yogurt or angel food cake. You can even use it to give a unique twist to roast chicken or pork. Although there are many ways to enjoy the mango, from condiments to drinks, many people think it is at its juicy best when simply opened up and eaten. If you try a juicy-ripe mango, you will understand why people in the Caribbean recommend eating it in the bathtub!

Serves 4; ¼ cup per serving

Nutrient Analysis (per serving)

Calories 132
Protein 1 g
Carbohydrate 26 g
Cholesterol 0 mg
Sodium 41 mg
Total fat 3 g
    Saturated 1 g
    Polyunsaturated 1 g
    Monounsaturated 1 g

1 ripe mango, peeled and diced
¾ cup no-sugar-added pineapple juice
1 tablespoon acceptable margarine
2 tablespoons honey
1 tablespoon rum or ¼ teaspoon rum extract
1 tablespoon fresh lime juice
2 teaspoons cornstarch
4 teaspoons water
1 teaspoon grated lime zest
¼ cup frozen low-fat whipped topping, thawed
    (optional)
4 sprigs mint (optional)

Place mango in a blender or the work bowl of a food processor fitted with a metal blade and process until smooth.

In a small saucepan, bring the pureed mango, pineapple juice, margarine, honey, rum, and lime juice to a simmer over high heat. Reduce heat to medium-low and cook mixture for 10 minutes, stirring occasionally.

Place cornstarch in a small bowl. Stir in water. Add cornstarch-water mixture to the saucepan and cook over medium heat until mixture is thickened, about 2 to 3 minutes, stirring occasionally. Stir in the grated lime zest and remove from heat. Serve sauce warm or chill for later use.

If serving sauce over angel food cake, you may want to pour the sauce over each piece of cake, then top each serving with a tablespoon of whipped topping and a sprig of mint.

COOK'S TIP ON CUTTING MANGOES: To cut a mango, place it on its flattest side. Using a sharp knife, make a horizontal cut to slice off approximately the top half of the mango. (The large, flat pit in the center doesn't "let go" of the flesh; you can't cut the fruit exactly in half.) Turn the mango over, pit side down; slice off the top part of the second side, near the pit. Trim off all peel from the three pieces. Trim off any flesh remaining on pit. Dice all the flesh.

Sweet Stuffed Cornmeal

Duckanoo

JAMAICA

This fun dessert is usually tied in banana leaves and steamed. Corn husks or aluminum foil are convenient North American substitutes, unless you are growing a banana tree in your backyard!

28 dried corn husks or banana leaves or 24 5-inch squares aluminum foil
2 cups cornmeal
¾ cup firmly packed brown sugar
2 tablespoons raisins
½ teaspoon ground cinnamon
¼ teaspoon ground allspice
⅛ teaspoon salt
¾ cup skim milk
½ cup cooked and mashed sweet potatoes (about 1 small)
1 teaspoon molasses
½ teaspoon vanilla
⅛ teaspoon coconut extract

Serves 12; 2 packages per serving

Nutrient Analysis (per serving)

Calories 160
Protein 3 g
Carbohydrate 36 g
Cholesterol 0 mg
Sodium 40 mg
Total fat 0 g
  Saturated 0 g
  Polyunsaturated 0 g
  Monounsaturated 0 g

With your fingers, tear 4 of the husks into 6 strips each, forming 24 strips. They will tie the bundles. Place the remaining husks in enough cold water to cover. Let soak for 15 minutes.

Meanwhile, in a large mixing bowl, combine the cornmeal, brown sugar, raisins, cinnamon, allspice, and salt. In a separate mixing bowl, combine the remaining ingredients. Add this mixture to the dry mixture and stir until just combined.

Remove one corn husk from the water, shaking off excess water. Spoon about 2 tablespoons of the cornmeal mixture onto the middle of the husk. Fold the sides of the husk toward the middle, then fold the ends into the middle to completely enclose the filling. Tie with a corn-husk strip and set aside. If using foil, spoon filling onto the center and fold foil in half, crimping edges to seal. Repeat with remaining filling.

Place a steamer rack in a large stockpot. Add water to just below the rack. Heat over high heat to simmer. Place the duckanoo "packages" in the stockpot on the steamer rack. Water should not touch the packages. Cook, covered, over low heat for 45 minutes.

Carefully remove packages from pan and let cool slightly. Unwrap and serve warm or cold.

To store, place packages in an airtight container. They will keep for 5 days in the refrigerator or 2 months in the freezer. Reheat over steaming water for 5 minutes, or place 6 at a time in the microwave and heat for 30 to 60 seconds on 100% power (high) (if using foil, remove duckanoo from package before reheating in microwave).

Piña Colada Shake

PUERTO RICO

*I f you crave something frosty and sweet, this shake
is for you! The popular piña colada is traditionally
made with rum, pineapple juice, coconut cream, and
crushed ice. With smart substitutions of sherbet, skim
milk, and flavoring extracts, you can get the flavor
without the fat. Serve these at your next party and
make your guests feel as if they're on a tropical
island!*

**½ cup fresh pineapple chunks or pineapple
  chunks canned in fruit juice with no sugar
  added**
1 lime, cut into thin slices
3 cups pineapple sherbet
1½ cups skim milk
¼ teaspoon rum extract
¼ teaspoon coconut extract

Drain juice from pineapple. Discard juice. Thread a
few of the pineapple chunks and lime slices onto
each of 4 wooden skewers and set aside.

In a blender, combine the remaining ingredients
and blend until smooth. You may have to scrape the
sides with a rubber spatula occasionally. Pour shake
into 4 wineglasses or other festive-looking glasses.
Place a pineapple-lime skewer in each glass. Serve
immediately. Shakes will keep for 30 minutes in the
refrigerator when stored in the capped blender
pitcher.

VARIATION: If desired, add 4 ounces of rum
to the other ingredients in the blender and process
as directed.

**COOK'S TIP ON CHOOSING PINE-
APPLES:** When looking for a fresh pineapple,
choose one that gives slightly when gently pressed
with your fingertips. Also, when you pull on a top
inner leaf, it should come out easily. Color does not

Serves 4; 1¼ cups
per serving

Nutrient
Analysis
(per serving)

Without rum

Calories 248
Protein 5 g
Carbohydrate 52 g
Cholesterol 9 mg
Sodium 114 mg
Total fat 3 g
  Saturated 2 g
  Polyunsaturated 0 g
  Monounsaturated 1 g

With rum

Calories 312
Protein 5 g
Carbohydrate 52 g
Cholesterol 9 mg
Sodium 114 mg
Total fat 3 g
  Saturated 2 g
  Polyunsaturated 0 g
  Monounsaturated 1 g

indicate ripeness, but the pineapple should not be dull or have mold growing on it. Fresh pineapple cubes freeze well when packed in a rigid container. You can sprinkle a small amount of sugar over the cubes if desired. They will keep for 6 to 8 months in the freezer.

ASIAN CUISINE

Eggplant Dip
Seafood Terrine with Shrimp and Asparagus

Forest Mushroom Soup
Hot-and-Sour Soup

Spicy Skewered Shrimp

Chicken in Garlic Sauce
Cilantro-Lime Turkey Breast

Savory Ginger Beef Barbecue
Shredded Beef with Bok Choy and Carrots
Barbecued Pork Roast

Vegetarian Fried Rice

Green Beans in Spicy Sauce
Eggplant Hunan-Style
Cold Noodles with Sesame Sauce

Koi-Pond Pudding
Almond Diamonds

Fiery Pickled Vegetables

The flavors of Asia are incredibly diverse, and we're still discovering them, a plateful at a time. Japan's foods, such as the Seafood Terrine with Shrimp and Asparagus on page 221, are delicate. Recipes are designed to emphasize seasonal foods and to focus attention on the natural flavors of the foods themselves. Sake, which is a Japanese rice wine, and sugar are popular as flavoring agents. Mirin, a sweetened, low-alcohol rice wine, takes the place of both in many recipes.

The Japanese believe that the choice of tableware and the placement of the foods on the plate are integral parts of the meal. This attention to detail is an art form in Japan. Garnishes are designed to complement the food. They can range from a few carefully placed pine needles to elaborately carved fruits and vegetables—no parsley sprigs here!

China boasts the most diverse styles of cuisine within a single country. Many of the mild dishes we often think of as classical Chinese come from Canton. The oriental restaurants many of us grew up with were Cantonese, and as the dishes were adapted to American tastes, more and more meat was added and the vegetables were demoted to second place.

Then Szechwan and Hunan provinces gave us a wake-up call. Chinese food doesn't have to be bland! We learned we could use meat as a flavoring condiment instead of the primary component in a dish. Classic Szechwan and Hunan flavors of hot pepper, ginger, and garlic became popular.

A World–Class Condiment

The first thing many Americans think of when they hear "Asian food" is soy sauce. Brewed from the soybean, a primary protein in most Eastern cultures, soy sauce varies from country to country. Chinese soy sauce is the saltiest and most intense, and Japanese soy sauce, or shoyu, is the mildest. For the recipes in this section, the American Heart Association recommends using reduced-sodium soy sauces (even they contain a lot of sodium). In any language, less salt is your heart's best bet.

Soy sauce reigns in the north, but fish sauces are king in southern and southeastern Asia. Fish-based sauces, such as nam pla and nuoc nam, haven't become nearly as popular in the United States as soy-based sauces. The Western version of fish sauce is Worcestershire, which is made from fermented fish but tempered with fruits and spices from India. In a pinch, you can substitute Worcestershire for fish sauce, but you'll want to add less to the dish and be sure to taste it before adjusting.

In all its forms, the soybean has a firm place as a staple protein. Buddhism prohibits red meat consumption, leaving fish and fowl among the few proteins permitted. As a result, tofu, a high-protein soy product that's inexpensive and easy to produce, became the meat substitute for millions. Soy milk, which is basically liquid tofu and is high in calcium, became the dairy substitute. Over time, the use of milk as a food for both children and adults has virtually disappeared in Asian cultures. An Oriental child usually tastes milk for the last time when he or she is weaned.

Centuries of genetic adaptation are reflected in the fact that most adult Asians are lactose intolerant—they can't digest milk—because they've lost the ability to produce the enzymes needed to do so. Even in western Asia, where milk is still used, it is seldom drunk. Instead, it is consumed in the form of yogurt and cheese, which are easier to digest.

Rice Is the Heart of Life

Sticky or fluffy, seasoned or plain, rice is the basis of every meal in all Asian cuisines. It might simply be steamed as a subtle contrast to the flavors of the accompanying dishes. But sometimes rice is highly seasoned to make a statement of its own. Rice has achieved almost-sacred status, so in many cultures it is a sign of great disrespect to leave any of it on the plate. In several languages, the word for *food* is *rice*. You might be invited for the most sumptuous of meals with the simple words, "Have you had rice?"

Most meals are served family style, presented in communal bowls or plates from which you serve yourself. You are expected first to take a full bowl, or serving, of rice and only about two to three tablespoons of the other dishes. If you finish your portion, including the rice, politeness dictates that you first take more of the rice and the vegetable dishes, which are usually offered in abundance. You take more of the special meat dishes only after everyone else has had a share.

Inform your guests of Asian etiquette if that's the way you'll be cooking and serving. Serve the meal family style or bring out individual servings of food in traditional Asian bowls. But bring on lots of rice!

When cooking and eating Asian food, you may want to contemplate these words found in an old text:

The wise man eats simply of simple foods, and his comfort lies in moderation rather than excess. Nevertheless, he should delight in the eating, so however simple, the food should be prepared with respect and care, as if for a king.

Eggplant Dip

Kachi

KOREA

S erve this flavorful dip with lightly toasted strips of Afghan bread, pita bread, or crackers.

Serves 12 as
an appetizer;
about 2½ tablespoons
per serving

Nutrient
Analysis
(per serving)

Calories 25
Protein 1 g
Carbohydrate 3 g
Cholesterol 0 mg
Sodium 101 mg
Total fat 1 g
    Saturated 0 g
    Polyunsaturated 1 g
    Monounsaturated 0 g

Eggplant(s), about 1 pound total (small ones preferred)
2 tablespoons reduced-sodium soy sauce
4 teaspoons grated fresh gingerroot
1 tablespoon chopped green onion
1 tablespoon mirin
2 teaspoons rice vinegar
1 clove garlic, minced
1 tablespoon fragrant toasted sesame oil
4 drops chili oil
Chopped fresh cilantro

Preheat oven to 400° F.

Pierce the eggplant(s) several times with a fork and place on foil laid directly on an oven rack. Bake in middle of oven for 45 minutes to 1 hour, or until very soft when pierced with a knife. Remove from oven and let cool for about 5 minutes.

Cut eggplant(s) in half lengthwise and scoop the pulp onto a cutting board. Finely chop the pulp and transfer it to a medium serving bowl. Set aside.

In a small saucepan, simmer the soy sauce, gingerroot, green onion, mirin, vinegar, and garlic until the liquid is reduced to about 1 tablespoon. Reduce the heat to low, add the sesame and chili oils, and continue to cook for about 30 seconds, stirring constantly. Carefully stir the hot soy mixture into the chopped eggplant until well combined. Garnish with chopped cilantro. Cover bowl tightly and refrigerate for 1 hour or more, until ready to serve. This dip can be made the day before and refrigerated overnight in an airtight container.

Seafood Terrine with Shrimp and Asparagus

Hampen

JAPAN

H ampen *makes an elegant appetizer or light
lunch, depending on portion size. You can make
it several hours, or even a day, in advance. Just before
serving, arrange slices on a serving platter with
parsley and lemon wedges for a beautiful
presentation.*

10 ounces bay or sea scallops
5 ounces flounder, sole, or other mild white fish
  fillets
1 tablespoon cornstarch
1 tablespoon water
1 egg white
1 teaspoon mirin
1 teaspoon white miso
¼ teaspoon salt
7 large raw shrimp, rinsed, peeled, and deveined
5 to 7 stalks fresh green asparagus, woody bases
  snapped off and discarded
Parsley (optional)
Fresh lemon wedges (optional)
Reduced-sodium soy sauce (optional)*
Wasabi (optional)*

Serves 16 as
an appetizer;
1 slice per serving
Serves 4 as an
entrée; 4 slices per
serving

Nutrient
Analysis
(per appetizer
serving)

Calories 36
Protein 7 g
Carbohydrate 1 g
Cholesterol 16 mg
Sodium 116 mg
Total fat 0 g
  Saturated 0 g
  Polyunsaturated 0 g
  Monounsaturated 0 g

Rinse the scallops and drain on paper towels. Rinse
the fish, pat dry with paper towels, and cut into
small pieces. Place scallops and fish in a blender or
the work bowl of a food processor fitted with a
metal blade and process until smooth. Place cornstarch in a small bowl. Stir in water. Add cornstarch-
water mixture to fish mixture and process.

Add the egg white, mirin, miso, and salt. Process
until smooth.

Dip a microwave-safe glass loaf pan into cold
water, then pour the water out. With a rubber
spatula dipped in cold water, fill the dampened loaf

pan with the seafood mixture, laying in the shrimp and asparagus as you go. Keep in mind how they will look in cross section when the finished loaf is cut. You may want one, two, or even three layers of the asparagus and shrimp to achieve the look you like best.

Press gently to make sure no air bubbles are trapped in the mix. Gently rap the dish on a counter to free any remaining air bubbles. Smooth the top of the loaf with the rubber spatula dipped in cold water.

Cover the pan with plastic wrap and poke several small holes in the plastic wrap to allow the steam to escape.

Cook the terrine in a microwave oven on 50% power (medium) for 3 minutes. You may have to adjust the cooking time based on the wattage of your microwave oven. Test for doneness by inserting a toothpick or cake tester in the center of the terrine; the implement should come out clean. If the terrine is not done yet, continue cooking it, a minute at a time, until it tests done.

Let the terrine sit, still wrapped, for 2 to 3 minutes; it will cool a bit and shrink from the sides of the pan.

Remove the plastic wrap, pour off any accumulated liquid, and invert the terrine onto a serving plate. Cover it again with plastic wrap and chill it for at least 30 minutes before slicing with a sharp knife.

Garnish with parsley and serve with lemon wedges, if desired. Or for a more traditional taste, serve with soy sauce and wasabi for dipping. Each diner puts a dab of wasabi (it's hot!) and about a teaspoon of reduced-sodium soy sauce in a small dipping bowl or saucer.

COOK'S TIP: If the asparagus spears are large and tough, they won't cook evenly in the terrine. Microwave them, without any added water, in a covered dish until they are just tender. Proceed as directed above.

* Because both reduced-sodium soy sauce and wasabi are high in sodium, go easy on these optional ingredients if you're close to the 2,400-milligram recommended maximum today.

Forest Mushroom Soup

Yuk-Tong

CHINA

This simple soup brings out the warm earthiness of the mushroom. Feel free to use shiitake for all the mushrooms if you enjoy their strong, rich flavor. The homemade chicken stock in this recipe can also be used in other recipes, such as Hot-and-Sour Soup (page 226). If you don't want to take the time to make homemade broth, use the commercial low-sodium variety.

Stock

3 pounds chicken parts, such as wings, necks, backs, ribs, and breastbones
1 green onion, cut into 4 pieces
2 slices fresh gingerroot, each about the size of a quarter

Soup

2 fresh or dried shiitake mushrooms
6 cups chicken stock
2 tablespoons reduced-sodium soy sauce
1 teaspoon fragrant toasted sesame oil
3 tablespoons dry sherry (optional)
3 tablespoons cornstarch (optional)
3 tablespoons water (optional)
2 to 3 drops chili oil
6 to 8 fresh medium mushrooms, any variety, sliced
2 green onions, thinly sliced diagonally

Serves 6; 1 cup per serving

Nutrient Analysis (per serving)

Calories 41
Protein 3 g
Carbohydrate 3 g
Cholesterol 0 mg
Sodium 257 mg
Total fat 2 g
   Saturated 0 g
   Polyunsaturated 1 g
   Monounsaturated 1 g

Rinse the chicken parts and pat dry with paper towels. To prepare the stock, place the chicken parts in a large stockpot and add water to cover. Add the green onion pieces and the gingerroot. Bring to a simmer over medium heat, then reduce heat to maintain the simmer.

Skim off and discard the foam that rises to the top in the next few minutes. When the foam thins and lightens in color, partially cover the pot, leaving a small vent. Adjust the heat to maintain the barest simmer. Cook for about 4 hours.

Remove the stock from the heat. Strain the stock over a large bowl without pressing on the chicken parts. (Pressing on them causes the stock to be very cloudy.) Discard the chicken parts and chill the broth, tightly covered, overnight. By morning, all the fat will have risen to the top of the jellied broth. Remove and discard the fat.

To assemble the soup, soak dried shiitake mushrooms, if using, in a small amount of boiling water for about 15 minutes, or until soft. Drain. Cut off the woody stems and slice the caps very thinly.

Meanwhile, heat 6 cups stock in a large saucepan over medium heat. Add the shiitake mushrooms, soy sauce, and sesame oil, and the sherry, if using. Simmer gently for 5 minutes. If you want a slightly thicker soup, place cornstarch in a small bowl. Stir in water. Add cornstarch-water mixture to the simmering soup. Stir constantly until it reaches the desired thickness. Add the chili oil a drop at a time, tasting after each addition. Add the fresh mushrooms and sliced green onions. Stir once and serve.

COOK'S TIP ON BUYING AND BONING CHICKENS: If you buy whole chickens and bone them yourself, you can save money in two ways. You can store the bones in your freezer to use in making virtually fat-free chicken stock, and you get skinless, boneless chicken meat at about half the store price.

Hot-and-Sour Soup

Sze-Suan-Tong

CHINA

Don't get too caught up in the kinds and amounts of vegetables and the amount of tofu in this very adaptable soup. The "handful of whatever's handy" method works just fine. Snow peas, broccoli florets, shredded carrots, canned water chestnuts, or bamboo shoots would all be good substitutes in or additions to the recipe. The vinegar and black pepper give this delightful dish its kick. To make it a little less spicy, cut back a bit on the pepper. You might then want to reduce the amount of vinegar as well.

8 cups low-sodium chicken broth
¼ cup cornstarch
3 tablespoons water
1 cup thinly sliced green cabbage or bok choy (about 3 ounces)
1 cup sliced fresh shiitake, cloud ear, or other mushrooms
½ cup sliced green onions (about 6)
2 tablespoons reduced-sodium soy sauce
2 tablespoons minced fresh gingerroot
½ pound firm reduced-fat tofu, cut into strips
1 cup white vinegar or to taste
1 tablespoon black pepper or to taste (freshly ground preferred)
Egg substitute equivalent to 2 eggs, or 2 eggs lightly beaten
1 teaspoon fragrant toasted sesame oil

Serves 8; 1 cup per serving

Nutrient Analysis (per serving)

Calories 111
Protein 9 g
Carbohydrate 11 g
Cholesterol 0 mg
Sodium 235 mg
Total fat 4 g
  Saturated 1 g
  Polyunsaturated 2 g
  Monounsaturated 1 g

Bring the broth to a boil in a large stockpot over high heat.

Meanwhile, place cornstarch in a small bowl. Stir in water. Set aside.

Add the cabbage, mushrooms, green onions, soy sauce, and gingerroot to the boiling broth. When the broth mixture returns to a boil, stir in the cornstarch-water mixture. Let the mixture boil for about 3 minutes.

Add the tofu strips, vinegar, and pepper. Taste and add more pepper or vinegar if desired. Reduce heat to a simmer.

Slowly drizzle the egg substitute into the simmering soup, stirring gently. Remove from the heat, stir in the sesame oil, and serve.

Spicy Skewered Shrimp

Ebi no Kushi-Yaki

JAPAN

T his delight can be found on every other street corner in Japan. Mobile carts appear in the evenings so that office workers can snatch a quick bite on the way home.

32 medium shrimp, with shells and tails

M a r i n a d e
2 tablespoons sake or lemon juice (optional)
2 tablespoons reduced-sodium soy sauce
2 tablespoons mirin
2 teaspoons grated fresh gingerroot
1 green onion, finely chopped
2 to 3 drops fragrant toasted sesame oil
   or chili oil

Rinse the shrimp and pat dry with paper towels. Set aside.

Combine the marinade ingredients in a medium mixing bowl. Add shrimp to the marinade and toss well to coat. Leave the shrimp in the mixture, covered, for up to 12 hours in the refrigerator.

About 10 minutes before cooking time, place eight 8-inch bamboo or wooden skewers in water to cover. Prepare grill or preheat broiler.

Remove shrimp from the marinade. Pour marinade into a small saucepan and bring to a boil over high heat. Reduce heat and slowly boil marinade for 5 minutes.

Meanwhile, thread 4 shrimp onto each skewer. Grill over hot coals or broil for 1 to 2 minutes on each side, 3 to 4 inches from the coals or broiler. Brush the shrimp with some of the marinade and grill or broil for another minute or so, until the shells look chalky with just a little char. Serve hot, at room temperature, or cold.

Chicken in Garlic Sauce

Shiu Heung Gai

CHINA

If you don't want this dish spicy, you can reduce the amount of chili paste or replace it with ketchup.

1 pound chicken pieces
1 egg white, lightly beaten
2 teaspoons cornstarch
1 teaspoon dry sherry (optional)
2 teaspoons cornstarch
1 tablespoon water
2 tablespoons reduced-sodium soy sauce
2 teaspoons sugar
2 teaspoons white vinegar
1 teaspoon chili paste or hot bean paste
2 tablespoons dry sherry (optional)
3 teaspoons canola or peanut oil
1 teaspoon minced fresh gingerroot
1 tablespoon minced garlic (about 3 large cloves)
2 green onions, sliced into 1/4-inch pieces
1 cup snow peas (about 6 ounces)
1 teaspoon fragrant toasted sesame oil

Serves 4; 3 ounces per serving

Nutrient Analysis (per serving)

Calories 236
Protein 27 g
Carbohydrate 9 g
Cholesterol 68 mg
Sodium 396 mg
Total fat 10 g
  Saturated 2 g
  Polyunsaturated 3 g
  Monounsaturated 4 g

Remove skin from chicken. Rinse chicken and pat dry with paper towels. Trim off all visible fat; remove bones. Cut chicken meat into bite-size pieces.

Mix the egg white, 2 teaspoons cornstarch, and 1 teaspoon sherry, if using, in a medium mixing bowl. Add the chicken, tossing to coat well. Cover and refrigerate for about 30 minutes.

Place 2 teaspoons cornstarch in a small bowl. Stir in water.

Combine the soy sauce, cornstarch-water mixture, sugar, vinegar, and chili paste and the 2 tablespoons sherry, if using, in a small mixing bowl. Set aside.

Heat a wok or large, heavy skillet over high heat until hot and drizzle with 2 teaspoons oil. Immediately add the chicken and stir-fry for about 2 minutes. Remove wok from the heat. Transfer chicken to a bowl and set aside.

Add another teaspoon of oil to the hot wok; add the gingerroot, garlic, and green onions. Stir-fry for a few seconds, taking care not to burn the garlic. Return chicken to wok and add the snow peas and sesame oil. Stir-fry for a few seconds to warm the ingredients.

Pour in the soy sauce mixture, stirring constantly, and cook for about 30 seconds, or until the sauce thickens and lightly coats the food. Serve immediately.

Cilantro-Lime Turkey Breast

Chilmyanchi

THAILAND

*T*hai cooking features robust flavors from fish
sauce, garlic, chili peppers, and lime. The
*mildness of turkey combines deliciously with all
these flavors in this easy-to-make main dish.*

1 cup uncooked Thai fragrant rice or basmati rice
1 pound boneless, skinless turkey breast or
chicken breasts, all visible fat removed
½ cup water
¼ cup firmly packed light brown sugar
1 tablespoon fish sauce
2 cloves garlic, minced
1 to 2 hot chili peppers, such as serrano, Scotch
bonnet, or habañero, finely chopped*
1 tablespoon finely chopped fresh cilantro
1 teaspoon grated lime zest
Fresh cilantro leaves (optional)

Serves 4; ½ cup
turkey and ¾ cup rice
per serving

Nutrient
Analysis
(per serving)

Calories 392
Protein 31 g
Carbohydrate 56 g
Cholesterol 67 mg
Sodium 327 mg
Total fat 4 g
    Saturated 1 g
    Polyunsaturated 1 g
    Monounsaturated 1 g

Cook the rice according to package instructions.

Meanwhile, rinse turkey and pat dry with paper
towels. Cut turkey into bite-size pieces. Set aside.

In a medium saucepan, combine the water,
brown sugar, and fish sauce. Cook and stir over
medium-low heat for about 5 minutes, or until
sugar dissolves. Add garlic and chili peppers. Bring
to a boil over medium-high heat. Continue to boil
for about 5 minutes, stirring occasionally.

Lower heat to medium. Add turkey to sauce.
Cook for 5 minutes, or until turkey is tender and
no longer pink, stirring occasionally. Stir in the
cilantro and lime zest.

Serve turkey mixture warm with rice. Garnish
with cilantro leaves, if desired.

*Wear rubber gloves when handling hot peppers or
wash hands thoroughly after handling. Skin, especially
around the eyes, is very sensitive to the oil from peppers.

Savory Ginger Beef Barbecue

Chichi-Gogi

KOREA

This dish is traditionally cooked at the table on a grill that looks like an overturned shallow bowl set on a portable stove. Both the grill and the portable stove can be purchased in ethnic groceries, gourmet shops, and larger department stores. This is a very forgiving recipe, however, so don't let the lack of a Korean grill stop you from trying it. You can use an outdoor grill or even a skillet. Just be certain that whatever you use is heated before the meat is added.

2 pounds lean sirloin tip roast or any other lean, boneless cut of your choice, such as sirloin steak, all visible fat removed
2 tablespoons oyster sauce
3 tablespoons dry sherry (optional)
2 green onions, finely chopped
4 cloves garlic, crushed or minced
1 tablespoon hoisin sauce
1 tablespoon fragrant toasted sesame oil
1 teaspoon grated fresh gingerroot
1 teaspoon smoke-flavored liquid seasoning
1/2 teaspoon sugar
Black pepper (freshly ground preferred)
Dash of red hot-pepper sauce, or to taste

Freeze the meat slightly for easier cutting, then slice across the grain into strips about $1/8$ inch wide. Place in a glass dish. Combine the remaining ingredients in a small mixing bowl and pour over the meat slices, tossing well to coat. Marinate meat, covered, in the refrigerator for about 1 hour.

Cook to desired doneness on a hot Korean grill at the table, on a preheated outdoor grill, or in a hot skillet over medium-high heat for about 1 minute on each side. Turn only once or the meat will become dry and tough.

Serves 8; 3 ounces per serving

Nutrient Analysis (per serving)

Calories 133
Protein 23 g
Carbohydrate 1 g
Cholesterol 60 mg
Sodium 214 mg
Total fat 4 g
    Saturated 1 g
    Polyunsaturated 0 g
    Monounsaturated 1 g

Shredded Beef with Bok Choy and Carrots

Hung-Gao-Yuk

CHINA

This is so good that you may want to double the recipe and have leftovers. Steamed rice is a good accompaniment.

1 pound beef flank or skirt steak, all visible fat removed
1 tablespoon reduced-sodium soy sauce
2 teaspoons grated fresh gingerroot
2 to 3 cloves garlic, crushed or minced
$^{1}/_{2}$ teaspoon red chili paste
3 tablespoons dry sherry (optional)
6 stalks bok choy
5 medium carrots
$1^{1}/_{2}$ teaspoons canola or peanut oil
$1^{1}/_{2}$ teaspoons canola or peanut oil, if needed
$^{1}/_{2}$ cup low-sodium beef broth
1 tablespoon cornstarch
2 tablespoons water

Serves 6; about $^{3}/_{4}$ cup per serving

Nutrient Analysis (per serving)

Calories 173
Protein 17 g
Carbohydrate 8 g
Cholesterol 43 mg
Sodium 185 mg
Total fat 8 g
  Saturated 2 g
  Polyunsaturated 1 g
  Monounsaturated 4 g

Slice the meat across the grain into slices about $^{1}/_{8}$ inch wide and place in a large mixing bowl. Place the soy sauce, gingerroot, garlic, and chili paste and sherry, if using, in a small bowl and mix thoroughly. Pour marinade over the meat and set aside for about 10 minutes.

Meanwhile, thinly slice the bok choy; slice the carrots into matchstick-size strips. Set aside.

Remove the beef from the marinade and discard the marinade.

Heat a wok or deep, heavy skillet over high heat, add $1^{1}/_{2}$ teaspoons oil, and stir-fry the drained beef until just cooked, about 2 minutes. Remove the meat with a slotted spoon and set aside.

Add another $1^{1}/_{2}$ teaspoons oil if the pan is dry, and stir-fry the bok choy and carrots for 2 to 3 minutes over high heat. When the vegetables are almost cooked but still crunchy, add the reserved beef and the beef broth. Place cornstarch in a small bowl. Stir in water. Add cornstarch-water mixture to the beef mixture, stirring constantly. Cook until the sauce thickens, about 1 minute, and serve.

COOK'S TIP ON SLICING MEAT: Meat is easier to slice thinly when it is partially frozen.

Barbecued Pork Roast

Chia-Siu

THROUGHOUT ASIA

S liced thinly and served in small portions, this is
an old favorite. For a more Americanized version,
serve the remaining sauce with the meat. Prepare
enough roast to have leftovers for tasty sandwiches.
If you don't intend to serve the remaining roast,
however, simply halve all the ingredients. Steamed
rice is a good accompaniment.

Vegetable oil spray
1 teaspoon paprika
½ teaspoon chili powder
5-pound boneless pork loin roast, all visible fat
    removed

Barbecue Sauce
1 teaspoon fragrant toasted sesame oil
1 cup chopped onion (about 2 medium)
1 teaspoon minced garlic
1½ cups water
1 cup ketchup
2 tablespoons brown sugar
2 tablespoons cider vinegar
2 tablespoons Worcestershire sauce
1½ teaspoons chili powder
1 teaspoon paprika
½ teaspoon red hot-pepper sauce

Serves 22; 3
ounces per serving

Nutrient
Analysis
(per serving)*

Calories 193
Protein 23 g
Carbohydrate 5 g
Cholesterol 66 mg
Sodium 189 mg
Total fat 8 g
    Saturated 3 g
    Polyunsaturated 1 g
    Monounsaturated 4 g
*Assuming all sauce is
consumed

Preheat oven to 325° F. Spray rack and shallow
roasting pan with vegetable oil spray.

In a small bowl, mix paprika with chili powder
and rub into meat. Place on the rack in the roasting
pan. Roast, uncovered, for about 1½ hours.

Meanwhile, prepare barbecue sauce. Heat oil in a
large saucepan over medium heat. Stir in onion and
garlic and cook until onion is translucent, about 3
to 5 minutes. Add the remaining sauce ingredients.
Bring to a boil over medium-high heat, then reduce

heat and simmer for 30 minutes, stirring occasionally. Place mixture in a blender or the work bowl of
a food processor fitted with a metal blade and
process until smooth. Set aside.

After the meat has roasted for about 1½ hours,
baste it with sauce, roast for 15 minutes more, baste
with sauce again, and continue roasting for about
15 minutes more, or until a meat thermometer
inserted in thickest part of meat registers 170° F.
Baste a final time. Remove roast to a warm platter
and let stand for 15 to 20 minutes before slicing.

Vegetarian Fried Rice

Chao-Fan

CHINA/JAPAN

This vegetarian version of fried rice gets a large protein boost from the tofu, making it a complete meal. You can leave out the tofu without compromising the flavor, however.

1 tablespoon canola or peanut oil
1 cup sliced mushrooms (about 3 ounces)
1 green onion, thinly sliced
1 cup bean sprouts (about 2 ounces)
6-ounce package firm or soft tofu, crumbled
  (optional)
½ cup frozen no-salt-added peas, thawed
  (about 3 ounces)
1 tablespoon reduced-sodium soy sauce
1 teaspoon fragrant toasted sesame oil
3 cups cooked rice, any kind (about 1½ cups
  uncooked)

Serves 6 as an entrée; 1 cup per serving
Serves 12 as a side dish; ½ cup per serving

Nutrient Analysis (per entrée serving)

Calories 156
Protein 5 g
Carbohydrate 26 g
Cholesterol 0 mg
Sodium 112 mg
Total fat 4 g
  Saturated 0 g
  Polyunsaturated 2 g
  Monounsaturated 2 g

Heat oil in a wok or large, heavy skillet over high heat. Add mushrooms and green onion and sauté for several minutes, until slightly wilted. Add bean sprouts and cook for another minute to wilt them slightly. Add remaining ingredients except rice, mixing well. Stir in rice and heat through before serving.

Green Beans in Spicy Sauce

Chau-Dau-Kok

SZECHWAN PROVINCE, CHINA

These tasty green beans can be served as a side dish or with steamed rice and ground pork (see variation below) as an entrée. The pork adds flavor but not a lot of fat, since such a small quantity is used.

Sauce

1 teaspoon cornstarch
3 tablespoons water
1 teaspoon canola or peanut oil
1 teaspoon reduced-sodium soy sauce
¹/₂ teaspoon sugar
¹/₂ teaspoon fragrant toasted sesame oil
¹/₂ teaspoon white vinegar
¹/₂ teaspoon dry sherry (optional)
Pinch of white pepper

Green Beans

1 teaspoon canola or peanut oil
12 ounces fresh green beans
1 teaspoon canola or peanut oil
2 small fresh red hot peppers, such as serrano chili peppers, minced
2 teaspoons minced fresh gingerroot
2 teaspoons minced garlic

For sauce, place cornstarch in a small bowl. Stir in water. Add the remaining sauce ingredients to cornstarch-water mixture and stir. Set aside.

Heat a wok or large, heavy skillet over high heat for 40 seconds. Add 1 teaspoon oil. When a wisp of white smoke appears, stir-fry the green beans for about 2 minutes, or until they soften. Remove green beans with a slotted spoon to a colander and set aside to drain.

Add second teaspoon of oil to wok. Over high heat, add red peppers, gingerroot, and garlic. Stir

Serves 4; ¾ cup per serving

Nutrient Analysis (per serving)

Without pork

Calories 74
Protein 2 g
Carbohydrate 9 g
Cholesterol 0 mg
Sodium 59 mg
Total fat 4 g
  Saturated 0 g
  Polyunsaturated 1 g
  Monounsaturated 2 g

Nutrient Analysis (per serving)

With pork

Calories 116
Protein 5 g
Carbohydrate 9 g
Cholesterol 14 mg
Sodium 67 mg
Total fat 7 g
  Saturated 1 g
  Polyunsaturated 2 g
  Monounsaturated 4 g

for about 1 minute. Return green beans to wok and stir-fry for another minute.

Make a well in the center of the green beans. Stir the sauce and pour into the well. Mix beans and sauce quickly and thoroughly. When sauce thickens, remove from wok and serve immediately.

VARIATION: Cook 3 ounces ground pork in a small skillet over medium heat for about 5 minutes, or until no longer pink. Place in a colander, rinse under hot water, and drain. Add to oil in wok with red peppers, gingerroot, and garlic, then proceed as directed. Serve with steamed rice.

Eggplant Hunan-Style

Hunan Naiqa

CHINA

Eggplant, an ancient vegetable, is popular throughout Asia. This spicy dish brings out its best.

1 tablespoon canola or peanut oil
1 pound Japanese or Asian eggplant, unpeeled, cut into 1-inch pieces
½ teaspoon canola or peanut oil
4 cloves garlic, minced
1 tablespoon chili paste
1½ teaspoons minced fresh gingerroot
½ cup low-sodium chicken broth
1 tablespoon reduced-sodium soy sauce
2 teaspoons sugar
2 teaspoons sake, mirin, or dry sherry (optional)
1 tablespoon rice vinegar
2 tablespoons chopped green onion
1 teaspoon fragrant toasted sesame oil

Heat 1 tablespoon oil in a nonstick wok or large, heavy skillet over medium heat. Add eggplant and stir-fry until soft, about 3 minutes. Remove with a slotted spoon and set aside.

Add ½ teaspoon oil to wok and stir-fry garlic, chili paste, and gingerroot for about 15 seconds over medium heat. Add broth, soy sauce, and sugar and sake, if using. Bring to a boil. Add vinegar and eggplant and cook until eggplant has absorbed most of the sauce, about 1 minute. Add green onion and sesame oil and toss well. Remove eggplant with a slotted spoon. Serve hot.

VARIATION: Add 3 ounces ground pork for a main-dish variation. Cook pork in a medium skillet over medium heat for about 5 minutes, or until no longer pink. Place in a colander, rinse under hot water, and drain. Add to oil in wok with garlic, chili paste, and gingerroot, then proceed as directed.

Serves 4; 1 cup per serving

Nutrient Analysis (per serving)

Without pork

Calories 96
Protein 2 g
Carbohydrate 12 g
Cholesterol 0 mg
Sodium 208 mg
Total fat 6 g
 Saturated 1 g
 Polyunsaturated 2 g
 Monounsaturated 3 g

Nutrient Analysis (per serving)

With pork

Calories 138
Protein 5 g
Carbohydrate 12 g
Cholesterol 14 mg
Sodium 216 mg
Total fat 8 g
 Saturated 2 g
 Polyunsaturated 2 g
 Monounsaturated 4 g

Cold Noodles with Sesame Sauce

Dongji Mame

CHINA

For a change, add the sauce without cooling the noodles and serve the dish warm.

¼ **pound Chinese noodles**
2 tablespoons reduced-sodium soy sauce
2 tablespoons peanut butter
1 tablespoon fragrant toasted sesame oil
1 tablespoon rice vinegar
2 teaspoons chopped green onion
1 teaspoon grated fresh gingerroot
1 teaspoon sugar
½ **teaspoon minced garlic**
⅛ **teaspoon chili oil**
Chopped green onions
Sesame seeds

Serves 4; ¾ cup per serving

Nutrient Analysis (per serving)

Calories 155
Protein 3 g
Carbohydrate 19 g
Cholesterol 0 mg
Sodium 339 mg
Total fat 8 g
    Saturated 1 g
    Polyunsaturated 3 g
    Monounsaturated 3 g

Cook noodles according to package directions. (Don't add oil or salt, however.) Drain noodles and place in ice water to cool. Set aside.

Place soy sauce, peanut butter, sesame oil, rice vinegar, 2 teaspoons green onion, gingerroot, sugar, garlic, and chili oil in a blender or the work bowl of a food processor fitted with a metal blade. Process until smooth. Drain noodles thoroughly and pour sauce over them. Toss, adding a little cold water if needed for consistency.

Sprinkle with chopped green onions and sesame seeds. Serve immediately or refrigerate for up to 3 days.

Koi-Pond Pudding

Goigua Cheung Hap

CHINA

This attractive Chinese dessert looks its best when served in clear glass bowls so that you can see the "goldfish" (koi) swimming in the pond. You can vary it by using pastel-colored tapioca pearls, available at many Asian markets.

½ **cup water**
¼ **cup sugar**
½ **cup small pearl tapioca**
2 large oranges
2 cups water

Mix ½ cup water and the sugar in a medium mixing bowl, stirring until the sugar is dissolved. Add the tapioca and let soak for about 30 minutes to soften.

Meanwhile, use a sharp knife to cut the rind and the pith from the oranges. Working over a bowl to save the juice, separate orange sections and remove all membrane from the sections. If sections are very large, cut them into smaller pieces. Set aside.

In a large saucepan, bring 2 cups water to a boil over high heat; slowly stir in the tapioca mixture. Lower heat to medium and cook, stirring constantly, for about 5 minutes, or until pudding thickens. Add the orange sections along with their juice and stir just until the mixture boils again.

Remove from heat and allow the pudding to cool for about 5 minutes before serving.

Serves 4; ¾ cup per serving

Nutrient Analysis (per serving)

Calories 156
Protein 1 g
Carbohydrate 40 g
Cholesterol 0 mg
Sodium 1 mg
Total fat 0 g
   Saturated 0 g
   Polyunsaturated 0 g
   Monounsaturated 0 g

Almond Diamonds

Hunyun Dow-fu

CHINA

This unusual dessert is light and refreshing after a spicy meal, and the leftovers make a pleasant breakfast. Good fruit choices include melon, strawberries, bananas, oranges, pears, star fruit, and kiwifruit. An adult variation would be to marinate the fruits for a few hours in a few teaspoons of your favorite liqueur.

3½ cups cold water
3 envelopes unflavored gelatin
½ cup evaporated skim milk or skim milk
¼ cup sugar
2 to 3 teaspoons almond extract, to taste
6 cups fresh fruit, any combination, cut into
    bite-size pieces
750-ml bottle cold champagne, sparkling apple
    juice, or alcohol-free champagne

Pour cold water into a medium saucepan. Sprinkle with the gelatin. Bring to a boil over medium heat, stirring until the gelatin dissolves. Reduce heat to low and add milk, sugar, and almond extract, stirring until sugar dissolves. Taste the mixture, adjusting the sugar and extract if needed.

Pour mixture into shallow 8- or 9-inch square glass baking dish(es); it should be about ½ inch deep. Refrigerate until firm. (Recipe can be prepared to this point a day in advance.)

To serve, place fruit in an attractive serving bowl. Cut almond jelly into 1-inch diamonds and add to the fruit. Add the champagne and stir gently. Serve in small glass bowls with a little of the liquid.

COOK'S TIP: If the stark whiteness of the diamonds doesn't appeal to you, add a drop or two of food color to the mixture after the sugar dissolves. Choose a color that contrasts nicely with your choice of fruits.

Serves 12; ¾ cup per serving

Nutrient Analysis (per serving)

Calories 124
Protein 3 g
Carbohydrate 18 g
Cholesterol 0 mg
Sodium 21 mg
Total fat 0 g
  Saturated 0 g
  Polyunsaturated 0 g
  Monounsaturated 0 g

Fiery Pickled Vegetables

Yang-Bechu

KOREA

The poor in Asian countries literally live on rice and pickled vegetables, with some tofu now and then. Napa, or Chinese, cabbage is the easiest to grow, and therefore the most common, vegetable. Feel free to vary the amount and types of vegetables in this dish to suit your own preferences.

1 small head napa cabbage, cut into pieces
1 pound carrots, peeled, cut into 3-inch pieces,
   and quartered
1/2 pound green beans, cut in half
1 medium turnip, cut into 1/4-inch squares
2 cups white vinegar
1 cup cider vinegar
4 dried chili pods
1 ounce fresh gingerroot, sliced
2 cloves garlic, chopped
1 tablespoon sugar
1 tablespoon salt
2 tablespoons Chinese "white liquor," vodka,
   grain alcohol, or lemon juice
1 teaspoon whole black peppercorns

Serves 30; 3 tablespoons per serving

Nutrient Analysis (per serving)

Calories 23
Protein 1 g
Carbohydrate 5 g
Cholesterol 0 mg
Sodium 245 mg
Total fat 0 g
  Saturated 0 g
  Polyunsaturated 0 g
  Monounsaturated 0 g

Put the cabbage, carrots, green beans, and turnip in a 2-quart glass jar with a tight-fitting lid. Set aside.

Place the remaining ingredients in a medium mixing bowl and stir well to combine. Pour liquid mixture into the jar, making sure the vegetables are covered with the liquid (prepare another batch of marinade if necessary). Put the lid on the jar and shake the jar until the salt and the sugar are completely dissolved.

Let stand for two days at room temperature before refrigerating.

To serve, remove the desired amount of pickles from the jar and drain well. Arrange them in small bowls or serving dishes.

COOK'S TIP: You can add a fresh batch of vegetables to the marinade after you drain it from the pickles. The pickles keep for weeks, and many Asians think the marinade needs a few pickling cycles before it really gets good. Remove the chili pods if the marinade gets too spicy for your taste.

COOK'S TIP ON GINGERROOT: You don't even have to peel the ginger for this dish (though you do for most other recipes). Just wash the gingerroot and cut it into very thin slices. For a stronger ginger flavor, make the slices about $\frac{1}{4}$ inch thick; for a milder ginger flavor, make the slices about $\frac{1}{8}$ inch thick.

Select gingerroot with smooth skin and a spicy fragrance. Leftover ginger, unpeeled, will last about a week on the counter. Or wrap the ginger in a paper towel and refrigerate it in an airtight plastic bag for up to 3 weeks. For longer storage, place peeled ginger in a small jar with a tight-fitting lid and cover ginger with dry sherry, Madeira, or vodka. Refrigerate for 2 to 3 months. The liquid will be infused with flavor, making it great for cooking.

APPENDIXES

American Heart Association Dietary Guidelines

Whether your menu contains exotic ethnic cuisines or traditional all-American favorites, eating for a healthy heart is universal. The American Heart Association recommends the following dietary guidelines for all healthy people over age two. These guidelines can help you reduce blood cholesterol and prevent or control high blood pressure.

AHA Dietary Guidelines

1. Keep your total fat intake to less than 30 percent of your daily calories.
2. Keep saturated fat to less than 10 percent of your daily calories.
3. Keep polyunsaturated fat to 10 percent or less of your daily calories.
4. Your cholesterol intake shouldn't exceed 300 milligrams per day.
5. Carbohydrate foods should make up at least 50 percent of your daily calories. Most of these foods should be complex carbohydrates.
6. Protein foods should provide the rest of your daily calories.
7. Your sodium intake shouldn't be greater than 2,400 milligrams a day.
8. Drink no more than 1 to 2 ounces of pure alcohol (ethanol) per day. One ounce of pure alcohol equals 8 ounces of wine, 24 ounces of beer, or 2 ounces of 100-proof whiskey.
9. Eat enough total calories to maintain your recommended body weight.
10. Eat a wide variety of foods to get a balance of nutrients.

Some people misinterpret the first guideline. They think it means that each food or each recipe should have less than 30 percent of its calories coming from fat. Not true. The guideline applies to the *total* calories you eat in one day. If you apply it to single foods, the "30 percent of calories from fat" guideline will exclude many foods that fit into a well-balanced eating plan.

Examples of these foods include oil and margarine (100 percent of calories from fat); regular and low-calorie salad dressings (70 to 100 percent of calories from fat); dark chicken meat without skin (43 percent of calories from fat); salmon (36 percent of calories from fat); lower-fat meats, such as turkey ham (34 percent of calories from fat); and many nuts and seeds (75 to 90 percent of calories from fat). Applying the 30 percent standard to single foods would greatly limit the variety of foods in your eating plan. The only way to maintain the balance, variety, and enjoyment of the AHA eating plan is to interpret the guideline with emphasis on the word *total*.

HOW TO FOLLOW THE AHA DIETARY GUIDELINES

Your passport to staying young at heart is issued the day you learn how to create a low-fat, heart-healthy eating plan. Take a look at this breakdown of the nutrients you consume on a daily basis. It will show you the potholes on the road to success, and it will help you make smart choices in each category. We've also included some tips on eating a balanced diet and the importance of getting regular exercise.

Fat

There are three main types of fat in the foods you eat: saturated, polyunsaturated, and monounsaturated. Your body can use all three types in small amounts. Eating too much fat, especially saturated fat, is not healthful. To stay at your healthiest, the AHA recommends limiting your total fat intake to less than 30 percent of your daily calories. When you're planning your daily meals, divide that 30 percent this way:

1. *Saturated fats:* Make saturated fats contribute less than 10 percent of your daily calories. The fat in meat, poultry, lard, butter, and coconut oil is saturated. These fats also are in palm and palm kernel oils, which are often used in commercially baked goods.

2. *Polyunsaturated fats:* Up to 10 percent of your calories can come from polyunsaturated fats. Many foods contain more polyunsaturated fats than other types of fat. Some examples are walnuts, corn oil, safflower oil, and fish.

3. *Monounsaturated fats:* The rest of your fat intake should come from monounsaturated fats. They are predominant in olives, olive oil, canola oil, peanut oil, and avocados.

Cholesterol

Excess cholesterol and other substances accumulate on the inner walls of your arteries and clog them, which can lead to a heart attack. You can't cut out all the cholesterol—your body produces it. That's why it's a good idea to eat fewer than 300 milligrams of cholesterol a day. Watch out for foods that tip the cholesterol scales, such as egg yolks, organ meats, cream, and cheese. Remember: Cholesterol found in foods comes only from animals. Vegetable-based foods contain no cholesterol, although they may contain fat.

Carbohydrates

Think *complex.* If you eat more complex-carbohydrate foods (such as fruits and vegetables, grains, potatoes, whole-grain breads, rice, and pastas), you'll probably eat less fat. Be sure to leave off the butter and the fatty sauces that simply add fat to these healthful foods. In general, it's a good idea to increase the amount of carbohydrates in your diet to at least 50 percent of your daily calories.

Protein

Protein is considered your body's construction material. It is the main source for growth and tissue repair. But very little protein is needed to do the job. The fact is, most of us eat about twice as much protein as we need. Only about 15 percent of our total daily calories needs to come from protein. Some excellent low-fat protein choices are dried beans, grains, and seeds. Unfortunately, most of us tend to eat high-fat protein foods, such as meats, poultry, seafood, and dairy products.

Sodium

Sodium is vital in helping your body maintain a balance of fluids. The AHA's recommended guideline of no more than 2,400 milligrams of sodium per day applies to most adolescents and adults. If you have high blood pressure or there's a history of it in your family, however, your doctor may recommend even less sodium. Examples of high-sodium foods are salt (which is about half sodium), soy sauce, Worcestershire sauce, pickles, and canned chicken broth.

Alcohol

Alcohol has no nutritional value. It contains only calories with no nutrients. Too much alcohol can lead to a host of medical and social problems. Although wine and beer play a large role in certain ethnic cuisines, you can substitute nonalcoholic versions of these beverages in cooking.

Calories

Calories measure energy—the energy your body uses and the energy in the foods you eat. You need a certain number of calories to support body functioning, such as breathing, digestion, and physical activity. If you consume more calories than your body needs, you gain weight. If you eat fewer calories than your body needs, you lose weight. So, naturally, if you eat the same number of calories that you burn, you maintain your weight. Your doctor or a dietitian can help you figure your ideal weight and whether to reduce, increase, or maintain your caloric intake.

Variety

Variety, balance, and moderation are the keys to a well-planned, palate-pleasing, and healthful diet. It's important to choose heart-smart foods that you *enjoy* and that fit into your lifestyle. Why? Because if an eating plan doesn't fit your likes and needs, you probably won't stick to it. In this book, you'll find a world of recipes that will fit perfectly into your heart-wise eating agenda.

Exercise

Studies show that people who exercise the most, in addition to eating nutritious, low-fat foods, are simply healthier. In fact, people who are fit are less likely to die early from any cause—including cardiovascular disease. Fortunately, you don't have to run marathons to get this protection. Regular moderate exercise will do it.

A good way to get started is by doing modest activities, such as gardening and light housekeeping. Gradually work up to 30 to 60 minutes of activity three times a week. Eventually, you can add low-impact aerobic activities, such as walking, swimming, or biking. That's all it takes. If you're over forty or if you have any medical problems, check with your doctor before beginning any exercise program.

From New Delhi to New Zealand to New Orleans, following these guidelines when planning your menus will keep you on the road to good eating and good health.

MEAL PLANS
AND SHOPPING

PLANNING HEALTHFUL MEALS

Although it may seem easier to plan an all-American meal than one from a foreign country, it really isn't. With our mix-and-match recipes, we've made it easy to put together healthful but delectable international meals in minutes.

Turn to the recipe sections. You'll find that each cuisine includes recipes for salads, vegetables, seafood, meats, poultry, and desserts. Sometimes we included appetizers, soups, meatless entrées, sandwiches, and beverages. All you have to do is write down the entrées you want to try during the next few days or even a week. Then pencil in ideas for soups or salads, vegetables, side dishes, and desserts. This will help you plan more-nutritious meals and save you time and money in the supermarket. Plus, you won't repeat the same main dish or meal very often when you plan ahead. Once you get in the habit of planning your meals, it will become second nature.

When planning your menus, include the following for each adult:

- ♨ No more than 6 ounces of meat, seafood, or poultry a day;

- ♨ Dried beans, peas, lentils, or tofu in place of meat a few times a week;

- ♨ Whole-grain or enriched bread or cereal products each day;

- ♨ Three or more servings of fruit and three or more servings of vegetables each day (include one serving of citrus fruit or vegetable high in vitamin C and one serving of dark-green leafy or deep-yellow vegetables);

- ♨ Two or more daily servings of nonfat (skim) milk or nonfat or low-fat milk products (three to four servings for children and adolescents);

🔥 Five to eight teaspoons of polyunsaturated and monounsaturated fats and oils in the form of margarine, cooking oil, and salad dressing each day (the amount may vary according to your caloric needs).

THE SHOPPING LIST

Get ready for an out-of-this-world treat. Shopping for international foods is almost as much fun as eating them.

Most of the ingredients for the recipes in this book can be found in your supermarket, especially if you live in a major city. If you can't find an ingredient at the grocery, try a gourmet or ethnic grocer in your area. Finally, we've included a list of mail-order sources on page 281 in Appendix H. Simply contact one of these sources and place your order. It's an exciting world we live in when salsa or the rarest spice is just a phone call away!

Take a look at the recipes you've chosen. Chances are you'll find them light on fat and salt but heavy on spices. That's one of the ways we kept the flavor and taste but lost the heart-hampering results. You'll want to stock your pantry with the spices you use most often. Try spices in place of salt as flavor enhancers.

Armed with your ingredients list, you can shop with confidence, avoiding those not-so-healthful impulse purchases. Start your list when you plan your meals, then add to it as you think of other items. Get creative: Mix and match tastes, textures, and colors. It's all part of shopping with your heart—and your taste buds—in mind.

SHOPPING FOR A HEALTHY HEART

At the grocery store, you'll find foods in just about every aisle that are waiting to sabotage your healthful shopping outing. So take heed. Here are a few guidelines to help you avoid those heartbreaking temptations and fill your cart with foods that will do your heart good.

Meat

Be picky as you make your choices at the meat counter. The three grades of beef you'll find in the grocery store most often are prime, choice, and select. Prime meat contains the most fat, referred to as *marbling*. Select contains the least amount of fat. We give a thumbs-up to select grades of round steak, flank steak, sirloin tip, and tenderloin and to extra-lean ground beef. For all whole cuts of meat, look for fat that you can trim off.

Choosing the leanest ground beef available is as easy as reading the package label at the meat counter. Look for a label that indicates extra-lean or 90 percent lean (or 10 percent fat). In some stores, you can even buy a ground-beef product that is 95 percent lean. This product uses water and plant-derived ingredients to replace some of the fat and maintain moisture during cooking. Better yet, select *well-trimmed,* lean steak, stewing beef, or chuck roast and ask the butcher to grind it for you.

Thanks to modern-day pig farmers, pork is much leaner than it was just thirty years ago. That means you get more meat and less fat if you choose the right cuts of pork. Choose lean pork, such as tenderloin, loin chops, rib or loin roasts, low-fat and low-sodium ham, and Canadian bacon.

If you love Middle Eastern food, you'll find lamb a cut above the rest. Most lamb from the United States is marketed fresh, although a small amount may be frozen. When buying lamb, look for finely grained texture and reddish pink or dark red color. The leanest portion is the leg. Other lean cuts include leg sirloin chop, center roast, center slice, and shank. If leg chops aren't available, use rib chops instead. With all cuts of lamb, be sure to trim away the heavy covering of fat on the outside before cooking.

Veal is the young, tender meat of a calf that has not yet put on adult fat. That makes it a good choice for healthful eating. The most expensive, tenderest cuts come from milk-fed veal. It has a creamy pink, almost white, velvety appearance. Grain-fed veal comes from calves that have had grass or grain added to their diets, making the meat rosier in color. It has a slightly stronger flavor and a coarser texture. The leanest cuts of veal are leg cutlet, arm steak, sirloin steak, rib chop, loin chop, and top round.

Some wild game is very lean. Venison, rabbit, squirrel, and pheasant are examples of low-fat game. Duck and goose are not.

Processed meats should be eaten only if they contain no more than 10 percent fat, or 3 grams of fat per ounce. Be aware that many processed meats are high in sodium. Eat high-cholesterol organ meats—such as brains, liver, kidney, and sweetbreads—only occasionally.

Seafood

It's universal: Fish is an excellent low-fat choice. Lean varieties include, cod, haddock, halibut, flounder, sole, red snapper, and orange roughy. All fresh and frozen fish are healthful options.

Canned fish, such as tuna, should be packed in water. For a nice alternative to tuna, choose canned salmon. The boneless and skinless variety will save you time in the kitchen.

Shrimp, lobster, crab, crayfish, and most other shellfish are low in fat. But ounce for ounce, some varieties contain more sodium and cholesterol than poultry, meat, or fish. Choose these occasionally, and they can fit into the guidelines of 300 milligrams of cholesterol and 2,400 milligrams of sodium per day.

Some fish are high in omega-3 fatty acids, which may help lower the level of triglycerides, one type of lipid (blood fat). Choose from Atlantic and coho salmon, albacore tuna, mackerel, carp, lake whitefish, sweet smelt, and lake and brook trout.

Poultry

If you're looking for a tasty, versatile, and nutritious food, poultry is an international cook's wish come true. All you have to do is remember that poultry *skin* harbors a great deal of fat and cholesterol. So when roasting a whole chicken or turkey, remove the skin before eating. When cooking chicken or turkey pieces, be sure to buy skinless poultry or remove the skin before cooking. When buying ground poultry, be sure to select the kind ground without skin.

Look at the type of poultry you're choosing. Light meat is leaner than dark meat, so choose it first. Biggest is not necessarily best with poultry. Larger, older birds, such as roasters and capons, are fattier than smaller and younger birds. Finally, avoid goose and duck—they're high in saturated fats.

Dairy Products

Many international cuisines are famous for cream sauces and rich cream-based desserts. The good news is you can still have them. All you have to do is make a few healthful substitutions. For example, instead of whole milk, put nonfat (skim) or 1% milk on your grocery list. It's the world's best low-fat, high-calcium drink. Cross light cream off your list and add evaporated skim milk. It's a flawless low-fat substitute for cream in cooked sauces. Don't forget buttermilk. Although its name sounds like high fat, buttermilk actually is made with cultured skim milk or low-fat milk.

Choose cheeses that are lower in fat, such as part-skim mozzarella cheese, farmer cheese, part-skim ricotta cheese, sapsago cheese, or Parmesan cheese. Check the dairy case for specially made nonfat and low-fat versions of Cheddar and other hard cheeses that are usually high in fat. Light cream cheese, Neufchâtel cheese, and nonfat cream cheese are heart-smart stand-ins for cream cheese.

For dessert, reach for ice milk, nonfat or low-fat frozen yogurt, sherbet, and fruit ices.

Avoid dairy substitutes that are high in fat and saturated fats. Nondairy coffee creamers, canned sour-cream substitutes, and whipped-cream substitutes often contain coconut or palm kernel oil, which are high in saturated fats. Read labels carefully and choose dairy products and substitutes that are low in fat and saturated fat.

High-fat cheeses—such as France's famous Brie and Camembert and whole-milk cheese spreads—can wreak havoc on a low-fat diet. Leave them in the dairy case.

Eggs

Egg yolks are loaded with cholesterol. One large yolk contains 213 to 220 milligrams of cholesterol, which is almost your entire daily allowance. Try to limit your consumption of egg *yolks*. The whites, however, are cholesterol and fat free. You can eat as many egg *whites* as you like. They're an excellent source of protein.

In cooking, you can usually substitute two egg whites for one whole egg. Or use egg substitutes, which contain little or no cholesterol. To avoid the possibility of salmonella poisoning, never eat raw eggs.

Fats and Oils

A big part of heart-healthy cooking is to limit the amount and kind of fat you eat. Of course, you do need *some* fats. Just make them polyunsaturated or monounsaturated oils. That should be easy, since some of the cuisines in this book use olive oil, a monounsaturated fat, as their primary cooking oil.

Always buy margarine in place of butter. Look for margarines that list liquid vegetable oil as the first ingredient. These usually have no more than 2 grams of saturated fat per tablespoon. Diet margarines, which contain water, are fine as spreads and in some cooking, such as sautéing vegetables. There are also several reduced-fat margarines that are great for sauces. Baking is iffy, however, with either of these types of margarine. Use nonstick vegetable oil sprays in place of butter or margarine for some cooking or for coating baking pans.

Select vegetable oil made from safflower, corn, sesame, sunflower, soybean, olive, or canola oil. Avoid coconut oil, palm kernel oil, and palm oil, because they contain high amounts of saturated fats.

Supermarket shelves are well stocked with a vast array of salad dressings, ranging from high fat to no fat. Look for reduced-calorie, low-calorie, nonfat, or no-cholesterol dressings. Some are extremely high in sodium, so be sure to read the nutrition label if you're watching your sodium intake.

Vegetables and Fruits

Most fresh vegetables and fruits are a heart-healthy cook's idea of perfection. They contain little or no fat, are low in sodium, and are high in fiber and vitamins. The exceptions are coconut meat and avocados. Coconut meat (shredded or flaked) is high in saturated fat, and avocados are high in unsaturated fat. Eat these only occasionally.

Canned and frozen fruits are healthful alternatives to fresh. For less sugar and fewer calories, choose frozen fruits without added sugar and fruits canned in water or their own juice.

Scan the frozen-food aisle and read the label of any frozen vegetables you're considering. Try to buy no-salt-added frozen vegetables, and avoid any prepared with butter or sauces.

Breads, Cereals, Pasta, and Starchy Vegetables

From whole-wheat pita to hearty pumpernickel, you can choose from a world of delicious breads. Look for enriched breads, such as whole-grain, whole-wheat, rye, pumpernickel, cracked-wheat, French, and Italian. Most contain lots of nutrients with relatively few calories.

Avoid products made with whole milk and egg yolks. Bypass most commercially baked products—such as muffins, croissants, and doughnuts—since they are high in fat. One exception is angel food cake. It is made with egg whites and is fat-free.

If you're baking rather than buying, select a variety of tasty whole grains, such as brown rice, bulgur, millet, and wheat berries. They are low in fat and high in fiber.

Dried beans and lentils make an excellent substitute for meat in casseroles, stews, and soups. To save preparation time, choose canned beans. Just be sure to rinse them well and drain them first to wash off some of the sodium. Better yet, if you're watching your sodium, look for varieties without added salt.

Don't forget about hot cereals, pastas, and rices. They are low in fat and, unless they're the instant type, contain almost no sodium. Omit the salt (and butter) when cooking.

Cold cereals are relatively low in fat but may be high in sodium. Read the labels to help you make a healthful choice.

Snacks

Of all the world's cultures, America seems to be the mecca of snacking. Fortunately, healthful snacks are easy to find, thanks to the growing variety of nonfat and low-fat crackers and cookies. Be sure to read the labels and keep a close eye on sodium and calories, though. Nonfat and low-fat crackers and cookies are often as high in calories as their high-fat counterparts, so don't assume they will help your waistline along with your heart.

Nuts and seeds make tasty natural snacks. Choose unsalted, dry-roasted versions to cut down a little bit on fat and sodium.

Most chips are high in fat and sodium. Look for low-sodium baked chips.

Hands down, the best snacks are fresh fruits and vegetables.

Miscellaneous Foods

The recipes in this cookbook may contain items you're not familiar with, such as plantains, nopales, chayote squash, semolina, and grape leaves. Check your supermarket or gourmet shop, or use our list of exotic food sources on page 281.

If you're creating luscious homemade soups from the recipes in this book, great. If not, choose canned soups that are low in fat and sodium. Look for them in the grocery aisle with other soups.

We've included beverages here from a variety of cultures. But you can also wet your whistle with other healthful beverages, such as 100 percent fruit juices and bottled water. Be sure to read labels to avoid beverages high in sodium. If you drink alcohol, it's best to limit your intake to one to two drinks per day.

On the lookout for sodium? Then watch out for the following salty foods: soy sauce, steak sauce, ketchup, chili sauce, monosodium glutamate (MSG), meat tenderizer, pickles, relishes, seasoning salts, bouillon granules or cubes, and salad dressings. Use them in moderation, and also look for the low-sodium versions.

NUTRITION LABELING

When shopping for healthful foods, take time to read labels. It's easy to find heart-healthy foods today, thanks to the nutrition label found on most foods in the supermarket. Most American-made foods must have a nutrition label and an ingredients list. You can buy with confidence, since claims such as "low cholesterol" and "fat-free" can be used legally only if a food meets standards set by the federal government.

Some of the international ingredients you'll need won't have nutrition labels, because the foods were manufactured in other countries or are sold only in gourmet shops or ethnic shops.

Reading a label is like looking inside the package without opening it. Ingredients are listed in order by weight, the largest amount first.

You'll also find other important information on a nutrition-facts label:

1. *Serving size:* The serving size for all similar foods must be consistent, allowing you to compare their nutritional values easily.

2. *Calories and calories from fat:* The label will list the number of calories per serving and the number of calories from fat.

3. *Daily values for nutrients:* This section will show you how a food fits into your overall daily diet. These values tell the food's nutritional content based on a 2,000-calorie-per-day diet. The nutrients listed are total fat, saturated fat, cholesterol, sodium, total carbohydrate, dietary fiber, vitamins A and C, calcium, and iron.

4. *Maximum and minimum amounts of daily values:* The label also lists six nutrients and the maximum and minimum amounts of each that you should try to eat every day. These amounts are based on a daily intake of 2,000 calories. If your caloric intake is less or more, these values will change.

Key Words on Food Labels and What They Mean

When you see certain words on a food label, you can rest assured they mean what they say, as defined by the government. For example:

Key Words	What They Mean
Fat-free	Less than 0.5 gram of fat per serving
Low-fat	3 grams of fat or less per serving
Lean	Less than 10 grams of fat, 4 grams of saturated fat, and 95 milligrams of cholesterol per serving
Light (Lite)	One-third fewer calories than the higher-calorie, higher-fat version, no more than half the fat of the higher-calorie, higher-fat version, or no more than half the sodium of the higher-sodium version.
Cholesterol-free	Less than 2 milligrams of cholesterol and 2 grams or less of saturated fat per serving

Labeling Regulations About Health Claims

To Make Health Claims About . . .	The Food Must Be . . .
Heart disease	Low in fat, saturated fat, and cholesterol
Heart disease (in relation to fruits, vegetables, and grain products)	A fruit, vegetable, or grain product that is low in fat, saturated fat, and cholesterol and contains at least 0.6 gram soluble fiber, without fortification, per serving
Blood pressure and sodium	Low in sodium

Other claims may appear on some labels.

APPENDIX C

COOKING FOR A HEALTHY HEART

If you've been stewing over how to cook these inspired international recipes without sacrificing the flavor along with the fat, take a look at the following heart-healthy cooking tips. They'll help you serve delicious, authentic, and traditional ethnic foods as good for your attitude as for your arteries.

- ♨ Broil meats and poultry, letting the fat drip away from the food as it cooks. Check it out on our Gyros on page 110.

- ♨ Poach in a nonfat or low-fat liquid—a great way to cook chicken, fish, or eggs. Poaching keeps the food moist and flavorful and doesn't add fat. See for yourself—poach your favorite fish, then top it with the sensational salsa you can make from the Gazpacho recipe on page 147 (see the Cook's Tip on page 148).

- ♨ Bake meat, poultry, and fish. Baking can be a fat-free or low-fat form of cooking that'll do your heart good. Love Italian food? Try Baked Fish Steak with Capers, page 9.

- ♨ Braise and stew meats. These wonderful slow-cooking methods will tenderize tough cuts of meat. Try Sauerbraten from Germany, page 82.

- ♨ The fat in many soups, stews, and gravies cooks into the liquid and rises to the top when chilled. Then the fat is easy to remove. That's why it's best to cook these foods a day ahead and chill them overnight. Try Forest Mushroom Soup, page 224, to see just how easy it is.

- ♨ Steam fish or vegetables. Steaming is a perfect way to cook food without fat while retaining the food's natural flavor, vitamins, and minerals.

- Sauté or stir-fry meat or vegetables. You'll cook food quickly over high heat with little or no fat. Here's where a nonstick finish on your skillet or wok comes in handy. Start with Shredded Beef with Bok Choy and Carrots, page 233.

- Grill meats or vegetables. Grilling adds a new flavor dimension to cooked meats and allows the fat to drip away from the meat as it cooks. Want evidence? Try Germany's Grilled Pork with Caraway-Horseradish Sauce, page 85. Grilling is also a simple way to prepare seafood. Crisp-tender grilled vegetables can be low-fat and full of flavor, as can grilled fruits.

- If you don't have nonstick cookware, try using vegetable oil spray.

- For sheer ease, try microwave cooking. It dries food less than conventional cooking, so it requires little or no added fat. A good example is Seafood Terrine with Shrimp and Asparagus, on page 221.

FRESH IS BEST

Here are several tips for keeping foods fresh and flavorful during storage.

- Always cover food to be refrigerated. Otherwise, bacteria can attack it, changing its flavor and composition.

- Store milk in its original container in the refrigerator, and close the carton after each use.

- Store eggs in the refrigerator the same way they were purchased—in their cartons with the large end of the egg up.

- Refrigerate poultry in its original wrapping and use it within 1 to 2 days after purchasing. Freeze it for longer storage.

- Let bananas ripen at room temperature and then refrigerate them. The cold will darken the skin, but the flavor will be fine.

- For best flavor, store cantaloupe at room temperature for 2 to 4 days.

- Store all-purpose flour and cereals at room temperature in tightly covered containers in a dry place. This keeps out dust, moisture, and insects. Store whole-wheat flour in your refrigerator to keep it from becoming rancid.

- Keep vegetable oils tightly sealed and store them at room temperature. For longer storage, place them in the refrigerator. Most oils stay clear when chilled, but olive oil becomes thick and cloudy.

Refrigerate homemade salad dressings in a jar with a tight-fitting lid for up to 2 weeks.

HEART-SMART SUBSTITUTIONS LIST

To help you convert your own international and ethnic favorites to more heart-healthful fare, look to this substitutions list.

Food	Substitution
Whole milk (1 cup)	1 cup skim milk in most recipes. For added richness, stir in 1 tablespoon unsaturated oil.
Heavy cream (1 cup)	1 cup evaporated skim milk or a combination of $\frac{1}{2}$ cup nonfat or low-fat yogurt and $\frac{1}{2}$ cup nonfat or low-fat cottage cheese.
Sour cream	Nonfat or light sour cream; blended nonfat or low-fat cottage cheese, or ricotta cheese made with skim or low-fat milk (thinned with a little skim milk or buttermilk, if necessary).
Cream cheese	Nonfat cream cheese, Neufchâtel cheese, or light cream cheese; 1 cup blended dry nonfat or low-fat cottage cheese and $\frac{1}{4}$ cup acceptable margarine (thinned with skim milk, if necessary). Season with herbs and seasonings, if desired.
Butter (1 tablespoon)	1 tablespoon acceptable margarine or $\frac{3}{4}$ tablespoon polyunsaturated oil.
Shortening (1 cup)	1 cup (2 sticks) acceptable margarine.
Eggs (1 egg)	1 egg white plus 2 teaspoons unsaturated oil; cholesterol-free egg substitute used according to package directions; 3 egg whites for 2 whole eggs; 2 egg whites for 1 whole egg in baking.
Unsweetened baking chocolate (1 ounce)	3 tablespoons unsweetened cocoa powder or baking carob powder plus 1 tablespoon polyunsaturated oil or margarine.

APPENDIX D

DINING OUT

You'll probably want to hang up your apron occasionally and go to dinner at an international restaurant. So how can you eat at Marcel's and avoid those rich cream sauces? At Luigi's and steer clear of cream cake? At the China Pagoda or Juan's without loading up on fried foods?

It's easy! All you need to know is how to place your order for a low-fat lifestyle. The good news is that almost every cuisine boasts delicious help-your-heart foods. Here are some hints for choosing healthful meals when dining out.

CHINESE

Arguably the most popular ethnic food in America, Chinese food can be healthful and satisfying. Simply ask the cook to use less oil in stir-fries and to leave out the soy sauce, MSG, and salt. Portions are often huge—if you're dining with others, you could order fewer entrées and save your money along with your hearts. Or ask for a container for the leftovers. If you think your resolve might crumble like a fortune cookie, ask for the container *before* you start to eat.

Tips

♨ Choose entrées with lots of vegetables.

♨ Ask to substitute chicken for duck in recipes.

♨ Skip the crispy fried noodles so often provided as free munchies.

Instead of:	Choose:
Egg drop soup	Wonton or hot-and-sour soup
Egg rolls or fried wontons	Steamed dumplings
Fried entrées	Boiled, broiled, steamed, or lightly stir-fried entrées
Dishes with fried meats	Dishes with lots of vegetables
Dishes with cashews	Dishes with water chestnuts
Fried rice	Steamed rice
Lobster sauce (egg yolks); oyster, bean, and soy sauce (high sodium)	Sweet-and-sour sauce; plum or duck sauce

FRENCH

Although traditional French cooking starts and ends with butter, the nouvelle cuisine in many of today's French restaurants offers lighter, more healthful fare.

Tips

♨ Avoid rich entrées, desserts, and sauces.

♨ Choose simple dishes with sauces on the side.

♨ Stick with nouvelle cuisine or Provençal tomato-and-herb-based entrées.

♨ Ask the chef to use margarine instead of butter or to cook without either.

Instead of:	Choose:
Appetizers with olives, capers, or anchovies	Steamed mussels or a salad
Pâté	Steamed mussels
French onion soup	Mixed green salad with vinaigrette dressing
Croissants	French bread
Rich, heavy entrées	Lighter nouvelle cuisine
Hollandaise, Mornay, béchamel, or béarnaise sauce	Bordelaise or other wine-based sauces
Creamy au gratin potato dishes	Lightly sautéed, crisp vegetables
Chocolate mousse	Flambéed cherries
Crème caramel	Peaches in wine

GREEK AND MIDDLE EASTERN

Although some Greek and Middle Eastern dishes are swimming in olive oil, others are prepared with a minimum of oil or none at all.

Tips

- Ask the chef to use less oil.

- Ask the waiter to serve high-sodium foods, such as feta cheese and olives, on the side.

- Avoid phyllo pastry dishes. They usually contain lots of butter.

- Watch out for Greek desserts. They're often high in fat. If you want to splurge, split dessert with a friend.

Instead of:	Choose:
Meat-stuffed appetizers	Appetizers with rice or eggplant
Fried calamari	Dolmas (rice mixture wrapped in grape leaves)
Baba ghanouj (eggplant appetizer)	Tzatziki (yogurt and cucumber appetizer)
Moussaka (lamb and beef casserole) and other creamy or cheesy entrées	Roast lamb; shish kebab; couscous or bulgur wheat with vegetables or chicken
Gyros (beef or lamb rolled in pita bread with a yogurt-based cucumber sauce)	Chicken pita sandwich
Spanakopita (spinach pie with egg and cheese)	Plaki (fish cooked in tomatoes, onions, and garlic)
Pastries	Fruit

INDIAN

Indian cuisine is both heaven and hell for your heart. On the plus side, it emphasizes carbohydrates and spices and plays down protein. Also, it uses lots of legumes and vegetables. On the downside, dishes in this cuisine are often prepared with ghee (clarified butter) or are fried or sautéed.

Tips

- Choose salads or yogurt with chopped or shredded vegetables as appetizers.

- Pick chicken or seafood rather than beef or lamb dishes.

- ☙ When ordering entrées for two people, order one protein and one vegetable dish to share. That way you can cut down on fat and calories.

- ☙ If you're watching sodium, steer clear of the soups.

Instead of:	Choose:
Samosas (stuffed and fried vegetable turnovers)	Papadum or papad (crispy, thin lentil wafers)
Korma (braised meat with rich yogurt cream sauce)	Chicken or beef tikka roasted with mild spices; or chicken or beef tandoori (these are basted with margarine instead of butter)
Curries made with coconut milk or cream	Curries with a vegetable or dal base; shish kebab; or tandoori chicken or fish
Pakora (deep-fried dough with vegetables)	Gobhi matar tamatar (cauliflower with peas and tomatoes)
Saaq paneer (spinach with cheese cubes and cream sauce)	Matar pulao (rice pilaf with peas)
Sauced rice dishes	Fragrant steamed rice
Fried or stuffed breads	Chapati (thin, dry, whole-wheat bread) or naan (leavened, baked bread topped with poppy seeds)

ITALIAN

Italy's famous pasta is low in fat and great for your heart—as long as you leave off the pesto and cream sauces. Go for the marinara sauce instead.

Tips

- ☙ Choose pasta as a main dish rather than an appetizer.

- ☙ Ask for grated Parmesan cheese, bacon, olives, and pine nuts to be left off.

- ☙ If you want pizza, ask for toppings such as spinach, mushrooms, broccoli, and roasted peppers.

Instead of:	Choose:
Fried calamari	Roasted peppers or minestrone soup
Cheese- or meat-filled pastas or casseroles	Pasta primavera (with sautéed garden vegetables) or pasta with white or red clam sauce

Pasta with butter or cream
  sauces (such as Alfredo sauce)

Pasta with marsala or marinara sauce

Any scaloppine or parmigiana
  (floured, fried, and baked
  with cheese) dish

Marsala and piccata dishes

Italian pastries, such as
  cream cake

Italian ices

JAPANESE

The Japanese have made low-fat cooking into an art form. Except for tempura and other fried dishes, Japanese cuisine highlights rice and vegetables and uses little or no cooking oil or fat. All you have to do is choose low-fat foods, so go with chicken and seafood rather than beef, for example.

Tips

ఢ Ask the cook to prepare your food without high-sodium marinades, sauces, and salt.

ఢ Ask for sauces on the side.

ఢ Avoid deep-fried, battered, or breaded foods.

Instead of:	Choose:
Vegetable tempura (lightly battered and fried vegetables served with sauce)	Steamed vegetables
Shrimp tempura	Fish or vegetable sushi
Pickled fish	Sashimi (fillet of fresh, raw fish served with wasabi and dipping sauce)
Tonkatsu (breaded pork cutlet)	Nabemono (casseroles); yosenabe (seafood and vegetables in broth); shabu-shabu (sliced beef and noodles cooked and served at the table with dipping sauce)
Oyako domburi (chicken omelet over rice)	Sumashi wan (clear soup with tofu and shrimp)
Chawan mushi (chicken and shrimp in egg custard)	Chicken or beef teriyaki (grilled)

MEXICAN

Mexican food can be fresh, low-fat, and flavorful. It can also be fried with lard, topped with cheese, and loaded with fat. It's up to you to learn which Mexican foods will do your heart good.

Tips

- Ask your server not to bring fried tortilla chips to the table.

- Ask the chef to leave the sour cream and guacamole off entrées. Use salsa for flavor instead.

- Choose veracruz or other tomato-based sauces. Avoid the creamy or cheesy ones.

- If you order a taco salad, don't eat the fried shell.

Instead of:	Choose:
Flour tortillas (which usually contain lard)	Corn tortillas (made with almost no fat)
Nachos	Seviche (raw fish soaked, or "cooked," in lime or lemon juice for several hours)
Carnitas (fried beef or pork) or chorizo (sausage)	Grilled fish or chicken breast
Refried beans	Frijoles a la charra or borracho beans; Spanish rice
Sour cream, cheese	Salsa, pico de gallo, cilantro, jalapeño peppers
Guacamole	Salsa
Quesadillas (tortillas filled with meat and cheese)	Chicken fajitas (marinated chicken grilled with vegetables and served with tortillas)
Chalupas and tacos	Taco salad or fajita salad (don't eat the tortilla shell)
Flautas (tortillas stuffed with shredded meat, fried and topped with a sauce); chimichangas (flour tortillas filled with meat and cheese, fried, and topped with tomato sauce); burritos (flour tortillas filled with beans or meat and topped with cheese)	Chicken or beef enchiladas with red sauce or salsa

THAI

Thai food is gaining in popularity because it's a terrific blend of the fresh and the spicy. It tends to go easy on fats, meats, and sauces, relying primarily instead on vegetables, noodles, and rice.

Tips

- Choose the lighter, stir-fried dishes.
- Avoid heavy sauces and deep-fried entrées.
- Ask the chef to cook with vegetable oil rather than coconut oil or lard.
- Choose chicken over duck.
- Limit your portions of meat, poultry, and seafood.

Instead of:	Choose:
Fried spring rolls	Fresh spring rolls
Dishes with coconut milk, peanuts, cashews, and peanut sauce	Stir-fried dishes
Tom ka gai (chicken in coconut milk soup)	Tom yam goong (hot-and-sour shrimp soup)
Gaeng keow wan gai (curry chicken with eggplant)	Nuea pad prik (pepper steak)
Fried rice	Steamed rice
Gluay kaeg (bananas dipped in coconut batter and fried)	Khao newo kaew (sweet sticky rice)
Coconut ice cream	Fruit ice

VIETNAMESE

One of the world's oldest and most exquisite cuisines, Vietnamese food is a blend of East Asian with French cooking. Many of the dishes are low in fat.

Instead of:	Choose:
Banh michien voitom (fried shrimp toast)	Canh chua tom (spicy and sour shrimp soup)
Cha gio (fried spring rolls)	Goi cuon (fresh spring rolls)
Vit quay (roast duck)	Bo xa lui nuong (grilled beef with lemon grass in rice paper with vegetables)

Heo xao chua ngot
(sweet-and-sour pork)
Ca-ri ga (curry chicken)

Banh dua ca ra men
(coconut flan with
caramel)

Ca hap (steamed whole fish)

Ca kho to (fish steamed with caramel
sauce in clay pot)
Lychee
(fruit in syrup)

General Tips for Eating Out

- Order foods that are steamed, broiled, grilled, stir-fried, or roasted. Or ask the chef to prepare the food with very little or no butter or oil.

- Ask for foods to be prepared without salt and MSG. Ask for margarine or vegetable oil instead of butter.

- Drink two full glasses of water before your food arrives.

- Avoid foods described in the following way: buttery, buttered, fried, pan-fried, creamed, escalloped, au lait, or à la mode.

- Ask the chef to remove the skin from poultry or remove it yourself at the table. Trim all visible fat from meat dishes.

- If you decide to eat sauces or salad dressings, ask for them on the side. Then use them sparingly.

- Good bread-basket choices are melba toast and whole-grain rolls. Avoid muffins and croissants, and skip the butter or margarine.

- Be selective at salad bars. Choose fresh greens, raw vegetables, fresh fruits, garbanzo beans, and low-fat dressing. Avoid cheeses, marinated salads, pasta salads, potato salad, and fruit salads with whipped cream.

- Skip dessert, order fresh seasonal fruit without whipped cream or a topping, or choose fruit ices, sherbet, or nonfat frozen yogurt.

MENUS

ITALIAN CUISINE

Fennel-Orange Salad
Pasta Primavera
Tuscan Peasant Bread
Tiramisù

FRENCH CUISINE

Mixed Baby Greens with Creamy Dressing
Beef Burgundy
French Bread*
Crêpes Suzette with Raspberries

ASIAN CUISINE

Forest Mushroom Soup
Cilantro-Lime Turkey Breast
Green Beans in Spicy Sauce
Almond Diamonds

*Recipe not included.

GREEK CUISINE

Marinated Tomato Salad
Aegean Baked Fish
Sautéed Summer Squash
Orzo*
Dried Fruit Compote with Vanilla Yogurt

HISPANIC CUISINE

Jicama Slaw
Paella
Whole-Wheat Rolls*
Flan
Sangría

CARIBBEAN CUISINE

Tropical Fruit Salad with Cherimoya Dressing
Jerked Chicken
Calypso Rice
Piña Colada Shake

GERMAN CUISINE

Chilled Asparagus with Lemony Garlic Dressing
Bundled Trout and Vegetables
Noodles*
Black Forest Cake

MIDDLE EASTERN CUISINE

Lemony Cucumber with Yogurt Salad
Couscous with Lamb Stew
Pita Bread
Walnut-Semolina Cake

*Recipe not included.

CONTINENTAL DINNER

(Italian and French)
Chicken Piccata
Roasted Asparagus with Dijon Vinaigrette
Fettuccine Alfredo
Chocolate-Strawberry Meringue Shells

MEDITERRANEAN FEAST

(Greek and Middle Eastern)
Mixed Fruit Salad*
Roast Chicken with Artichokes and Tomatoes
Garlic Potatoes
Lemon Cream

DINNER BY THE POOL

(Hispanic and Caribbean)
Gazpacho
Skewered Steak Supper
Steamed Zucchini*
Coffee Cooler

*Recipe not included.

EQUIVALENTS

Weights and Measures

Dash	= 2 to 4 drops		
3 teaspoons	= 1 tablespoon	= $\frac{1}{2}$ fluid ounce	= 15 ml
4 tablespoons	= $\frac{1}{4}$ cup	= 2 fluid ounces	= 59 ml
16 tablespoons	= 1 cup ($\frac{1}{2}$ pint)	= 8 fluid ounces	= 237 ml
2 cups	= 1 pint	= 16 fluid ounces	= 473 ml
2 pints	= 1 quart	= 32 fluid ounces	= 946 ml
			= 0.95 l
4 quarts	= 1 gallon	= 128 fluid ounces	= 3785 ml
			= 3.8 l

Beans

	Dried	Cooked
Kidney beans	1 pound ($2\frac{1}{4}$ cups)	$5\frac{1}{2}$ cups
Lima beans	1 pound ($2\frac{1}{2}$ cups)	$5\frac{1}{2}$ cups
Navy beans	1 pound ($2\frac{1}{3}$ cups)	$5\frac{1}{2}$ cups
Soybeans	1 pound (2 cups)	$4\frac{1}{2}$ cups

Rice, Wheat, and Pasta

	Dry	Cooked
Rice	1 pound ($2\frac{1}{2}$ cups)	8 cups
Macaroni	1 pound ($3\frac{3}{4}$ cups)	9 cups
Spaghetti	1 pound ($4\frac{1}{2}$ cups)	9 cups
Bulgur	1 pound ($2\frac{3}{4}$ cups)	8 cups

Flour

	Weight	Volume
Enriched white	1 pound	4 cups sifted
Enriched cake	1 pound	4½ cups sifted
Whole-wheat	1 pound	3⅓ cups stirred
Whole-wheat pastry	1 pound	4½ cups sifted

Citrus Fruit

	Juice	Grated Zest
1 lemon	3 tablespoons	2–3 teaspoons
1 lime	1½ tablespoons	1½ teaspoons
1 orange	⅓ cup	1–2 tablespoons

Miscellaneous

	Weight	Grated
Cheese	1 pound	4 cups

APPENDIX G

GLOSSARY

allspice   Allspice comes from an evergreen pimiento tree. The fragrant berry got its name because it tastes like a combination of many spices, such as cinnamon and cloves.

baker's peel   A baker's peel is a wooden paddle used to transfer dough to and from the oven. You can substitute an upside-down baking sheet. A cutting board also will work, though its thickness may make it a little harder to manage.

bok choy   The entire bok choy plant is edible, so use all the green, plus as much of this mild vegetable's stems as you like for crunchy contrast. Wash and slice bok choy as you would celery.

capers   Capers are the pungent flower buds of a Mediterranean bush. Usually available in supermarkets in small jars of brine, capers should be rinsed to remove excess salt.

chanterelle   This wild mushroom, orange-yellow in color and trumpet shaped, has a mildly nutty flavor. Choose plump, spongy chanterelles.

cherimoya   This fragrant, delicious fruit has an interesting indented pattern covering its surface. When ripe, the cherimoya feels slightly soft if gently pressed near the stem. A cherimoya should be green with no blemishes. The large black seeds aren't edible.

chili oil   Chili oil is also known as hot chili oil, and for good reason. Hot red chilies give sesame or vegetable oil both its fire and its color.

citrus peel or zest   Grated citrus peel is also known as zest, which is the citrus peel without the bitter white part just beneath it. If you don't have a grater, you can use a special tool called a zester or a vegetable peeler to remove the zest, then finely mince it. Grated citrus zest provides a burst of flavor, especially welcome when you are cutting back on fat and sodium.

couscous   Made of semolina, couscous cooks in about 5 minutes. It usually is served as a side dish or with meat and vegetables in a stew.

Cuban red bananas   Cuban red bananas are ripe when they feel soft and their skin turns dark. If unpeeled before their time (which is hard to do, since an unripe banana of this type is almost impossible to peel), they will have a bitter taste. When ripe, however, they are delicious.

eggplant   Smaller versions of this vegetable have a milder, more complex flavor and smaller seeds than their larger counterparts. Just remember to choose a plump, smooth-skinned eggplant without soft spots. The vegetable should feel heavy for its size.

farina   Farina is a flour or meal made from wheat and rich in protein. Most often cooked as breakfast cereal, farina can also be used for pudding.

fava beans   Also known as broad beans, fava beans are a popular ingredient in Middle Eastern and Mediterranean dishes. Fava beans can be purchased dried, canned, and, occasionally, frozen.

fish, drawn   A drawn fish has had only its organs removed.

fish, dressed   A dressed fish has had its organs, scales, head, tail, and fins removed.

guava   When ripe, this small, oval fruit will feel soft when gently squeezed and will have a fragrant aroma. The color varies among the many different varieties. Generally, when guavas are green, they are not ripe, but a few days on a counter away from sunlight will ripen them. Remove the hard seeds from the middle.

hearts of palm   Hearts of palm are the inner portion of certain varieties of palm trees. You'll probably have to use the canned variety, frequently placed near the canned artichoke hearts at the grocery store. Hearts of palm have a delicate flavor somewhat like that of an artichoke.

hot chili peppers   Tiny red or green "bird" chilies and serrano, Scotch bonnet, and habañero chili peppers are some of the hottest chili peppers. If you want to tone down the heat, remove the membrane and seeds before chopping the peppers. Boiling the pepper in a small amount of water for 2 to 3 minutes will help to mellow the heat even more. Wear rubber gloves when handling hot peppers or wash your hands thoroughly after handling. Skin, especially around the eyes, is very sensitive to the oil from peppers.

jícama   Jícama is a large, light-brown root with a sweet, nutty taste. Sometimes called the "Mexican potato," it can be eaten raw or cooked. The white flesh is crisp and crunchy.

kalamata olives   These flavorful olives are oblong and slightly soft, with a smooth purple skin. They come from Greece.

kosher salt   Coarse grained and additive free, kosher salt is preferred by many cooks for its texture and flavor.

leeks   Leeks, which look like overgrown green onions, have a subtle onion flavor. Smaller leeks are more tender than larger leeks.

mirin   A sweet rice wine that is low in alcohol, mirin is related to sake. One of mirin's many uses is to enhance the flavor of marinades.

miso   Miso, or bean paste, is available in a variety of colors and flavors. Made of fermented soybeans and grains, it is high in protein. Leftover miso keeps well in an airtight container in the refrigerator.

mortar and pestle   A bowl-shaped mortar and a club-shaped pestle are used together for grinding or pulverizing substances such as herbs and spices.

nopales   These are the leaves (or pads) of the nopal (prickly pear) cactus. When cooked, they have a delicate, slightly tart flavor and can be used in foods ranging from pickles to pies.

orzo   Orzo is a tiny pasta that looks like, and is a good substitute for, rice.

oyster sauce   Thick and rich, oyster sauce is made of oysters, brine, and soy sauce. It is popular in Asia as a condiment and as a seasoning in cooking.

pastina   Pastina is any variety of tiny pasta. It is used primarily in soups.

portobello mushrooms   Portobello mushrooms are very large and have a pronounced meaty taste. The caps are flat and the gills are exposed.

radicchio   Slightly bitter tasting, radicchio is a member of the chicory family and is used primarily in salads. It ranges in color from purple to red, with white accents.

rose water   A popular flavoring in Middle Eastern and Chinese cuisines, rose water is distilled from rose petals and retains their delicate fragrance. It is used primarily in desserts, syrups, and candies.

saffron   The dried stigmas of the crocus, saffron is the highest-priced spice in the world. It is noted for its bright orange-yellow color. Turmeric is often used as a substitute.

semolina   Semolina is coarsely ground, or cracked, wheat. It is often used in making pastas.

sesame oil   Oriental, or fragrant toasted, sesame oil is a deep, rich brown or red oil with a delightful aroma missing from the light golden sesame oils often found in grocery and health-food stores. If it doesn't have "that smell," it's the wrong oil for Asian recipes!

strippers   A stripper is a small, wedged tool that shaves strips of peel from citrus fruits or firm vegetables, leaving an indented strip.

turmeric Though this spice does impart a slight flavor to foods, it is best known for its bright yellow-orange color. Many cooks substitute turmeric for the more-expensive saffron to provide color.

ugli fruit This Jamaican specialty is at its best when it looks its worst. It has a loose-fitting skin, which sometimes looks bruised. Once you peel it, you will discover a very juicy fruit with a flavor between grapefruit and orange.

vanilla beans Vanilla beans can be found in most large supermarket spice sections or at gourmet food stores. Although vanilla beans are more expensive than extract, they really do impart a more intense flavor.

wasabi Also called Japanese horseradish, wasabi is available as a paste or in powder form. It takes only a dab of reconstituted wasabi for plenty of fire power.

yuca Yuca is a root that has a tough, slightly wrinkled brown skin and looks similar to a potato. Yuca is usually 4 to 12 inches long. It is also known as cassava or manioc.

zester When pulled across the surface of citrus fruit, the zester creates threadlike strips of peel. The zester removes only the colored portion (zest) of the peel, leaving behind the bitter white pith.

Mail-Order Sources

Note: Listed below are mail-order companies that specialize in international foods and hard-to-find ingredients. Inclusion in this list does not constitute an endorsement, implied or otherwise, by the American Heart Association. This list is *not* comprehensive. Many other companies offer similar products. The details provided are based on information that was current at the time of publication.

The Baker's Catalogue
King Arthur Flour
P.O. Box 876
Norwich, VT 05055-0876
800-827-6836

   Baking ingredients, including flours, grains, yeasts, salts, spices, oils, flavorings, flower waters, dried fruits, nuts, sugars, molasses, and kitchenware

Dean & Deluca
Attention: Catalog Department
560 Broadway
New York, NY 10012-3938
800-221-7714
Fax 800-781-4050

   Oils and vinegars, olives, dried mushrooms, chilies, pastas, rice, beans, grains, herbs, spices, dried fruits, nuts, and kitchenware

Pendery's Inc.
1221 Manufacturing
Dallas, TX 75207
800-533-1870
Fax 214-761-1966
    Chilies, herbs, spices, pastas, oils, vinegars, nuts, dried fruits, dried and powdered vegetables, sauces, salsas, and kitchenware

Penzeys, Ltd. Spice House
P.O. Box 1448
Waukesha, WI 53187
414-574-0277
    Herbs, spices, seasonings, flavorings, chilies, and vanilla beans

Rafal Spice Company
2521 Russell
Detroit, MI 48207
313-259-6373
    Herbs, spices, flavorings, dried mushrooms and tomatoes, rice and rice blends, beans, cooking wines, olive and other oils, vinegars, Asian specialties, sauces, seasonings, and kitchenware

Todaro Bros.
555 Second Avenue
New York, NY 10016
212-679-7766
    Olive oils, olives, vinegars, dried mushrooms, dried beans, grains, pastas, condiments, and pine nuts

Vivande Porta Via
Italian Pantry Products
2125 Fillmore Street
San Francisco, CA 94115
415-346-4430
Fax 415-346-2877
    Oils, vinegars, flours, dried beans, pastas, rices, herbs, spices, seasonings, dried and powdered mushrooms, olives, and dried and canned tomatoes

Watkins Incorporated
150 Liberty Street
P.O. Box 5570
Winona, MN 55987-0570
800-533-8018
    Herbs, dried and liquid spices, flavorings, and seasonings

World Variety Produce, Inc.
P.O. Box 21127
Los Angeles, CA 90021
800-588-0151
    Dried fruits, nuts, dried beans, grains, dried mushrooms, fresh fruits and vegetables, dried chilies, corn husks, grape leaves, spices, herbs, seasonings, and tofu

American Heart
Association Affiliates

For further information about American Heart Association programs and services, call 1-800-AHA-USA1 (1-800-242-8721) or contact us online at http://www.americanheart.org.

National Center

American Heart Association
7272 Greenville Avenue
Dallas, TX 75231-4506
214-373-6300

Operating Units
of National Center

Office of Public Advocacy
Washington, DC

American Heart Association, Hawaii
Honolulu, HI

Affiliates

Desert/Mountain Affiliate
Arizona, Colorado, New Mexico,
   Wyoming
Denver, CO

Florida/Puerto Rico Affiliate
St. Petersburg, FL

Heartland Affiliate
Arkansas, Iowa, Kansas, Missouri,
   Nebraska, Oklahoma
Topeka, KS

Heritage Affiliate
Connecticut, New Jersey, New
   York City, and Long Island
New York, NY

Mid-Atlantic Affiliate
Maryland, Nation's Capital, North
   Carolina, South Carolina, Virginia
Glen Allen, VA

Midwest Affiliate
Illinois, Indiana, Michigan
Chicago, IL

New England Affiliate
Maine, Massachusetts, New
  Hampshire, Rhode Island,
  Vermont
Framingham, MA

New York State Affiliate
Syracuse, NY

Northland Affiliate
Minnesota, North Dakota,
  South Dakota, Wisconsin
Minneapolis, MN

Northwest Affiliate
Alaska, Idaho, Montana, Oregon,
  Washington
Seattle, WA

Ohio Valley Affiliate
Kentucky, Ohio, West Virginia
Columbus, OH

Pennsylvania Delaware Affiliate
Delaware, Pennsylvania
Wormleysburg, PA

Southeast Affiliate
Alabama, Georgia, Louisiana,
  Mississippi, Tennessee
Marietta, GA

Texas Affiliate
Austin, TX

Western States Affiliate
California, Nevada, Utah
Los Angeles, CA

INDEX

cholesterol-free, defined, 260
cilantro
    Cilantro-Lime Turkey Breast, 231
    storing, Cook's Tip on, 153
cinnamon
    Cinnamon-Nutmeg Hot Chocolate, 178
    Cinnamon Rice, 137
    use with tomato products, 97
citrus fruit, equivalents for, 276
Citrus Peel, Candied, 28–29
clams
    choosing and preparing, Cook's Tip on,
        155
    Paella, 154–55
    see also shellfish
coconut
    coconut milk, substitution for, 183
    Coconut Quick Bread, 207–8
    substitution for, 183
cod
    Fish Sautéed with Tomatoes and
        Cinnamon, 101
    see also fish
Coffee Cooler, 179
Cold Noodles with Sesame Sauce, 241
collard greens
    see greens
complex carbohydrates
    see carbohydrates, complex
cookies
    Biscotti, 27
cooking, tips for healthful, 261–63
cooking methods, healthful, 261–62
cooking oils
    see fats and oils
Cook's Tips
    on aluminum foil containers, making, 136
    on annatto (achiote seeds), 162
    on apples, varieties of cooking, 92
    on avocados, ripeness of, 150
    on bell peppers, freezing, 52
    on bell peppers, roasting, 83
    on bell peppers, smoking, 169
    on bread crumbs, soft, 45
    on cactus pads, preparing, 171
    on capers, sodium in, 115
    on chayote, preparing, 188
    on chicken bones, using in stock, 225

    on chicken tacos, preparing, 196
    on chili peppers, grinding dried, 159
    on chili peppers, smoking, 169
    on chili peppers, varieties of, 188
    on cilantro, storing, 153
    on clams, choosing and preparing, 155
    on crêpes, storing, 63
    on egg custard, preparing, 174
    on egg whites, beating, 65
    on fish, how to cook, 102
    on frozen Coffee Cooler, preparing, 179
    on gingerroot, preparing and storing, 245
    on green beans, choosing, 43
    on ground poultry, 38
    on herbs, grinding dried, 159
    on herbs, storing fresh, 55
    on mangoes, cutting, 210
    on marinating, 132
    on meat, slicing, 234
    on meringue shells, 65
    on mussels, choosing and preparing, 155
    on mussels, how to eat, 11
    on nonmetallic bowls, 190
    on onions, peeling pearl, 165
    on peas, frozen, 22
    on pineapples, choosing, 213–14
    on portobello mushrooms, 14–15
    on radicchio, 8
    on salsa, 148
    on shrimp, deveining, 194
    on soufflé dishes, 57
    on spices, grinding dried, 159
    on tomatoes, peeling, 172
    on tomato paste, 51
    on wine, cooking with, 114
    on yuca root, preparing, 204
Corn, Zucchini, and Tomatoes, 172
corned beef
    Black-Eyed Peas and Corned Beef, 201–2
    Meaty Black Beans and Rice, 160–62
Cornmeal, Sweet Stuffed, 211–12
Couscous with Lamb Stew, 133–34
crab
    Crab, Spinach, and Ham Soup, 186
    Seafood in Creole Sauce, 193–94
    Shrimp and Crab Legs with Spicy Tomato
        Sauce, 184–85
    see also shellfish